Creating
Extraordinary Joy

"Creating Extraordinary Joy *is a terrific tool for getting on with the rich, fulfilling life we were all meant to lead. Chris Alexander truly understands the magic of synergy, and how we can manifest true joy in life.*"

— Suzanne Falter-Barns, author of How Much Joy Can You Stand?

"*In* Creating Extraordinary Joy, *Chris Alexander takes us onto a new playing field in personal development and self-improvement, where we can be fully present, and fully aware of who we are and why we are here. Through Joy, Chris becomes our personal coach, helping us to realize that the true definition of success in this century is anchored in love, connection to others, and allowing our purpose for work to be driven by passion. Thank heavens someone has finally nailed it on the head!*"

— Diane Y. Chapman, talk show host, author, speaker

"*This is a beautiful book, both inspiring and practical, full of wonderful insights and ideas to make your life a shining experience.*"

— Brian Tracy, author of Maximum Achievement and The 100 Absolutely Unbreakable Laws of Business Success

Ordering

Trade bookstores in the U.S. and Canada, please contact:
Publishers Group West
1700 Fourth Street, Berkeley CA 94710
Phone: (800) 788-3123   Fax: (510) 528-3444

Hunter House books are available at bulk discounts for textbook course adoptions; to quali-
fying community, health care, and government organizations; and for special promotions and
fundraising. For details please contact:

Special Sales Department
Hunter House Inc., PO Box 2914, Alameda CA 94501-0914
Phone: (510) 865-5282   Fax: (510) 865-4295
E-mail: ordering@hunterhouse.com

Individuals can order our books from most bookstores, by calling **(800) 266-5592,**
or from our website at **www.hunterhouse.com**

To Beverly,

Creating

Extraordinary

Joy

A GUIDE TO AUTHENTICITY, CONNECTION, AND SELF-TRANSFORMATION

Go with Peace, Love & Joy!

Chris Alexander

Chris Alexander

Hunter House
PUBLISHERS

Hunter House Inc., Publishers
PO Box 2914
Alameda, CA 94501-0914

Library of Congress Cataloging-in-Publication Data

Alexander, Chris, 1948–
Creating extraordinary joy : a guide to authenticity, connection, and self-transformation /
Chris Alexander.— 1st ed.
p. cm.
Includes bibliographical references and index.
ISBN 0-89793-335-4 — ISBN 0-89793-334-6 (pbk.)
1. Success—Psychological aspects. 2. Joy. I. Title.

BF637.S8 A396 2001
158—dc21   2001026467

Project Credits

Cover Design: Peri Poloni, Knockout Books
Book Design and Production: Hunter House and Jinni Fontana
Developmental Editor: Lori Covington
Copy Editor: Laura Harger
Proofreader: Lee Rappold
Indexer: Nancy D. Peterson
Acquisitions Editor: Jeanne Brondino
Associate Editor: Alexandra Mummery
Editorial and Production Assistant: Emily Tryer
Sales and Marketing Assistant: Earlita K. Chenault
Publicity Manager: Sara Long
Customer Service Manager: Christina Sverdrup
Warehousing and Shipping: Lakdhon Lama
Administrator: Theresa Nelson
Computer Support: Peter Eichelberger
Publisher: Kiran S. Rana

Printed and Bound by Publishers Press, Salt Lake City, Utah
Manufactured in the United States of America

9 8 7 6 5 4 3 2 1   First Edition   02 03 04 05 06

Contents

Foreword

When I first learned that Chris Alexander was writing this book, I thought to myself, "what a great concept; I could sure use some tips on creating *extraordinary joy* in my life; even ordinary joy would be an improvement!" I began to take inventory of my life, and asked myself how much joy had I actually experienced, and how much joy was I missing? The resulting life assessment stunned me with the realization that I needed this book; I had needed it for many years.

My memories of experiencing joy in my early years centered on family outings, vacations, and the many hours of "playing." I remember singing about joy in church hymns and Christmas carols and certainly felt joy when I got the golden retriever puppy, the Barbie Dream House, and a new guitar. The environment I grew up in was very achievement oriented, where high standards were set and expectations of success were stressed. (Some of you may be familiar with my father, Denis Waitley, who wrote the best-selling program, *Psychology of Winning*.) I was taught that in order to live a fulfilling life, I would have to work hard and achieve financial success. As an adult, my life became a challenge to earn money to survive and earn more money to thrive, so that eventually I could do the things that brought me joy. Many of us become stranded in the "Someday I'll (Isle)." Someday, when I have more money...someday, when I've earned my degrees...someday when I retire...someday, when I reach the pinnacle of my career...I can live a more joyful life. My experience of joy was fleeting, sporadic, and usually created by circumstances outside of myself—getting the overdue promotion, taking a vacation, listening to my son's first words, watching my son's football games (usually more joyful if the team won, or he played well), or treating myself to a massage. Rarely could I access a sense of joy unless something good or exciting happened. Rarely did I awaken to a new day and feel the joy that comes from just being alive.

In *Creating Extraordinary Joy* Chris Alexander teaches us how to awaken to the joy that is inside us at any given moment; the joy that is our potential, our birthright, our destiny. We learn how to create joy through our ultimate connection with our "authentic self" so that our relationships (with ourselves, others, and the environment) are more loving and synergistic. A few years ago, I had the fortune of meeting Chris Alexander at a national booksellers convention and was invited to be a guest on his cable television show. I have yet to meet an individual who exudes the level of passion and joy for living that Chris does. In a time when we are bombarded with a multitude of "how-to" books written by so-called self-help gurus, Chris Alexander emerges as a true mentor, teacher, and guide for us all. He has integrated the methods and means for creating extraordinary joy into his personal and professional life.

If you have picked up this book and are reading these words, then you have now begun your journey to a more fulfilling, rewarding, and joyful life. If you are like me, then you are ready to break the shackles of fear, insecurity, and self-doubt that have held you back from experiencing the joy you deserve. This book is not about finding ways to have more joy in your life, it is about becoming the *creator* of joy in your life. As Chris says, "joy is a creative choice for freedom." The *extraordinary* thing about this newfound joy is that it becomes quite ordinary; in other words, you integrate it so powerfully into your daily life that fear and negativity become the exceptions. Living with extraordinary joy is not a luxury that we must earn or a state that is reserved for special, gifted, or "chosen" people. It is a choice that each and everyone of us can make for ourselves right this moment. Welcome to this glorious journey. May you begin living and always live your greatest dreams . . . a life you never thought possible . . . but is now yours!

Deborah Waitley, Ph.D.

VICE PRESIDENT OF THE WAITLEY INSTITUTE,
CONSULTANT AND AUTHOR

Preface

The deepest, most intimate yearning of the human spirit is connection, and in this book you will learn how to create the ultimate connections—with yourself, with nature, and with others.

How can I make such an extraordinary claim? I am sure about this because every week I see stressed, harried, and unhappy individuals reinventing their lives and finding extraordinary joy by applying the principles and teachings presented in this book.

For the last twenty years, my fascination with human behavior has led me to research interpersonal connection and its effects upon our ability to live our lives on purpose, with meaning and joy. Through this research, I discovered the phenomenon of synergy. At first, I didn't understand the power of unity and connection. Nor did I understand how important they are to the human condition. But I soon discovered that connection on a mental, emotional, and spiritual level is as important as physical touch.

Because I am an organizational behavior specialist, my search led me to many corporations that suffered from dysfunctional communication and conflict, resulting in lowered morale and productivity. In almost every situation, at the heart of the problem was fear that arose from a lack of communication.

As communication improved and connection became the goal, a synergistic effect began to permeate the organizations. Productivity increased, morale skyrocketed, and attrition decreased. Suddenly, everybody had a part in making something great and worthwhile. I too grew from these interventions and experiences. I began to notice the effects of synergy everywhere. When there was positive connection, the sum was always greater than the separate parts. In this book, I have carried that conclusion through to every level of our lives, to the physical, emotional, mental, and spiritual things that keep us truly alive.

Extraordinary joy is the result of synergy created by connecting with our true and authentic selves. When we drop fears and facades and embrace our true selves, we are free to create the ultimate connection: loving and being loved by others.

Creating Extraordinary Joy guides you through seven Synergy Life Mastery steps. These steps are grounded in the ancient teachings of the masters and the latest scientific research, and each of them is accompanied by practical applications for your daily life. I have been using Synergy Life Mastery for years with businesspeople who want to make their companies more effective, with people who have experienced mental illness and personal pain, and with ordinary people who want to experience a more purposeful, joyful stay on this earth. The steps work, and as you take each step, the results you create will encourage you to take the next one, transforming your life into one of extraordinary joy!

Chris Alexander

LAKE FOREST, CALIFORNIA

NOVEMBER 2001

Acknowledgments

It gives me great joy to acknowledge all the people who have contributed to this book in so many ways. Firstly, to my family for their never-ending encouragement. Without their support, this book would not have been possible. Secondly, to Madison McCord who assisted me with the editing of the original manuscript and to the editorial team at Hunter House—you are the most creative, inspiring team I have ever worked with. More specifically, I want to acknowledge Jeanne Brondino, Kiran Rana, and Lori Covington. Jeanne and Kiran, thank you for recognizing how important the 7 Synergy Principles are to creating extraordinary joy in one's life. Lori, I appreciate your dedication to simplifying my complex ideas and writings into a more acceptable, easy-to-read format. You are masterful, objective, and fun to work with. Finally, I salute all the prophets, teachers, authors, speakers, and visionaries of life, known and unknown. Your teachings, your struggles, and your collective consciousness have made this work possible. There were times when the words just flowed and I knew where they came from. Truly, we are all connected. Connection is vital to our existence. When we connect with one another intimately, soul-to-soul, we experience extraordinary joy, and instantly we realize that everything is connected and that synergy is a reality.

Introduction:
Who I Am

Like many modern people, I am independent and adventurous. I have always thought of myself as pretty much a self-made man, but when I started writing this book, I realized that my value system was built long ago; it reached back to my knowledge of my parents and grandparents. I wanted to include their stories in this book because I think my upbringing is an important part of how I learned about creating extraordinary joy.

In 1890, my grandfather, then a young man, went from South Africa to Mashonaland, a district of Rhodesia (now called Zimbabwe). He was attracted to Rhodesia by the British South African Company, which basically owned the whole country and offered men land in exchange for colonization. The goal of the British South African Company was to populate Rhodesia, the location of one of the richest mining operations in history.

My grandfather saw a business opportunity to transport goods to Rhodesia from the much more developed South Africa. Commodities were scarce and very expensive, so there was much money to be made in this line of business. He used an ox wagon to transport goods from Johannesburg and Kimberly in the Northern Cape Province of South Africa to Salisbury (now Harare) and Bulawayo, which were at that time Rhodesia's two principal towns.

My grandfather was a great team player and hard worker and encouraged the other transporters to group together. The road was long and hard, and they sometimes traveled in convoys. He learned these skills from my great-great-grandparents, who were among the very first settlers in the Cape of Good Hope and formed the first work groups and unions in protest against the treatment they received from the Dutch East India Company. The Cape of Good Hope colonies—made up of German, French, Dutch, and English settlers—were created to grow fresh fruit and vegetables and make wine for the ships that stopped at the Cape of Good Hope to replenish supplies on their way to India and the Far East. (The Suez Canal had not yet been constructed.)

Malaria, a mosquito-borne disease, was common in the area, and the medicines to counteract the ravages of this disease were scarce. My grandfather once traveled without a convoy and grew so sick from malaria that he became delusional and was stranded in the middle of the bushveld for eight days. He later said that it was the belief and positiveness of his Zulu assistant that prevailed and sustained him until other wagons arrived. He never attempted the great trek from South Africa on his own again. He believed in the power of unity over adversity, a belief learned from daily experience on his treks: for example, it often happened in the rainy season that more than one span of oxen was needed to pull a loaded wagon from the mud. My grandfather always spoke about the importance of working together and the need for faith and the belief that God would provide and deliver them from the ravages of the African terrain.

He continued the transportation business and also opened some trading posts. Business was brisk, with cattle traded and bartered for blankets, coats, beads, and other goods that the local African people needed. Then came the great Rinderpest Plague, a cattle disease that put a halt to the cattle trade. Many transport companies changed over to mules, but my grandfather settled on a farm with his cattle, which were unaffected. He married and had a daughter—my mother. My grandfather, like many other Rhodesian settlers I know, had come to Africa to start a new life and discovered that Africa was abundant with life itself. He fell in love with Africa.

In the old days in Rhodesia, farming cattle and tobacco was pretty much the norm. However, my father was more interested in business, religion, politics, and hunting, and he was good at all those things. My father was ten years older than my mother. He provided well for us, he worked hard, and he really had our best interests at heart; however, he became angry and withdrawn from trying to solve his own inner turmoil.

I learned early that some people find the path to joy only through tragedy. It took an accident for my father to realize that he was in charge of his own thoughts and feelings. He fell twelve feet from a ladder, fracturing his pelvis, breaking a leg, and bruising his whole body. His brush with death may have been the best thing that ever happened to him—he changed from a terribly sad and insecure person into someone who could appreciate life on a whole new level. He became much happier and loving after his accident, and I finally started to feel close to him.

I've always taken it for granted that growing up in Africa was like growing up any place, but lately I've come to see how different my life would have been if I'd grown up somewhere else. There's something about Zimbabwe—the landscape, the weather and animals, the culture—that predisposed me to seek the joy of my childhood and to recreate it as an adult and share it with others. There is a saying in Africa: "Once you experience the red dust of Africa in your nostrils, you will always return." Once you experience joy, you will return to it again and again.

I was born in the farming community of Gatooma in the Hartley District of Zimbabwe, an incredible place to grow up. Many people believe that Zimbabwe is a modern term for the Shona phrase *dzimba dza mabwe* (houses of stone), which refers to the ancient city founded in this southern African country. Great Zimbabwe was home to some fifteen thousand people, and it still stands today—uninhabited. Towering stone walls, seventeen feet thick, are still held together by a clay and gravel mixture known as *daga*. Who built Great Zimbabwe? To this day, no one knows. It has been rumored since the sixteenth century that the fabulous stone structure was one of the cities of the Queen of Sheba.

I have great fondness, memories, and deep ties to the workings and collaborations of nature, all gifts to me from my childhood in Zimbabwe. My memories of early childhood are still vivid and always bring me a sense of joy. It was paradise for a curious, inquisitive, and rambunctious youngster. Although I don't remember it, I'm told that I experienced the full impact of nature for the first time when I was only three weeks old. My father took the whole family on safari and set up camp on the Umsweswi River, which became a joyful bathtub for me. I loved the feel of cool water, and I still do!

Ever since I can remember, I have loved to spend time outdoors, communing with nature. Growing up in Africa was very different from growing up in an industrial country, and I am thankful for the opportunities it gave me to connect with the world around me in direct and meaningful ways. I was never concerned about shoes because I never wore shoes. I ran around barefoot among the anthills and thorn trees—I had a ball! My toys were created by my imagination: whatever lay close by could be transformed into whatever I wanted it to be in my mind. Stones became Land Rovers, old clay bricks became trucks, and large thorn trees became the masts of great ships. My nickname at home and in the village was Christopher Columbus, and like most explorers, I lived life to the hilt. To this day, I have scars to support the memories of my childhood.

Living in Africa nourished the roots of my understanding of the incredible partnership we can create with life itself. My friends were varied and interesting, and I met new ones every day. I collected chameleons and watched them change to the color of whatever material I put them on. I saw African soldier ants eat pathways through the thickest grass, a million creatures cutting a single-minded, lawnmower-like swath. When we were out in the bush, we were close to elephants, rhinos, zebras, and giraffes. At night I could hear the lions roar and the hyenas laugh. It was scary and exciting at the same time. Looking back, I now realize how close I was to the original earth.

My favorite pet was a baboon we named Jaco. I had endless hours of fun playing with him and allowing him to affectionately search for dry skin on my scalp. It was a great experience. However, as he grew bigger and stronger, he became more independent, and we had to set him free to return to the bushveld. I was happy that he was free and sad that I might never see him again. But he returned often to see us. To this day, I believe animals should be free, and I will never understand why pets are cooped up in small backyards or in apartments. Freedom is the greatest gift we humans have, and we should afford that gift to all earth's inhabitants. From my childhood days, I have noticed that nature has a way of partnering humans and animals that is quite extraordinary.

Earlier, I mentioned that I didn't care about the shoes I wore. That mind-set stood me in good stead, because I was the youngest in my family. When I began school, like all of the youngest in families growing up in my era, I got the final hand-me-downs. My first pair of shoes had three previous owners—my brothers. Mr. Patel repaired our shoes, so they lasted much longer than shoes do now. I've never seen anyone who could fix shoes as well as Mr. Patel.

At elementary school, I felt confused about one particular boy who sat next to me. His name was Henry. Henry made imaginary binoculars with his hands, and he looked through them constantly. Henry was a Romanian refugee, and I found out later that his father watched through binoculars every day to protect his family before escaping to Zimbabwe to start a new life. I did not understand why any human would need to escape from another human being. The primitiveness of some human behavior still rocks the core of my being. I do not understand war. I do not understand violence. Nor do I understand those who say things such as, "Well, that's the world we live in." I'm sure that Henry found me strange, too, because in winter my mother insisted that I wear a bag of garlic around my neck. I must admit, I never got sick.

My first mentor was my geography teacher, Colonel Burke, who had traveled the world and was a gifted teacher. He was a colonel in the British Army, a gentle man *and* a gentleman. He insisted on courtesy; he always said that civility was the essence of humanity. Our classroom was decorated with python skins from Burma, tiger skins and elephant tusks from India, zebra and lion skins from Africa, and many more artifacts from all over the world. Each one was used for a lesson. I loved the idea of the whole world being connected in one classroom. My classmates egged me on to ask him about his exploits—a perfect opening for us to sit back and listen to exciting stories and allow our imaginations to fly. He was the first person to introduce me to Rudyard Kipling's writings, starting with the great poem "If."

I had lots of other people who called themselves teachers, but most of them probably just needed a job: they had no idea how to connect with an inquiring mind that wanted to connect with the world. For a number of years, I simply lost interest in what they had to say. Every time I asked a question that was out of the ordinary, I was told to be quiet. Many times I was sent out of the classroom. They didn't like me to question their reasoning, but it was hard for me *not* to question. Too many things didn't make sense. Even arithmetic did not make sense. It seemed too absolute. Once I asked the teacher: "Why does one plus one always have to equal two? Why can't it equal three or five or some other number for a change?" Well, that completely floored her! She made me feel like I was totally wrong and dumb to ask such a question. However, somewhere deep within, I knew I was right, because everything around me worked harmoniously, creating more than the sum of its parts.

In high school I loved to play rugby and enjoyed team activities: I excelled in swimming, cricket, and soccer. But I had great difficulty with conformity that made no sense to me and reduced me to an object. It was only later, in college, that I discovered that creativity and problem-solving, rather than conformity, were the real tools of life. I suppose that's why I gravitated toward playing in a rock band. I knew that the secret of playing well together was being in sync. Being in sync was created mainly by one's intention to be so. As a young person, I therefore realized that my attitude was reflected in everyone and everything around me.

After college, one of my mentors was a seventy-year-old pharmacist who put in a full day's work and could out-work any person in his organization. He taught me that the alternative to happiness is misery—and if you don't choose happiness, what are you left with? He encouraged me to start my first pharmaceutical business, and it was he who taught me that anything can be accomplished if you put your mind to it. My company grew at an incredibly fast pace and eventually was sold to a larger pharmaceutical house. During this time, I realized that my core competency was leadership and the ability to motivate people to reach their full and true potential. I now realize that my training to lead and motivate actually began in early childhood, when I learned nature's lessons about collaboration and cooperation.

The success of my pharmaceutical business gave me the opportunity to consult with many multinational companies. I conducted team-building workshops and seminars for many large corporations. That is where I learned that each and every one of us instinctively needs connection with others and that validation by others fills a deep, primal need. Following this realization, I became a student of organizational behavior. I truly believe that through synergy (the power of connection) and intentional choices, one can create extraordinary joy.

One of my strongest childhood memories is of a supper I shared with friends and the workers who lived in our village. The men built a campfire and hung an iron pot over the coals. The pot contained a stew of wild yams, meat, and tomatoes, and below, on the edge of the fire's ashes, rested another pot, filled with a stiff dough made of cornmeal called *zasd-zsa*, the staple food of most tribes in Zimbabwe. My friends and I sat around the fire with the men, and each of us took a handful of the dough. It was so tough that it could be worked into a sort of scoop that rested in the palm. Using these cornmeal ladles, we dipped into the communal stew pot. I remember the smell of burning wood and the laughter of the men, who were only part-way through their evening's work. My friends and I listened to their stories and shared their dinner, and although we were black and white, young and old, the feeling was one of peace and connection.

My mother didn't mind when I didn't come home to supper, and she didn't worry that I might be in trouble when I stayed out at all hours. I was always with other kids, and the adults in the community all watched over us. It was like having dozens of parents instead of just two. I think that, if you have such a deep and satisfying experience of connection as a child, you spend the rest of your life trying to recreate it. My work in helping people connect in all sorts of organizations is a way to recapture the peaceful sense of community I enjoyed as a boy. Moving from organizational behavior into the behavior of families was the most natural thing in the world, for every family is an organization, made up of people who have different needs and desires but who all work within the same culture.

Since I began working to help people create synergy and joy in their lives, I have found my own life's purpose. One of my strong beliefs is that I am the product of the process I teach, and my happiness and success contribute directly to the happiness and success of the people who study Synergy Life Mastery. Synergy Life Mastery is more than a set of skills; it is a process that strengthens, enlivens, and energizes your life. I wanted to write this book because there are only so many people I can reach with workshops and seminars—I want everyone to benefit from these timeless, and timely, teachings.

STEP ONE

Understanding Synergy

All things are interwoven with one another;
a sacred bond unites them; there is scarcely one
thing that is isolated from another. Everything is
coordinated, everything works together giving
form to the one universe. The world order is
a unity made up of multiplicity.

MARCUS AURELIUS

Ordinary Joy and Extraordinary Joy

This book is about creating and accessing extraordinary joy in your everyday life. This kind of joy is extraordinary because it sustains you from day to day and is created and perpetuated by your awareness and attention to what matters. You don't hear people talk much about joy; we tend to hear about pleasure or happiness or thrills. There's nothing wrong with those things, but they tend to be fleeting. Ordinary types of joy are like a window that opens briefly, showing you a marvelous sunny landscape that you never saw before. *Extraordinary* joy is about opening the door to that landscape and walking outside into the sun.

The difference between ordinary and extraordinary joy is also one of participation. Moments of pleasure or happiness often come unexpectedly; they are things that "happen to us." Extraordinary joy is an intention and a way of life. You learn to focus on joy as an ongoing presence, and you learn ways to access that presence any time you want. If ordinary joy falls like an occasional rain shower on our heads, extraordinary joy is a stream rushing past us; any time we are conscious of it, we can dip our hands into it, splash it on our faces, and revel in its freshness. You may learn enough about joy to wade right into the stream and make it the force that carries you through the world. Extraordinary joy is always new and clean, fast-moving but never-ending. All you have to do is remember that it's there!

When you went to school, you studied math and grammar and social studies, but I'll bet you never had a class on how to achieve happiness. Considering that that's the one thing all people want, isn't it strange that it isn't a course option? Unless we're blessed by growing up in that rarity called the happy family, we have no models for happiness besides what we see on TV. On TV, people become "happy" by acquiring new, improved possessions. The right dish soap can inspire 30 seconds of bliss. Wait a minute; the right pants also inspire 30 seconds of bliss. The DeBeers engagement ring and all that it implies is worth (in TV land) 30 seconds of bliss, too (45 on Super Bowl Sunday). So we learn two messages from advertising: any new product can make you ecstatic, and each ecstatic moment lasts around 30 seconds.

So it's no surprise that we think of true happiness, extraordinary joy, as something that's outside our control. We have nothing to measure it by. We have no skills with which to acquire it. Does it surprise you to hear that you can live in extraordinary joy by learning new skills, just as you would take a class to master new software or learn to cook? These relatively mundane goals can be achieved by taking a class, sure, but extraordinary joy must require years of dedicated study, direction, prayer, and meetings with wise elders, right?

Actually, that's not right. Joy is a stream flowing through the universe. It lies just on the other side of your consciousness, but it's close enough to touch as the 9/11 attack demonstrated. Catastrophe and suffering reintroduces us to the preciousness of a (joyful) life. And you don't have to spend your life in an ashram or a church to know joy. You can simply learn some new skills and practice them in the course of your everyday life. As in any learning experience, as you increase your skills, your awareness begins to change. It's the most natural thing in the world to become more sensitive to the things that interest you. Soon you start to see the stream of joy, to hear it splashing by. You begin to trust that it's always there, and it becomes part of your life.

You have the potential to live a meaningful and joyous existence. You have the right to expect to achieve your purposes and to do it happily, without struggle. Synergy Life Mastery is a step-by-step process of clarification. It both starts and finishes with increasing your awareness!

The set of skills you will learn from *Creating Extraordinary Joy* is called Synergy Life Mastery. Practicing Synergy Life Mastery will change your awareness and positively impact your spiritual existence. The goal is to bring extraordinary joy into your life!

Synergy Life Mastery

Heavy words for a terrifically light concept! Synergy Life Mastery may sound like work, but it is really about learning to play; to splash into life like a teenager off a high dive: exuberant, unencumbered, and confident of the depth and warmth of the water that welcomes your body. Synergy is the energy and force that propels you into life and makes things easy. Mastering your life is not about molding yourself, but about refashioning your reality, making your life the way you want it to be—the way you *know* it should be.

You approach Synergy Life Mastery through a series of steps that bring you into closer and closer contact with your true self. This contact enables you to grow closer to others, too, to have happier relationships and a more meaningful daily life. This book contains examples to inspire you, exercises to stretch your capacity for joy, and journalizing entries that allow you to discover for yourself the things that matter most to you. Useful tools such as the Workshop of the Mind and Relax-Action help you target specific areas of your life that you want to change and to effect the changes you desire. Each chapter of this book explains a step of Synergy Life Mastery.

Step One, **Understanding Synergy,** teaches you the basic lesson of Synergy Life Mastery—what synergy is, how it is useful to you, how you can become aware of it, and how to create it.

Step Two, **Seeing All the Choices Before You,** helps you look at the role of choice in your life and opens up your possibilities for making better decisions, directly multiplying your happiness.

Step Three, **Cleansing Your Inner Ecology,** explains how daily life creates byproducts we don't want and tells you how to replace them with healthful alternatives.

Step Four, **Making Authentic Choices,** helps you understand what you need and how to get it through the minute-to-minute, life-changing choices you make.

Step Five, **Expressing Your True Self and Your Higher Purpose,** teaches you to honor and act on your true self's desires: the direct route to a fulfilling life.

Step Six, **Reaching Extraordinary Joy by Achieving Your Goals,** shows you how the simple task of goal setting can turn your dreams into reality.

Step Seven, **Staying Connected—with Joy,** is about maintaining a joyful lifestyle. It offers advice on how to get back in touch with the important things in your life, and provides reminders that old age can be the most vital and exciting time to be alive.

In the middle of the book are three "Synergy Interludes," the refrain of which is synergy—in choice, in loving, and in family and community. As you journey through the book, you'll find that the theme of synergy is developed through practical applications that you can use to find synergy in your true self, your relationships with others, and your impact on the world.

Each chapter of the book contains exercises designed to help you think about ways of living a more joyful life. Titled "My Synergy Journal," the exercises consist of questions that challenge you to rethink the ways of being that you've always taken for granted. You may find yourself trying out new ideas and behaviors, and you may uncover some things about yourself that you never suspected were there. Use your Synergy Journal to better your life: don't beat yourself up about things you discover, but revel in the idea of knowing yourself better. If an exercise makes you uncomfortable, never mind—we all change and grow in different directions, and something you avoid this month may later suddenly become relevant to you. Use these synergy exercises to strengthen and support yourself, to stretch into new and happier ways of relating with others.

You Are Perfect

We are made up of so much more than our physical bodies: we are the sum of our experiences, our learning, our culture, and our family. We are masses of indecision, confusion, uncertainty, and insecurity. Everything that happens to us from birth onward is stored somewhere within ourselves: in memories, bodily sensations, mysterious feelings, or outright hang-ups. I'm a mess, and so are you!

But we are also perfect. The essential you is flawless, needing nothing extra, having nothing in excess. Before you were born and after you're dead, you are the same person, a spirit, an energy pure and strong as sunshine, and as endless. In a way, people are just the opposite of perfume. In perfumery, a plant is subjected to heat and pressure, which extracts the juices, made up of water and essential oils. The liquid is distilled, and the essential oils are considered the concentrated plant—its "soul," in a way.

When we're born, we are already at that pure "soul" stage—in fact, that's just about all we are! As we grow, life dilutes us. We develop layers of experience, the different faces we wear around other people, various shells to try to protect ourselves from pain. But for all the changes we create, our true selves remain. In the way that a plant contains its essential oils, you contain—and always will contain—your true self.

How many times throughout your life have you heard the words "You are perfect"? When you read them now, are you inclined to believe them? I don't expect you to believe them now, but I do ask you to consider the possibility of your innate perfection. In fact, this is a great exercise for starting your Life Mastery journey.

You are perfect! Take a minute to close your eyes and savor the idea. Repeat the words "I'm perfect" to yourself, and enjoy how they sound. Don't let feeling silly stop you, and don't worry too much about all the implications; just go with the good feeling of knowing you're all right. Do this exercise today, and if you can make that sort of commitment, practice it twice a day for the next few days. See whether you notice a change in your energy level, your motivation, and your enjoyment of life. This is your first-hand experiment with accessing joy through a simple, powerful affirmation. Now, wasn't that easy?

Remember your true self—we're going to come back to it again and again in this book, because uncovering and expressing your essence is your key to happiness—and your rightful inheritance.

Your essential being rests like a peaceful aquifer under rocky layers of negative habits. In Synergy Life Mastery, you practice ways of accessing and acting from your true self. It's not mysterious, and it's not hard work. It's just something you start doing and, seeing success, continue doing.

There are two parts of Synergy Life Mastery: synergy and choice. Synergy Life Mastery helps you reclaim your true self by teaching you to practice synergy and make good choices. The two are interdependent; as you increase synergy in your life, the world of choice opens up to you. As you start to make, and continue making, your best choices, synergy comes to you in a cycle of positive feedback. When you are conscious of synergy, making choices for a more joyous life becomes a natural state of mind. Expressing your true self through your daily activities and relationships becomes simple once you've accessed synergy.

As I noted above, this book is separated into seven steps, with three "Synergy Interludes" in the middle. The chapters are geared to help you focus on recognizing and creating synergy, see the wide range of choices available to you, use them to improve your life, get rid of the negative feelings and ideas that clutter your internal landscape, choose your own path in the world, and follow the desires and demands of your true self to their logical outcome—success. The final section discusses ways to reconnect with joy throughout your life, so you will always have the resources necessary for maintaining a life filled with purpose and delight.

Synergy Defined

Synergy is a natural phenomenon—you see it all around you, and you use it unconsciously in your daily life. When two or more things combine, creating something larger than the sum of those individual things, the phenomenon is called synergy. In synergy, the result of combining ingredients is more complex than one would expect from those ingredients alone. Synergy is what turns flour and water into bread, something greater and completely different from either flour or water. Bread nourishes us in a way that flour or water alone cannot: in synergy, the separate ingredients of yourself blend into a single, harmonious, and remarkably more effective whole.

You experience synergy within yourself when your mind, body, and spirit are all focused on the same purpose at the same time. Using all the parts of yourself to accomplish the tasks of daily life is infinitely more effective than using just one part.

Dr. Robert Ornstein, of the University of California, did research on how the logical left brain and creative right brain work together. He discovered that when both sides of the brain are engaged in a project, the result is much greater than simply twice that of either half—in fact, it's five to ten times greater.

Sports psychologists have found that when an athlete exercises while concentrating on the muscles she is working (or the result she wants to see), she physically, measurably achieves more than when she is exercising with her mind on other things. Using the power of their minds in conjunction with their bodies, using two types of intention rather than one, athletes can actually increase their physical abilities. In this book, you will use your mind, body, and spirit to accomplish your goals with more success than you've ever expected before.

Synergy in Nature

Connecting with nature teaches us life-enhancing lessons about the importance of collaboration and the beauty of symbiotic relationships. When we pay attention to nature, we learn spiritual lessons without being consciously "taught." Anyone who has sat for hours in a blind watching for a wild animal, or rowed on a silent lake, or searched for mushrooms and wild herbs, experiences the magic of patience and tolerance and the power of silence in the natural world.

An energy runs through the universe, working and building, growing and creating every day. This connecting energy creates partnerships that result in more than the sum of their individual parts. Synergy, often expressed as symbiosis (the partnering of animals or plants in a mutually beneficial relationship), is the essential functioning of nature.

Partnerships are the most natural thing on earth. They thrive in our own backyards. Bees, hummingbirds, and flowers are all working together in creative alliances. Weaverbirds in Southern California build their nests on the lower branches of trees, just above a wasps' nest, so that rattlesnakes can't reach them. For some strange reason, one of the few things feared by rattlers are wasps! Wasps act as security guards for the weaverbirds, whose eggs are now protected. When the birds migrate, the wasps move into the vacated birds' nests. The hunt for real estate, like the desire for a safe place to house your young extends to animals as well as people. Many trees produce a sugary nectar that ants feed on. These trees also produce little fruit bodies, full of protein, which are sufficient to satisfy the ants' protein needs. What do the ants do for the trees? They fell small seedling trees, which ensures that larger trees will have more space in which to grow.

Redwood trees in North America's rain forests create synergy with tiny fungi. The fungi are tubular and store water, minerals, and nitrogen. They feed the tree by wrapping themselves around its roots, protecting the roots from heat and providing extra water. The fungi feed on sugar from the tree.

Another example of an interspecies synergistic collaboration is the one between the people of Mauritania and dolphins. Mauritania is on the coast of Africa, where the Sahara Desert meets the Atlantic Ocean. Every year, late in November, fishermen gather at the shore to beat the ocean with long, flat sticks. This beating of the ocean is a signal, a request for assistance that echoes into the deepest corners of the underwater world. Dolphins hear it and unfailingly arrive, forming a solid barrier a few hundred yards from the shore. The fence of dolphins traps thousands of mullets, which race to the shore in fear. Fishermen wade into the water with their nets and bring home the much-needed, protein-rich food. The dolphins get their share of mullet, too, as they feed off the rich bounty concentrated between themselves and the beach. Over centuries, villagers have come to understand that a team effort between themselves and the dolphins is possible. And the dolphins seem to agree.

A lot of us are pretty far away from nature. We live in cities and towns surrounded by asphalt, and even the landscape of what we still call the countryside may have been completely altered by farming a hundred years ago. We don't think much about our impact on the environment until our houses slide into the ocean or catch fire in lightning-sparked summer fires. A few years ago, a new office building went up near my home, and the next season, thousands of ducks arrived at the building's parking lot. They were looking for their pond, but someone had paved it. I guess they forgot to tell the ducks.

I went to Shanghai recently. It's a big, ultra-urban city, very industrial and totally removed from nature. But Shanghai's getting into quality-of-life issues, and someone has created a wonderful People's Park and planted it with grass. I watched while children came to the new lawn. They didn't run and roll and play Frisbee, like a lot of kids would. These children sat down and with gentle fingers they stroked the grass, marveling at the softness of it. When you grow up with trees and grass, you tend to take them for granted, but to these kids it was miraculous to see velvety, green plants in the middle of their city.

Monarch butterflies migrate to Morro Bay each year, but they're never the same individuals that came the year before. Something in the very cells of each monarch tells them where to go each season. The group knows because the knowledge is bred into them. What sort of understanding are we breeding into the cells of our future generations? How many generations will it take before we can all live in joy as naturally and unconsciously as the butterflies migrate?

Synergy and Flow

You've probably had the experience of being totally involved in an activity that requires high levels of concentration and skill. You might be painting, singing, biking, writing, doing a craft, or gardening, but the feeling is the same—pure enjoyment, satisfaction, and the sensation that time has stopped. When you do finally look at the clock, you're amazed at how the hours have flown by. This peak experience, researched and documented by Mihaly Csikszentmihalyi *(Flow: The Psychology of Optimal Experience)*, is called *flow*, and it is the perfect example of synergy within the self. When you are in flow, the world feels right and perfect. You are challenged but not frustrated, wholly immersed in the experience and glad to be where you are. You wouldn't trade Right Now for anything else!

Synergy is the tool you have unconsciously used to get into flow. Your mind, body, and spirit have been engaged in a single purpose, and the feeling is a high no drug can match. When you look back on a flow experience, you might see it as a miracle, an aberration, or something that happens only once in a blue moon. In fact, when you consciously strive to attain synergy in your everyday life, you increase the number of peak experiences you have, and you increase their duration. Like any skill, the more you use synergy, the better it will work for you. Use synergy daily and "day-to-day" will come to mean what it should: daily opportunities to multiply your happiness.

Synergy expands your opportunities for happiness by taking into account the whims of fate. When you think synergistically, you don't rail against misfortune; you find solutions that allow you to express yourself in the best possible way. Your integrated approach to achieving your purposes is pointed but flexible as you incorporate the current situation into your stream of synergy.

It's important to think of synergy as not only a natural phenomenon but also something you create. Synergy might happen *to* you once in a while, but you have the capacity to *make* it happen continuously in your life. All you have to do is change a few habits of thought, and the rest will follow naturally.

The exercises in this book are designed to help you reconnect with, reach, and sustain synergy. You start by synergizing yourself—using every part of your being to accomplish your personal goals. As you become more skilled in using synergy, you will find that your happiness changes your relationships with others. Soon, you will begin to use interpersonal (or group) synergy, combining your focused self with your friends, lovers, and colleagues to create more joyful, meaningful, and effective relationships. When synergy is used by a group of people committed to the same goals, the impact in the wider community is phenomenal. Your personal steps toward synergy can change your community!

Creating a Synergy Journal

If you're going to use synergy to achieve a happy life, it's important to recognize it when it happens, recall it when it's past, and plan for it by making choices that will lead you to synergistic experiences. You might keep a Synergy Journal, logging the events in your life created by (and re-creating) synergy. Many people use a diary to chronicle the painful occurrences in their lives, but research shows that focusing on happy events and memories perpetuates a positive cycle, creating more happiness. Write down the good things, too.

Entries in your Synergy Journal might look something like this:

Saturday: *We had a terrific conversation at the sushi bar. It was almost like being with a family, with Kenny laughing and joking with customers, and his little daughter sharing her crayons with a customer's child. People were laughing and flirting, and we talked about having kids and how we'd both like to wait so long that we may end up adopting instead of having our own—and that's okay with both of us!*

Sunday: *Spent the day working in the garden. Repotted the jasmine and a bunch of succulents, fertilized the roses, and watered everything. Worked until I nearly dropped and was as filthy as a kid playing in the mud. When I started, I thought, I'd just work a couple of hours, but it was almost four hours later when I got the last pot in place.*

Tuesday: The drive to work was beautiful, with the sun rolling the fog away as I drove into town. The sky was rosy and the air so fresh. I turned up the radio and sang my head off to the oldies!

Here's a set of questions to get you started on your own journal. Think of the last time you felt synergy working for you: that is, think of a time when you were doing something challenging and rewarding that completely absorbed you, and when you later looked at a clock, you were surprised at how quickly time had passed. The short questionnaire below will help you think about your experience of synergy.

What were you doing?

_____

How did you decide to do this activity? Was it planned? Were other demands competing for your attention while you were doing it?

_____

When you started, how long did you plan to do this activity?

_____

How much time did you actually spend doing it?

_____

Was anyone else with you? (If yes, who?)

_____

How did you feel while doing it? (List at least four feelings.)

_____

How do you feel now, thinking about it?

_____

What other activities inspire (or might inspire) synergy in you?

_____

Do you ever experience synergy at your job?

_____

Synergy Between People

"We just clicked," "Time flew by," "We're on the same page": these are the things people say about one another when they have experienced synergy together. In the same way that using your body, mind, and spirit together helps you achieve greater goals, working in a cooperative, intuitive, mutually sustaining relationship with someone else brings you both great satisfaction and outstanding results. Much of what has been written about teamwork in the workplace is based on the idea of group synergy—two or more people wholeheartedly acting in concert to achieve a common goal. When it happens, it's a thing of beauty, but for many people the workplace is so fraught with personal danger, cooperative work isn't even a dream. We're Americans, and we value The Best! And you can't have a Best without having a bunch of runners-up (otherwise known as "losers"). But synergy doesn't run on competition. Competition not only stymies individual creativity, it also ruins the chance of achieving synergy at work.

Volunteer projects are a good place to experience group synergy. If you've ever taken part in a community project, such as cleaning up a beach or park, you may have felt what it's like to work with a group of people to make a plan, visualize the goal, encourage one another on to success, and celebrate afterward. It is much like the synergy experienced by individuals, but the achievement may be larger—after all, two dozen people can repaint a church in a weekend, but one person might take a month. The other payoff of group synergy is its relational aspect—any time you co-create synergy with other people, you are making friends and building community—two activities most people sorely need.

We are an isolated people. Our jobs tend to be technical, detail-driven, and solitary. Our culture places great value on having plenty of individual space, so that the more money we have, the more bedrooms our houses have and the greater chance we have of avoiding our children when they're noisy, or of sleeping alone after a lovers' spat. We can watch TV alone, and may forget how to do things such as tell stories or make conversation. We often don't know our neighbors and move far away from our families. And we like it that way! We think, "I want my own bathtub and TV, my family drives me crazy, and knowing my neighbors means they may ask me to dog-sit on their next vacation. Connection with other people is a tremendous commitment of time and resources, and I just don't have the energy." But sometimes, a voice inside us may say something like this:

> *But I'm lonely. I've been lonely since childhood, so I've almost gotten used to it. I'm not going to tell anyone this, because I learned early that being lonely means I'm weak. Unlovable. Other people don't feel this emptiness; they aren't weak. I don't want anyone to know those things about me. I cope. I watch TV, which lets me vicariously experience family life without having to actually live it. The Internet allows me the perception that I connect with other people: I can log in and chat; I can look at other people's websites, I can play with ideas about how my life might be different. I have a cell phone so people can reach me when I'm away from home, in case someone not connected with my work decides to call me. Maybe we could get a beer, if someone would only call. . . .*

The loneliness in our culture is so accepted, we don't even notice it anymore. We have come up with excuses for loneliness—we work harder and longer than other cultures (but actually achieve no more than they do), we are "independent" and "free." We farm out our children to daycare and our parents to the old folks' home and return to an empty apartment each night bedraggled from work and empty of personal satisfaction. To achieve meaning, we have to express the true self, but expressing the true self requires someone to perceive us, react to us, synergize with us. In short, for me to express my true self, I need you.

Co-creating synergy can be as simple as baking cookies with a nephew or as complicated as learning to tango. If you find that the above description of loneliness speaks to you, it's important that you rediscover yourself as the child who once wanted to play all day long. Like many lessons, the hardest part is getting started, so the activity below is geared to help you do just that!

A Synergy Lesson

Spend 10 minutes (set a timer) daydreaming about noncompetitive things you want to do that involve other people. As ideas come to mind, write them down, without stopping to think about possible expenses or drawbacks; just make a list of everything you can imagine.

Maybe you want to study improvisational acting, to cook Thai food, to quilt, to sail, to work on cars, to be a museum or park docent, to learn haircutting. Don't worry about choosing a "spiritual" pursuit (unless that's what you'd really like to do), and you don't have to run off and join the Peace Corps. The most important things are that this is your dream and that it involves experiencing and interacting with other people.

When you have your list (and your ten minutes are up), go over it and cross out the ones that simply won't work. You may come up with a substitute for an impossible dream. For example: if I write down that I want to visit Mars, but I'm not ready to devote my life to becoming an astronaut, I might settle for a trip to space camp or even the planetarium. Because my group synergy goal requires other people, I might choose to attend a stargazing evening sponsored by the astronomy department of the local junior college.

After you've crossed out the "impossible dreams," you probably will have several dreams left on your list. I won't ask you to narrow them down further—I want you to hold your dreams very close. They are direct expressions of your true self and should be cherished until they can be lived. Just choose one dream you can start to live within the next week or two. Then complete the following dream-planner:

Due today	**My group synergy activity is:**
In 2 days	To start my activity, I need to:
In 1 week	Groups/classes begin:
In 2 weeks	I attend my activity.

Your Dream Planner might look something like this:

Due today	My group synergy activity is: learning to contra dance.
In 2 days	To start my activity, I need to: find out where classes are offered, when, and the cost.
In 1 week	Groups/classes begin: May 2, at the Piedmont Adult School (and cost $45).
In 2 weeks	I attend my activity. Yippee!

Keep in mind that group synergy is like great sex—it hardly ever happens between strangers. It's hard to work in unity when no one knows the steps, and it takes time to build trust in your own competence and in the knowledge of others. But even in a new activity you may find a sort of synergy in group uncertainty and confusion—if you can go easy on yourself, be gentle with others, and keep your sense of humor.

When you've started living one dream, you may find that others follow along naturally, or you may take up one activity, finish it, and then have to remind yourself that there are others on your list. The important thing is that you spend some consistent time with other people during which you can start to experience group synergy and the relationships that grow from it. If you look back over your week and realize you haven't had a particular moment of connection with someone else, promise yourself that in the coming week you will put yourself in a place where group synergy can happen.

Synergy—Friends and Enemies

The conditions for synergy are simple, but modern life may not easily meet them. The list of friendly and unfriendly conditions below may help you target reasons why synergy is lacking at work or at home and think of ways to solve the problems of anti-synergy.

✦ FRIENDS OF SYNERGY

The qualities that permit synergy tend to be the same in many settings; whether it's the workplace or the home, the general atmosphere and the attitude of the people I spend time with determine whether synergy can flourish. In synergy-friendly places, I feel relaxed, expectant, and happy.

Words that describe such settings include: *cooperative, uncritical, intellectually or physically challenging, playful, friendly, supportive, easy-going, somewhat unstructured.*

✦ ENEMIES OF SYNERGY

The qualities of people and places that inhibit synergy also inhibit you: you feel tense; your joints, neck, back, and stomach ache; and you have trouble completing more than the bare minimum at your job. You feel stuck and bored, your energy is sapped, and you are often sleepy and irritable in places where synergy is stifled.

The words that describe this atmosphere include: *competitive, controlling, critical, demanding, strict, routine, plodding, hostile, tight-assed, too structured, or totally unstructured and chaotic.*

The Family Dinner—An Anti-Synergy Event

You might wonder why it's so hard to have a pleasant dinner with your teenage children. You plan the menu, buy the groceries, and tell everyone to be home on Thursday by 6:00. You wife calls at 5:30 to say she has an emergency meeting and won't be home until 6:45. Your daughter wanders in around 6:20, and you're already annoyed. You tell her to set the table, then listen to her slamming plates down on the table while she mutters to herself about what an uptight dad she has. The fifteen-year-old rushes through the screen door at 6:30 (the time you'd been planning to serve dinner), rides his skateboard across the kitchen floor, and gives you that "You're so dumb" look when you ask why he's late. "I dunno," he says.

It's almost 7:00 when you get everyone shepherded into the dining room, and your wife hasn't even had a chance to take off her pumps. You sit at the head of the table and glare around at your loved ones. The chicken's dried out, the peas are mushy, your feet hurt, and your blood pressure is up. Right now, you'd trade them all for a blonde and four days in the Bahamas. You hand the platter of chicken to your loving wife and, sounding like Clint Eastwood, demand of your oldest son, "How was your day?"

If you've had this experience, you know it goes from bad to worse. It seems that everyone in your family has conspired to ruin your plans for a "nice family dinner." People who have been planted in front of *Seinfeld* re-runs by 6:00 every weeknight for the last year suddenly have drum corps practice, study hall, and Swedish folk dancing classes. Your life partner, the mainstay of your support, calls in late. Then, when you attempt to make conversation at the table, people stare at their plates, glance at you as if you've never met, take up the last argument you had, or run crying from the room. You meant so well! What happened?

Let's look at the friends of synergy. The first word on the list is *coopera-tive*. When you work in a solo synergy situation, cooperation isn't relevant, but when you attempt a group synergy situation, you need the *willing* participation of the group. Everyone has to be ready, willing, and able to plan and take part in the activity. Now, if you have teenagers, you're shaking your head, certain that any attempt to create group synergy is doomed to failure from the outset. You've forgotten the primary lesson of leadership—the willingness to give up control! The failure of the family dinner is nothing more than a demonstration of the futility of attempting to control others. The harder you try, the worse it gets. So you stop trying. But that doesn't mean you should go into a depression, believing your family will never enjoy one another's company again! You don't stop trying to *have* happy family experiences, you stop trying to *control* happy family experiences!

Now, I see you folding your arms across your chest and looking at me. "Fine, you're so smart, what exactly should I do to have a happy family experience?"

✦ FAMILY OUTINGS THAT WORK

Mary and Mike faced just this quandary: they saw their teenagers at the refrigerator on Saturday mornings and at twice-weekly arguments about anything from laundry to curfews. Rather than calling a family meeting (practically guaranteed to pit parents and kids against each other), Mary sent an e-mail to all her kids and to Mike:

> *Dear family,*
>
> *I'm so bored with the same old dinner night after night! I'm still young, and I want to have some fun. If any of you are interested in planning a dinner out (I'll buy)—it could be at the beach, or a bar-becue in the yard, or at a local restaurant; whatever—I'll help set it up. You choose the day and time together and let me know what kind of menu you want and where you want to have it. The budget is fifty-five dollars! The only thing is, everyone in the family should be able to attend, so I'll let you guys figure out the schedule. R.S.V.P. me by e-mail with your ideas and suggestions.*
>
> *Thanks.*
>
> *Mom*

The following Wednesday night, the whole family took hot dogs, potato salad, sodas, and marshmallows out to a local park. Their son Brian brought his CD player and deejayed, and everyone sat around on blankets bundled up in sweaters (it was March) and watched the stars come out. The little kids stayed up a bit later than usual (and on a school night!), but everyone had a good time and agreed they should have dinner like that every month.

Letting go of control is scary when you rely on your children to make decisions. As you can see, Mary set a limit on the budget and made it a requirement that all her family attend. She kept control in those ways but let go in all others. She was there to help, but basically she left the choices up to her family, which resulted in some ideas that might test a parent's resolve to keep from controlling the process. First, the kids chose to have the dinner on a Wednesday so it didn't interfere with their weekend activi-ties, such as dates and sleepovers. Some parents might balk at having a cookout on a weeknight, usually from sheer fatigue at the thought of doing anything out of the routine. But if you check "Enemies of Synergy," above, you'll find the word *routine* on the list. Deviating from the weekly routine might take a little effort, but in fact it is the routine itself that's the problem. Break it with impunity! Since when are you too old to play a little hooky on a school night?

Another parent might argue that the meal was somewhat less than nutritious, but so what? One night a month, your family can break all the nutritional rules without the food police being called in. Your goal in the project is family togetherness, not culinary perfection.

✦ RULES FOR CREATING THE SYNERGISTIC FAMILY EVENT

Use these general rules to create your next family outing. Before talking to anyone else:

1. **Give up on perfection:** We all have the fantasy of the perfect family dinner, but we may focus on things such as the menu, the kids' Sunday-best clothes, the table linen (and table manners), and the ideal of a peaceful meal. That's a lot of pressure to put on a family of ordinary human beings! Perfection, in this case, means that everyone has a good time—nothing more is required!

2. **Decide what matters most:** Think about the end you want to achieve. Is it really dinner you want, or do you just want your family to have some fun together? You might decide a trip to an amusement park is just the thing. In the example above, Mary was bored with cooking dinner and wanted to be with her kids, but she didn't want to make a big deal out of it.

3. **Decide what you can't compromise on:** The shorter this list, the better your chances of succeeding at your goal. Your goal is to set as few limits as possible without creating a total free-for-all. Mary set a budget and wanted the whole family at the outing. Everything else was a possible compromise.

4. **Make sure there are payoffs for others:** The fact that you want to have a good time with your family is moot if your family is going to suffer for it. Mary's kids got to plan a party, eat what they want, and stay up late.

5. **Anticipate flaws in the design:** Sometimes a child will throw a monkey wrench into the plan by asking to bring a friend. There's something about planning a family party that makes parents highly resistant to this idea. Unless you're strongly wedded to the idea of a family-only outing, you might encourage your kids to each bring a friend. After all, adding friends is just an opportunity to expand the possibilities of group synergy! (You could bring friends, too.)

Parenting is such an awesome responsibility that it sometimes feels like it's all about to get away from you. A lot of parents are so protective that they get locked into the role of rule-maker and disciplinarian, making it difficult to also be a comforter and nurturer. They may use rules their parents used ("Clean your plate!"), which don't especially benefit their children or the parent-child relationship. They may use the same rules year after year, forgetting that children grow, become more self-reliant, and need different rules. Parenting would be so much simpler if, every so often, parents took time to consciously evaluate their rules, choosing what's important, modifying what could work better, and throwing away the rest.

Family rules should exist only to support your family, to protect your children, and to give the family something each member can count on. Every unneeded or illogical rule parents apply harms not only their children but the parents themselves by sapping their energy and reducing their credibility. Don't deprive your children of the chance to know you as a caring, supportive person, and don't deprive yourself of your kids' affection and trust. Getting closer to group synergy with your family means lightening up on unnecessary rules and regulations, being open to new possibilities, and giving other family members access to co-creating synergy with you.

Switching from the mind-set of a controlling parent (or lover or manager) to that of a true leader is greatly helped by positive thinking. The over-controlling person tends to think in terms of protecting herself from being undermined by others; the positive thinker doesn't worry about losing authority or face but tends to think about the possibilities of success in any goal she attempts. Thinking positively means you expect the best from others (not perfection, but the best they can give you)—expecting the best from others tends to significantly increase your chances of getting their best!

Right Thinking and Optimism

Although the idea is present in all religions, the phrase *right thinking* comes from Buddhism and is one of the moral precepts of that philosophy. It encompasses many ideas, but for our purpose, this one is the most important: Right thinking is about holding your mind in a correct place in relation to what you believe and paying attention to your values. It's about remembering honesty and integrity, even when it might be more convenient or comfortable to forget or when you're the only person at the table who is abiding by his principles. It might mean taking a loss to right a wrong. It means staying focused on what matters most to you, because that is crucial for your happiness. There may be all sorts of incentives to abandon your values, but they are lesser incentives than the goal we are striving for here—a joyous, integrated life. When you stick with what you believe, your self-respect is intact. You may be the only person who knows when a choice you make is "right" rather than "smart," but *you* will know, and that affects how you see yourself and the world.

An example of doing "right" instead of "smart" can be applied even to financial dealings. Say that you have to make a choice between mutual funds. One carries the standard choices of oil and gas companies, some mining interests, and tobacco companies. Historically, this fund has done quite well, and the outlook for it in the current political climate is good as the new president makes changes to support industry, turns government lands over to logging, and prepares to fund drilling in the Arctic. You could make some money with this fund.

The second fund is almost as successful as the first, but it's riskier. It depends on alternative energy companies, products from conservation-managed rain forests, and cruelty-free cosmetic companies. This fund has proven to be a good long-term bet, but it doesn't have the "get-rich-quick" appeal of the first one.

Doing right, in this case, means looking at more than how much money you can make. What some might consider the smart choice might gain you some quicker profits, but at an added cost to the environment, increased burden on the health-care system, and the heavy price of lung cancer spread across the generations. You can do right by thinking long-term and thinking of the whole world; in this case, doing right is doing smart as well, although other investors might not agree.

When you choose what's right, you are automatically doing what's smart: it may not be considered smart by those who equate smart thinking with self-promotion at all costs, or those who consider the acquisition of goods as the most important goal. In Synergy Life Mastery, the most important goal is the expression of your true and perfect self. When you think with synergy, you look at more than one outcome for your choices. Always, always, you must do what you believe is right, what you can be proud of. Whenever you go with your intuitive understanding of what's right, you are living from your true self.

In Synergy Life Mastery, right thinking is also about making a choice to be positive whenever possible. This is a tall order, since we are often surrounded by people who equate "rational" or "logical" thought with negativity.

After all, in a world as troubled as ours, it's only natural to be pessimistic, right? How about this idea instead: in a world as filled with possibility as ours, why not be optimistic? Daily miracles may not make the six o'clock news, but just look around! Babies are born, trees flower in the spring, snowflakes are perfectly constructed. Looking at nature is one way to connect with a positive attitude, to recapture some of the magic you knew as a child. Remember how excited you felt when it snowed? When was the last time you ran out into the snow and made a snow angel, had a snowball fight, sculpted something really magnificent using only your mom's favorite spatula and your own creative genius?

Optimism has lost its chic in contemporary culture, but that can change! In *Anatomy of an Illness*, Norman Cousins shows us that thinking positively and laughing often and hard can literally save our lives. Positive thinking is a vital part of living, and it's a requirement of the kind of synergy we want to create for Life Mastery. Synergy needs a medium in which to grow, and that medium is your optimistic mind-set.

If you're thinking, "Oh, I couldn't possibly become an optimist at this late stage," this book is perfect for you! That thought, like all our thoughts,

MY SYNERGY JOURNAL | *Optimism*

Things that annoy me	*Their potential to cause me joy*
1. _____	1. _____
_____	_____
2. _____	2. _____
_____	_____
3. _____	3. _____
_____	_____
4. _____	4. _____
_____	_____
5. _____	5. _____
_____	_____

is a habit, and habits are made to be changed. Often, changing a habit is a matter of making a firm, committed decision to do one small thing today and another small thing tomorrow. Start changing the negative-thinking habit right now!

Being grown up doesn't have to mean that snow becomes just another annoyance on your way to work. Like all of life, snow has other possibilities, one of which is the possibility of joy.

Stop right here and list five things above that may sometimes annoy you. Next, list their possibilities for causing you great joy.

Now you're thinking synergistically, using your creativity and intention to change your world! When you find another, more positive way to look at situations that previously have been uncomfortable, you expand your range of possible choices and increase your chances for happiness.

Hopefully, this chapter has given you more than just the definition of *synergy* and has provided you with some ideas on how to bring it into your life. Synergy is hard to write about because it's both a natural phenomenon and something we create. In the same way that one plus one equals three when a couple has a child, synergy turns intention and awareness into reality, thereby creating a new and exciting phase in your life.

Now that you can recognize synergy and know a bit about how it works, it's time to discuss the creative behavior that we all use but that only some of us use to its full advantage—the power of choosing. The next step in Synergy Life Mastery involves increasing your awareness of the decisions you make every day—and those you may make only once in a lifetime.

Seeing All the Choices Before You

Life does not give itself to one who tries
to keep all its advantages at once. I have often
thought morality may perhaps consist solely
in the courage of making a choice.

LEON BLUM

Choice

You have more choices than you realize. As children, we can't wait to grow up and choose our own clothes, toys, and ways of living. What no one can tell us is that even once we've reached the age of reason, we still have few clues that help us realize our true capabilities! Sure, you can choose your breakfast, but do you love your job—really love it? Is your spare time filled with TV and the Internet or with hobbies that thrill and inspire you? Is the time you spend with your family happy, "quality" time, or is it car-pooling? It's too easy to become trapped by the machinations of life, by routines and oppressive expectations from society or your past.

Synergy thrives in places where there are many possibilities, and one way to reach synergy is by making decisions that invite it into your experience. A large part of living is about becoming aware of our possibilities. One of this book's major purposes is to point out that there is always another choice. You may be unaware of it, which is perfectly natural. But it's there, and it's waiting for you! It may be covered up with old baggage, or it may be hidden by fear. (In later chapters, you will learn how to uncover your choices.) By becoming aware of your possibilities, you increase your access to synergy and become powerful and free.

JOHN'S STORY

John was diagnosed with paranoid schizophrenia when he was eighteen, and he attended my Synergy Life Mastery course eleven years later, after multiple hospitalizations and all sorts of treatments. We usually have around fifteen people at a time in these classes, and I noticed John right away: his eyes were glazed and he was clearly highly medicated. In the course's first meeting, we talk about the two general kinds of choices—the "must-dos" and the "can-dos." Must-dos are things such as taking medicine, obeying the law, keeping up with personal hygiene, and communicating with others. When we discuss can-dos, we talk about making choices and setting goals. It was at the goal-setting seminar that the lights went on for John. I could actually see the curtain in his eyes going up as he realized he could still set goals for himself.

The realization that you have the freedom and capability to set goals for yourself is empowering for anyone, but particularly so for people who have lived with mental illness. Institutional experiences tend to make people feel like they have no control, and mental illness, coming as it does from inside, feeds that feeling of helplessness. Discarding that helpless feeling unleashed something so strong and positive in John that his life was changed forever. Yes, he still has schizophrenia, but he uses alternative life skills from the Synergy Life Mastery course to accomplish his goals. He reduced his medications, went back to school and got his MBA, and is now an editor. Simply put, he reclaimed his life.

✦ EXPANDING YOUR POSSIBLE CHOICES— THROUGH AWARENESS

You've been driving all day and half the night, and you haven't eaten since breakfast. Ravenous, you walk into a restaurant, and the waiter hands you the menu. When you open it, you discover it contains only one item—a cheese sandwich. You don't want a lousy cheese sandwich! You want meatloaf and mashed potatoes and fruit salad and cheesecake (you're impervious to cholesterol)! But this is the only restaurant open in Fargo, North Dakota, at 10:00 P.M. on a Wednesday. And the waiter confirms that the one choice is all you have. So you sigh heavily and say, "I'll have the cheese sandwich."

And you go away feeling gypped and unsatisfied because you weren't really free to choose, were you?

Going through life with one set of choices is like eating a cheese sandwich every day of the week because you never get to see the whole menu. Who we are, what the world is like, how other people see us are concepts that we acquire by the time we're five years old. We learn from our families what the world is like, but in reality we learn only about what our family-world is like. The outside world has so many other items on the menu! The challenge is learning to say to yourself, "Okay, when I was five (or six or ten) and living in the world my family created, I would have reacted this way. But I'm not a kid anymore, and I live in the whole world. What other choices are available to me?"

Inhibiting Thoughts—Where They Come From

Much of what we carry around with us belongs to someone else: Mom and Dad, a brother, the school bully, or the person we used to be. Although I may have grown up on the outside, there is still a part of me that will always be a little kid. Things that happened to me then may stick around, whispering in my ears and causing me to interact with the world from an old point of view that's no longer relevant or useful to me.

We've all found ourselves in situations where we felt stupid, attacked, frightened, or incompetent, and in those situations we might have found that friends didn't understand why we suddenly became so defensive or quiet or tearful. Emotional baggage is heavy but invisible: you may forget you're still carrying it until it drops to the ground in a moment of awareness. A good clue that emotional baggage is influencing the way you feel in certain circumstances or around certain people is that, when you look back on the situation, you can see that things you assumed you understood could be perceived in a different way. It's possible that when your husband said, "That tight blue top looks great on you" (with a friendly leer), he wasn't saying, "Gee, you're fat!" But if you were a chubby kid, that may be just what you heard!

JENNY'S STORY

Jenny grew up with four older brothers who took turns protecting her and tormenting her with brotherly pranks. Her father, a cool, inaccessible man, occasionally tried to teach Jenny things he'd taught his sons, but she didn't pick up chess quickly, couldn't hammer in a nail straight, and never learned to change the oil in the car. Jenny grew up with the feeling that she was slower and more stupid than her brothers. Her mother, a quiet, ineffectual woman, was so mired in her own unhappiness that she didn't make the effort to get close to her daughter. From getting the piece of chicken she wanted at the dinner table to protecting herself from bullying, Jenny always felt on the defensive. Her brothers teased her incessantly, making sure she felt clumsy and backward, and her parents didn't seem to notice, which further reinforced her belief that she was inferior. Jenny grew up always feeling wrong, and she hated that feeling.

Now Jenny's grown up—at least on the outside—and she can't take even a little bit of mild criticism. She comes unglued, gets really defensive, and starts talking in a loud voice, trying to drown out what the other person is saying. This turns out to be a big problem at her new job, where people are generally laid back and share informa-

tion with each other informally. Anna, who is trying to train Jenny, has become frustrated because Jenny won't listen to her and thus keeps making the same mistakes over and over. Anna's management style is generally relaxed and easy-going, but her people get the job done, and she's never had an employee who behaves the way Jenny does. When she tries to correct Jenny's mistakes, the young woman blames others for failing to give her proper instructions or follow up with her on projects. She seems unwilling to take responsibility for her actions, and every meeting between the two women ends with Jenny arguing every point until Anna gets annoyed and sends her back to her desk. Anna is seriously thinking of firing Jenny because she just can't work with her.

Jenny doesn't know it, but she's in an ideal place to learn not only her job but also how to work easily with people, provided she can overcome her own fear enough to connect with them. Unfortunately, she has what I call Inhibiting Thoughts, which include things such as "If I ask questions, they'll know I'm stupid," or "I can't be wrong— not here, too."

Identifying and Replacing Inhibiting Thoughts

Our thoughts are like sunglasses we never take off. They form a layer between ourselves and the world. We use them to interpret our reality, to forecast the future, and to protect ourselves from harmful elements. They have the power to darken our view or make the colors of the world seem richer and deeper. It all depends on what we choose. When you buy a pair of sunglasses, you know you have a choice between brands, frames, and UV protection levels, but thoughts feel like things that arise naturally and unbidden, not like things you can control. The fact is, you can choose from a menu of options, choosing to be jolly rather than morose or hopeful rather than despairing. It's not easy, but neither is living with one set of options in a world that requires a full menu. Choosing healthy, happy thoughts takes practice and dedication, but the payoff starts as soon as you do, because those healthy thoughts influence your behavior, the situations you create in your life, and the kind of people you attract.

Inhibiting Thoughts act as a bridge between old memories and hurts that inhibit us and our immediate present: they interpret events that happen now through a filter based on old, painful experiences. We're all afraid of things that once hurt us, and Inhibiting Thoughts arise from the fear of making the same mistake twice. Unfortunately, they also feed that fear by robbing us of new experiences and keeping us frozen.

Here is a story about the Shona and Matabele tribes, of Northern and Southern Zimbabwe, respectively, who have a tradition of hating the chameleon. A chameleon is a small lizard whose skin changes color depending on its surroundings. Its eyes don't operate in tandem as ours do, but can each rotate 180 degrees, so when a chameleon looks at you, it can also look away from you—a helpful strategy for an animal hunted by so many predators! I collected animals, and every time I produced a chameleon from my pocket, members of both tribes would run in all directions. As a kid, this was a lot of fun for me!

One day, I asked a wise elder in the village why everybody hated chameleons. He told me that that the Great Spirit in the Sky once sent a rabbit to tell all the villages of each tribe where they could find large herds of fat buck that they could easily hunt in order to feed their women and children. The rabbit ran too fast and only reached one village. Tired and hungry, the rabbit decided to send a chameleon to the rest of the villages. But the rabbit didn't know that the Evil Spirit had cast a spell on this chameleon, making the chameleon take very slow, hesitant steps. It took the chameleon forever to reach the other villages. By the time the villagers got the message and reached the place where the herds were supposed to be, the animals had already moved on. Everyone went hungry because of the evil spirit existing in the chameleon. Today the Shona and Matabele believe that if the chameleon touches you, you will have bad luck and be hungry for the rest of your life.

I was raised to believe that chameleons were harmless toys and interesting creatures, and I didn't believe they brought me bad luck or hunger. If

I had been raised in the Shona or Matabele tribes, even accidentally touching a chameleon (which is an easy thing to do because they camouflage their skin to blend with whatever they're resting on at the moment) might have brought a powerful element of fear into my life. Some superstitions have reasonable beginnings: walking under a ladder can certainly upset it and bring down whatever—or whoever—is on top of it. We all have superstitious ideas about how lucky or unlucky we are as individuals, and the good ideas protect us by giving us an optimistic lookout. The bad ideas may cause us a lot more trouble than necessary because we react to them as if they're true. Things that are essentially harmless or maybe even wonderful are ruled out because of old ideas that stop us from seeing the possibilities before us. Inhibiting Thoughts are an example of how superstitious behavior can limit your capacity for enjoyment—just like all those Shona and Matabele kids who never had the pleasure of playing with a pet chameleon.

Originally designed to protect us from further harm by stopping us from making errors, Inhibiting Thoughts also stop us from trying new things, cause us to jump to conclusions about what's really going on, and basically act like fussy old aunts who say things such as, "Sit up straight," "Everyone will laugh at you," and "You'll never get into that college, so why even try?"

You may have heard that there are three ways to cope with fear—flee, freeze, or fight. Isn't it strange that we don't hear about the fourth, most productive way to handle fear—to face it? To really conquer fear, you must do the opposite of the other three strategies: rather than fleeing, stay where you are; don't freeze, but take action; and, finally, fighting is more of a last resort than a useful option, so never fight your fear—invite it to dance!

If your four-year-old is terrified of the monster under his bed, you could remove the child from the room, making that monster so real and scary that your child may always be frightened. You could force the child to stay in bed, as parents used to do, convinced that after endless nights of screaming, the child would become a "little man." Or you could "kill" the monster, but then the child might be trapped in the room with either a ghost or a corpse.

Facing this fear might mean crawling under the bed to talk with the monster, inventing a lonely monster who only eats dropped popcorn (not four-year-olds!), who likes to watch *Sesame Street,* and who wants more than anything to be friends with your four-year-old. You might make up a life for the monster, draw pictures of him, and invite him to birthday parties. Allowing the child to re-create the monster as a harmless being helps the child to take positive control over a frightening mental image and ultimately befriend it.

Inhibiting Thoughts are the monsters we create, and the more we allow them to roam our minds, the more power they have. They may be based on old history and unhappy memories, but they are no more real than the monster under the bed. And as easily as you can convert your kid's monster into an imaginary playmate, you can turn Inhibiting Thoughts into motes of dust to be swept away.

Think of fear as being like the surf close to the beach. It's rough, roiling, and noisy. But if you can swim under the crashing waves and get past that first turbulent zone, the water is calm, with gentle swells that buoy you up. Facing fear is like putting your head down and heading into that rough surf with a solid goal and firm intentions and plowing through it until you've reached the calm water.

✦ TAKING ACTION AGAINST INHIBITING THOUGHTS

There are three things you need to do in order to exchange heavy, old baggage for shiny, new, and optimistic thoughts: you need to identify your Inhibiting Thoughts, put them into words, and, finally, replace them with thoughts that are positive and self-affirming.

First, identify your hot spots, the places where you are most tender and most easily wounded. Sit down and make a list of the things you say to yourself, things you might have been told by parents, siblings, or teachers when you were a kid. I call these Inhibiting Thoughts because they are the things we learned to say to ourselves that stop us from living life as fully as we can. Inhibiting Thoughts may contain words such as *should* or *shouldn't*, *must*, or *ought to*. Words such as these tend to bring up guilt and make us feel inadequate, stopping us from taking risks and putting an abrupt halt to any sort of creative action. Inhibiting Thoughts may also include extremes such as *always* or *never*, which hurt because they're unfair. When couples use them, they're often fighting words, and when we say them to ourselves, we feel depressed and hopeless. After all, no one is *always* or *never!*

An example of a tender spot and its Inhibiting Thought from the Tight Blue Shirt example I recently mentioned follows. Think of a recent incident that jabbed you in the wrong place. Then fill in the first column, under "What she or he said." Try to use the exact words the person used, not how you interpreted them. Next, write down your interpretation, under "What I heard." Finally, in the space provided under "My Inhibiting Thoughts," write down your Inhibiting Thoughts, and try to identify your tender spots in the last column. Then think of three more such incidents.

MY SYNERGY JOURNAL | *Inhibiting Thoughts*

Example:

What she or he said: That tight top looks great on you.

What I heard: Gee, you're fat!

My Inhibiting Thoughts: I shouldn't eat so much. I'm fat and tacky-looking.

My tender spot: My weight

Incident 1

What she or he said _____

What I heard _____

My Inhibiting Thoughts _____

My tender spot _____

Incident 2

What she or he said _____

What I heard _____

My Inhibiting Thoughts _____

My tender spot _____

Incident 3

What she or he said _____

What I heard _____

My Inhibiting Thoughts _____

My tender spot _____

Incident 4

What she or he said _____

What I heard _____

My Inhibiting Thoughts _____

My tender spot _____

(Make copies of this format for additional incidents)

Ouch! We don't even like to think about these things when we're alone, but that doesn't stop us from repeating them to ourselves every minute of every day. But it doesn't have to be that way! Now comes the good part. It's time to say goodbye to Inhibiting Thoughts, to resolve to notice them when they arise, and to replace them with positive optimistic thoughts! Here's how.

Transfer your Inhibiting Thoughts from the table above to column one in the table on page 43. Next, pretend you are talking to someone you love very much (more than you love yourself!). How would you answer your favorite person when he says, "I'm so dumb, it's hopeless" or "I'm sure people are laughing at me when I talk. I should just learn to keep my mouth shut"?

Would you just sit there and let your friend say such awful, self-hating things? Of course not! You would find answers; you would argue with him and dispute his statements. You would do your best to bolster him, to end his suffering. We're not taught to befriend ourselves, but that's just what you are doing here. In replacing Inhibiting Thoughts, your goal is to apply the concern and compassion you feel for a friend to yourself.

In the second column, write at least two sentences that vigorously dispute the Inhibiting Thought in column one. We'll call these Healing

My Inhibiting Thoughts	Healing Thoughts
I shouldn't eat so much. I'm fat and tacky-looking.	I haven't been chubby in years. My weight is within normal range. And my husband thinks I'm cute.
I'm a terrible dancer. I'll never improve. I'm just clumsy.	My brother called me "klutz," but I don't trip over things or fall down or anything like that. I never learned to dance, but I know I could.

1. _____   _____

2. _____   _____

3. _____   _____

4. _____   _____

5. _____   _____

Thoughts because they encourage you to try things you've been avoiding, to have more adventures and fun, and to live a freer, more exuberant life. Two examples are included to start you off. The format above is just a suggestion; create one of your own in your journal.

The next part of this exercise is the hardest. It's also the part that makes it work, so don't skip it! Promise yourself right now that when these half-dozen Inhibiting Thoughts come up in your life, you will use the Healing Thoughts you just wrote down to overcome them. Read the Healing Thoughts over, say them out loud, and resolve that the very next time an Inhibiting Thought puts you in a straitjacket, you will promptly and vigorously replace it with your custom-made Healing Thought.

You may find that you have more than six Inhibiting Thoughts you would like to tackle. Don't try to take on too much—that's a great way to end up overwhelmed. Take your time, and rest assured that as you work on a few Inhibiting Thoughts at a time, you're also retraining your mind to think in healthier, more positive ways. Be patient with yourself.

Expanding your possible choices becomes infinitely simpler when you can identify and change the thought habits that stand between you and your true self. Inhibiting Thoughts are powerful solely because of their long-standing repetition, but they are just habits and, as such, are made to be changed! The way to change any habit is to replace it with a healthier one, which is the idea behind Healing Thoughts.

✦ THE OPTIMISM TEST

Take a look at the overall pattern of your thoughts. For each number, circle *a* or *b* for the item that most closely matches the way you think.

Am I…

1. a. focusing on my health and working to keep myself healthy?

   b. worrying about illness and focused on how sick I feel?

2. a. worrying about poverty and the possessions I lack?

   b. thinking about what I already have and feeling grateful to have it?

3. a. living with a degree of contentment and happiness?

   b. driving myself crazy because I'm not perfect?

4. a. thinking of a way out of meeting my responsibilities?

   b. looking for creative solutions that meet my responsibilities and make me happy?

5. a. thinking about things that make me feel alive and filled with energy?

   b. agonizing about how exhausted I am?

6. a. feeling impatient and frustrated?

   b. enjoying the moment?

7. a. spending time relaxing and feeling calm?

   b. feeling irritable and angry most of the time?

8. a. thinking of revenge and getting even?

    b. able to let go?

9. a. bothered by what others think of me?

    b. contented with the things I do and the way I am?

10. a. open to listening to others' opinions?

    b. trying to make people see things my way?

11. a. feeling cynical and critical most of the time?

    b. feeling easygoing and carefree most of the time?

12. a. trusting that most people are basically good?

    b. thinking people are out to get me?

Positive answers:
1–a, 2–b, 3–a, 4–b, 5–a, 6–b, 7–a, 8–b, 9–b, 10–a, 11–b, 12–a.

Count up the number of positive answers you gave. That's your score.

0–2: You are highly pessimistic. The world seems very hard and unfair. You get depressed frequently.

3–5: You are fairly pessimistic. You might call yourself a realist. You often feel down and discouraged.

6–8: You are on the fence between optimism and pessimism. Your feelings change with each situation, so you may feel uncertain. You may not trust your intuitions.

9–10: You are quite optimistic. Things generally turn out well, and you don't worry much.

11–12: You are highly optimistic. Things go well for you, and you feel confident that things are meant to go well. You may find it hard to understand pessimists, who seem to be trying to spoil your fun.

Optimism and pessimism are reactions to the way life treats us. If children start out with a loving family, enough to eat, and comfortable shelter, they may feel the world is a safe and stable place that has room for them. Starting out with a deficiency in love, attention, food, or shelter teaches children that there is no place for them in the world, creating a negative expectation that their world will always be one of want. Some people come to pessimism in reaction to traumatic life events, but others become optimistic—even happy!—after having survived a heart attack or a serious bout of cancer. Again, it's how we choose to interpret our lives that makes the difference in the quality of our lives. To one person, a heart attack may be a near-death experience signaling the beginning of the end, but to someone else, it may be a chance at a brand-new life. The interesting thing is that someone who was once hugely negative may be completely changed for the better by having a frightening brush with death.

TERI'S STORY

Teri was pretty, popular, sociable, and smart. She had a lot of friends in college and was having a lot of fun. One weekend she went to Big Bear for skiing, and on the way back, she and her friend were the last car to pass through before the road closed behind them because of the snow. Their car rolled over, and there was no one to come along and rescue them. The two young women were trapped under the car for four days.

Lying in the snow, Teri found a strength she never knew she had. She remembered things her father had said about "toughing it out," and while her friend quickly became hysterical and desperate, Teri managed to hang onto the idea of survival. It was an odd thing, she said later, when she was at my workshop, but she'd never really gotten along with her father. But when the chips were down, it was his attitude—his words—that helped keep her positive, focused, and alive.

When they were finally rescued, Teri's severe injuries caused her to lose both her legs. She'd always taken them for granted, and not being very athletic, she always thought of her legs as just the things that got her from one place to another. Now they were gone, and Teri had to start doing physical therapy. She got involved with a prosthetic service, learned to walk, and then started running.

Before the accident, Teri hadn't often needed to look inside and ask herself what she was good at. She was a social butterfly, and intro-spection didn't come easily. But after the accident, she discovered that she really loved to use her body. She became a professional ath-lete and a spokesperson for a major sportswear brand. With a lot of determination and inspiration, Teri turned a devastating event into a brand-new life.

✦ ACTING AS IF

While it's easy for us to imagine that negative people have negative things happen to them (in fact, we sort of like to think that that's what happens), it takes a different sort of thinking to understand that we create by our thoughts not only our internal reality, but an actual impact on the world as well. Psychologists have discovered that when people are unhappy, smiling actually makes them feel better. It seems that smiling (whether you feel like it or not) increases the levels of serotonin in the brain, making you feel hap-pier with one simple move. Therapists often teach their clients this idea, which is called acting "as if." It is a powerful example of optimism at work, for it takes only a few tries to learn that smiling with your face can make you feel like smiling with your heart. That's the internal magic. The external magic comes about when a consistent lifestyle of expecting good things draws good things into your life.

Teachers such as Leo Buscaglia and Deepak Chopra have told us that the way to success in any realm—the interpersonal, the financial, or the spiritual—involves the focused application of hope. By *hope*, they do not mean our wishes for material possessions but the sustained, courageous gut feeling that something good is happening Right Now. Leo Buscaglia was famous for hugging strangers, certain that they needed his love and willing to take the risk that they would hug him back. Sometimes he was rebuffed, but mostly he was not. He lived in an optimistic, cheerful world where any-thing was possible, even that two strangers might meet in a loving embrace.

His expectation, his hope that the world would be welcoming and caring created that welcome for him all over the world.

Leo Buscaglia had a rare courage; most of us don't have the ego reserves to risk being rejected on a daily basis. It's just too hard! But we can find our way to courage one small step at a time by targeting particular thoughts, changing some of our behaviors, and paying attention to the results we get, the results we feel. We can start by identifying the things that hold us back from taking risks. Why don't we hug more people? What thoughts keep us playing it safe? What are the worries that hold us back? In the next section, you'll learn how to pinpoint and change Inhibiting Thought patterns into your true self's expression of positive hope.

Patterns of Inhibiting Thoughts, and Their Antidotes

There are different types of negative thinking, and with the human capability for multitasking, many of us can do them simultaneously. Which ones do you find cropping up in your life again and again? Which ones are you free of? Which ones would you like to give up?

✦ NEGATIVE EXPECTATIONS

Chicken Little is a storybook hen who was convinced that the sky was falling. She ran to everyone she knew, screaming that the heavens would soon be crashing heavily onto their heads. The sky never did fall, but Chicken Little had to start taking anti-anxiety drugs and was in therapy for years. Negative thinking, whether we broadcast our views or keep silent, never makes the world a better place to live, and it frequently ruins a perfectly good day.

The Antidote: When you find yourself assuming the worst, stop immediately and replace the negative picture in your mind with something positive. When your boss says, "Step into my office," set aside "Oh, now what did I do?" and think, "I'll bet she noticed what a great job I did on the XYZ project."

SYLVIA'S SAD STORY

Sylvia was a classic conclusion-jumper, and she invariably assumed the worst. When her boyfriend invited her to dinner at the nicest restaurant in town, she became immediately apprehensive. She called her sister, wailing into the phone.

"Bob's taking me to Chez Panisse Saturday night," she moaned. "He's going to dump me, I can feel it." Her sister tried to console her, but Sylvia didn't listen to her. She stood Bob up that night, and when he called her for the sixth time, she finally answered the phone.

He was boiling. "Where the hell were you?" he demanded. "I waited for you for nearly an hour."

"What do you care?" she answered. "Maybe I didn't feel like letting you ditch me over dinner, so I ditched you first." There was a long silence on the other end, and then Bob started to laugh.

"You dope," he chortled. "I wasn't going to break up with you at Chez Panisse; I was going to ask you to go to Hawaii with me!"

Lucky for Sylvia, Bob had a sense of humor and knew her well enough to follow up with her.

✦ HELPLESSNESS

This particular thought pattern is insidious; we first encounter helplessness when we are children and really are fairly helpless. As adults, the daily news reinforces our helpless feelings. ("There are bad things happening and there's nothing I can do about it.") When we get into the habit of thinking helplessly, we open the door to hopelessness and depression.

The Antidote: Action is the cure for helplessness! It might mean pursuing a cause, perhaps donating your time to something you care about, such as the environment or community service. It might mean helping animals or other people. When you take action, even if it's stuffing envelopes for your favorite charity, you put your positive energy into the universe—and make a difference!

ROGER'S STORY

Roger was the king of helplessness. He had given up on everything: relationships, getting a decent job, working out, anything that would better his life. He ate corned-beef hash out of the can and fell asleep in his clothes night after night. He was always sick or tired or both, until one day he rescued a kitten from some boys who were tormenting it. He took the little thing home, fed it with an eyedropper and a tiny spoon, and made an appointment with the vet. He named his cat Ferdinand and watched the scrawny kitten grow into a plump, self-satisfied cat.

For his part, Ferdinand sat on Roger's lap, demanded attention at sunrise, and hung around the house doing cute feline things. Roger, seeing the difference he'd made in Ferdie's life, started volunteering as a placement coordinator at an animal shelter and found that he wasn't helpless at all. He found reserves of determination he'd never known he possessed. A year later, he received an award from the shelter for placing more animals than anyone before him had.

◆ JUDGMENT

Especially in the realm of the educated, judging others starts out as an entertainment but quickly becomes a nasty habit guaranteed to make judgmental people disliked by those they disdain. Sometimes people learn judging behaviors from perfectionistic parents. Some people act judgmentally because they themselves have something to hide, and accusing someone else seems like a safe hiding-place. Some people judge others from a position of privilege: because they are of a higher status or have more education than most people, they feel they have the right to dictate what's right and wrong.

The Antidote: Stop any judgmental thoughts as soon as they happen. Ideally, find something nice to say to yourself about the person whom you were just judging, but if you can't think of something nice, then picture yourself crossing out what you just said in your mind. If you're alone, you should do this out loud, saying something such as, "I don't want to be so mean about

So-and-So. I didn't mean what I just said." You might even mentally apologize to that person.

Prevent making judgments by actively seeking the best in other people. Be like Melanie in *Gone with the Wind*, who, when she was told that Scarlett was chasing all the men at the party (as well as Melanie's fiancé, Ashley), said something like, "Nonsense! She's just high-spirited, that's all!"

PAUL'S STORY

Paul had an opinion on everything, and he was never fazed by new situations. His wife and kids, who knew him best, knew that his snap judgments tended to turn into long-lasting prejudices. Some years ago, his older son, who attended college in a nearby town, arranged to bring his girlfriend to dinner to "meet the family." They had been dating for six months, and he was serious about the girl. But right after the introductions were made, his father mouthed off.

"So," he boomed, "Dan tells me you're going to be a psychologist! What's the matter—couldn't get into med school?"

Dan married his girlfriend a few years later, and Paul didn't understand why they brought his grandchildren by only on Christmas. He said his daughter-in-law was "standoffish." After he retired, he noticed more and more that he didn't really have friends and that it was hard to strike up conversations with strangers. His wife didn't listen to him anymore; she just nodded and said, "Okay, honey."

As for his sons, the "smart one" said he was too busy with work, and the "crybaby" had avoided his harsh criticisms since childhood. It hurt Paul's feelings that his sons didn't like to be with him, but he didn't know what to do about it.

✦ COMPETITIVENESS

Competition is the essence of the capitalistic society, and American children are taught to compete as a major part of their education. But competing means sometimes losing and always feeling on trial. Competitive thinkers have few real friends because they drive people away by always wanting to be the best at everything, the best in every crowd.

The Antidote: Remember how you felt the last time you lost at something, anything at all? You probably felt stupid, embarrassed, like a loser. Now, realize that when you insist on competing, you create those bad feelings in others. Avoid competitive entertainment, and catch yourself when you try to top someone conversationally or socially. Practice backing away from always having to win, and learn what it feels like to not be on top. Finally, practice cooperative arts, such as dancing with a partner. Working with someone toward a common goal is the best way to understand the value of cooperation.

RICHARD'S STORY

Richard used to be an extremely competitive guy, so competitive that he had lost important friendships over friendly games of poker. At work he was known as cutthroat and merciless to anyone who stood between him and the vice presidency. His attitude backfired when he was passed over because, as the president told him, "No one trusts you enough to work for you." That changed Richard's life. Suddenly he was faced with the realization that he couldn't be the best, because when it came to teamwork and cooperation, he was the absolute worst. He set about changing his ways.

He started by letting his eight-year-old son beat him at chess, something he'd never allowed to happen, reasoning that he didn't want to pamper the kid. When he saw the glow in his son's eyes, he realized what he'd been missing, and the two discussed the entire game with the passion of champions. Richard realized that his son didn't have to lose every game in order to learn from the experience.

Next, with the help of a good counselor, Richard started modifying his behavior at work. He learned to stop interrupting people at meetings, and he joined the company volleyball league even though he was awful at volleyball. He learned to be a gracious loser. He also started practicing supporting his coworkers when they had great ideas or successful strategies. Along the way, people started trusting him, and he discovered for the first time what it meant to work in a happy environment. He'd never realized before that his work had felt so draining because he'd always been on his guard and looking for weaknesses in others. Richard's life became more pleasant, and he was easier to get along with, which made his wife happy, too. Today, Richard laughs about it. "When I stopped playing by my old dog-eat-dog rules, I won the game!"

◆ BLACK-AND-WHITE THINKING

It's easy to fall into black-and-white thinking, because all of its rules are established; there's no need to grapple with the nuances of decision-making. That is an extremely seductive place to be—wouldn't we all love the simplicity of knowing what's right at all times? But this sort of thinking leaves no room for flexibility, for new situations, or for other people, who may have their own take on reality. Reality isn't easy, and one of the responsibilities of being human is that you must be able to change when the situation demands it.

The Antidote: Experiment with change! Shake things up a bit by having dessert first, by wearing mismatched socks, by varying your routine. Ask yourself, "What happens if I don't do my laundry on Friday? What if I decide to do it Wednesday instead?" or "What if I do let my kid stay up an extra half-hour instead of rushing her into bed right after I've done the dinner dishes?" By making small changes, you open yourself up to the possibility of big changes. Like any muscle, your mental flexibility may need slow stretching, and with gradually increasing exercise it will accomplish greater feats.

MONICA'S STORY

Monica's husband died last fall, and she moved into a smaller apartment. Soon she found that she wasn't sure what to do with her time—Harold had been in poor health for the past seven years, and her life had centered around taking care of him. Now she wandered around her apartment, trying to figure out what to do next. Her daughter asked Monica to come stay with her, with the idea that babysitting the grandchildren would keep Monica busy and happy, and Monica nearly said yes. But she took the time to sit down and think about what she wanted her life to be.

"I was married at twenty and kept house for Harold. Then the children came along, and we spent twenty years raising them. These past years, I was everything for Harold. It seems like I've spent my whole life taking care of other people. Is that how I want the rest of my life to be?"

It would have been so easy to go live with her daughter. They had a great relationship, and Monica liked her daughter's husband and adored her grandchildren. Taking care of others was what she was used to—what she'd always done. But it was too easy! She decided she needed a big change.

So Monica, at fifty-eight years of age, signed up for a two-year stint in the Peace Corps. She didn't go as a teacher or a social worker; she went as an agricultural technician and spent her days helping a small South American village plan and create a composting and irrigation system that doubled their maize crop. She lived with four other Peace Corps volunteers in a mud shack and participated fully in village life. She was greatly respected as an older women in the village and formed close ties with other women, who wondered what it would be like to pull up stakes and move to a new country with no family or friends around.

When Monica returned to the U.S., she entered the university to work on a degree in agriculture, with the specific goal of finding new ways to feed the hungry people of the Third World.

✦ MIND READING

We all attempt mind reading once in a while, and some of us are better at it than others. People from abusive homes are particularly good at discerning the mood of a room or an individual, as mind reading can be a highly effective safety tool for someone who might need to escape a potentially volatile situation. However, the habit of mind reading can be stressful and harmful, as we imagine the worst about someone else's thoughts and react to what we expect rather than what we may actually encounter. Mind reading rarely discerns the positive, and it is another form of expecting the worst.

The Antidote: Like negative thinking, mind reading is usually a case of making negative assumptions. Check your perceptions against reality by asking people you trust to confirm or disconfirm your ideas. For example, if a friend seems distant and you aren't sure why, don't automatically assume it's because of something you did. Ask her, "Are you mad at me?" and listen carefully to her answer. If the answer is "No, but I had a fight with my kid today, and the dog peed on the carpet, and I'm really tired," you can relax: it's not you!

Another antidote for mind reading is thought stopping. When you find yourself ruminating about what another person may think of you, tell yourself, gently and firmly, to stop. Turn your attention to something else. Do it again and again, and your habit will change.

✦ HANG IN THERE

Persistence is the essence of changing negative thought habits! Expect to challenge and change any one negative thought twenty times a day. Remember when you first started driving, and it seemed you would never learn all the rules, all the road signs, and all the quirky shifts of the car? But soon it became easier, and now it's automatic. Changing your thoughts is like learning to drive—you are acquiring a new set of skills, which you will build into a new habit: a habit that will empower you and make you happier. So keep at it, because success is just around the corner.

Losing the Victim Mentality

Words are fascinating because we consciously choose which ones to say, but once spoken, they act on a subconscious level. Speaking positively about life helps life actually become more positive because the things that we say remove our self-imposed constraints. When I say, "I have to walk three miles today or I'll get fat all over again," I'm treating myself as a victim of my weight. I'm trapping myself into walking three miles, and I'm planning to resent those miles. It takes little effort to turn that statement into something positive and empowered: "I get to walk three miles today and keep my trim figure!" That's a happier thing to say and it's also a truer thing to say. I'm not being forced at gunpoint to walk those miles; I'm making a choice to do something healthy for my body. I'm not a victim; I'm a purposeful being.

Everyone whines sometimes, and everyone feels sorry for himself once in a while, too. Sometimes it feels like the universe is conspiring to ruin your day. And some social systems encourage us to feel victimized by suggesting that we are entitled to feel like victims, and that there's some ultimate pay-off. There are millions of support groups and chat rooms where people gather to discuss just how hard the world has been to them.

Support is a fine thing when it's constructive and helps a person move past feeling or being victimized, but many people get stuck in the feeling of perpetual victimhood. From the first fairy tales we hear as children, we learn that the beautiful princess who lives in poverty is eventually rescued by the handsome prince, so it's no wonder that people who feel like victims get stuck—they're waiting for their ship to come in. The only catch is, they're waiting at the train station! Victimhood is the ultimate way to give up personal power, to lose sight of purpose, and to deny the true self. If the victim mentality becomes a habit, it guarantees a life of pain. If you sense that you feel victimized and speak in ways that encourage your own helplessness, it's time to start making different choices. Start with the way you talk.

MY SYNERGY JOURNAL | *The Victim Mentality*

Make a list of things in your life that you think were or are unfair to you. Then write a paragraph or so about the effects of that unfairness in your life. Next, find some positive effects, however tiny, that came from the initial unfairness, and write them down. Finally, write down something you can do now to move past feeling victimized. Here's an example.

What's unfair: *Poverty.*

The effects: *My parents were poor and had to work really hard just to keep us housed and fed. I wore ragged clothes, and the other kids made fun of me at school. My parents couldn't afford to give me a good education, and I barely graduated from high school. I feel like a dummy because I never went to college—I had to go to work instead.*

The positive effect(s): *I grew up pretty self-reliant. I'm a hard worker, which I learned from my folks. I don't need much to live on, so I'm freer than people who think that nice clothes and cell phones are necessities of life. And I'm closer to my dad since I started working. We hang out on weekends or go to ballgames and talk about our jobs. If I'd gone to college, I never would have been able to spend time with Dad—he was always at work.*

What I can do now: *The lack-of-education thing bothers me, and I know construction workers are usually pretty worn out physically by the time they hit forty. I could check into taking night classes at the local junior college—maybe get my B.A.*

Your life is precious—it's the one thing that is truly yours. You can control it, make something of it, give it to someone else, or give it up. Happiness is a choice you make every minute of every day. Don't let the outside world determine your choices or your capacity for joy.

Being happy takes determination and vigilance. A wonderful example of determined happiness is seen in the following story. You have to mow the lawn, so while you do it, you lock your puppy in the garage. At first, the puppy wants to be with you, where the action is. He whines and scratches at the door. After a while he might even start those ear-piercing yips or howls. Then he gets bored, goes into the house, and starts to investigate the kitchen. He turns over the trash and roots through it for a snack. He grabs the shirt you left hanging on the doorknob and tears it apart with playful teeth, shaking his head and growling. Periodically he remembers that he misses you and does some more scratching and howling. By the time you're done with the lawn, you're wiped out and the garage and house are wrecked. Your puppy's standing in the middle of chaos, delighted to see you. He's had a marvelous time.

Be like the puppy. If you find yourself locked into a situation you don't want, explore everything, scratch at all the doors, and find ways to amuse yourself until you can get free. Have a marvelous time.

Playbacks from Wayback

Inhibiting Thoughts are our attempts to gain control over events by preventing old stressors and bad past experiences from repeating themselves. Like overprotective parents, Inhibiting Thoughts try to stop us from wandering into bad situations, from taking chances or incurring emotional risks. Memories of things that went wrong in childhood inspire Inhibiting Thoughts, which act as policemen, saying "You can't, you shouldn't, remember when you tried this before?" So don't hate your Inhibiting Thoughts, and don't dislike yourself for having them, because they are just trying to take care of you in the only way they know. But you don't need them, and they get in your way. No one functions best in an atmosphere of fear and guilt, which is what Inhibiting Thoughts create. So when you encounter one, recognize it, thank it for its well-meaning advice, and replace it with a cheerful, present-focused Healing Thought.

Painful events from our past also give birth to what I call our Playbacks from Wayback. They cause worry, tension, sadness, and anger, as we relive unhappy moments over and over. In general, Playbacks come from events that took place when we were children, often with parents, teachers, or other kids. The greatest impact is made by parents, who effectively build a child's world and interpret reality for the child until the child is grown. Getting negative messages at home guarantees we'll leave home with a lot more baggage than we can fit into an old VW Bug!

Playbacks from Wayback are the antithesis to living Right Now, because they drag us kicking and screaming into the past. The Dalai Lama and Thich Nhat Hanh are two examples of masters who teach the importance of living Right Now. Thich Nhat Hanh, in *Peace Is Every Step*, teaches readers that the only real moment is the moment that happens now and that the path to contentment can be followed as simply as appreciating the moment. Remember how utterly possible it is to choose to return to the present. Participate in Right Now, and you will find yourself more centered and more satisfied. Stop reading, look around the place where you sit, and find something you like. It might be a flower or a postcard or the open window. Just take a minute to appreciate the colors, the sounds, and the smells that surround you right now. That is present-moment living, and it is the perfect antidote to Playbacks from Wayback.

JOE'S STORY

Joe was born to a military family that moved six times before he was eight. Every year, he was the new kid on the block, the new kid in school. He learned to fight on the playground, but he was still the target of every bully, so he fought a lot. His teachers never remembered his name and the other kids treated him like what he was—an alien. Joe was naturally shy, and as he got older, he stopped even trying to make friends, reasoning that he'd just move away and leave them anyway. His family continued to move until his father retired in Joe's second year of high school.

Suddenly, the family was settled. Joe's dad got a regular job, and his mom started buying furniture for the house they'd just bought. Joe had to figure out a new way to go to school, since his old strategies had been to keep to himself and do just enough to get by. Before, when he had had a problem with a teacher or another kid, he'd always had the security of knowing that the school year would end and he would move to another state, but now he was stuck. He solved his dilemma by studying hard and graduating early.

But Joe's first job mirrored his school experiences. He was once again the new kid. He was cool, standoffish, and self-sufficient. He was also lonely and scared, because he was sure people didn't like him. His Playbacks were in full force, and going to sales conferences vividly recalled the torture of being forced by teachers to introduce himself to his classmates. He felt his coworkers talked down to him or ignored him like kids did in high school, although in fact, they were trying to be helpful. When he reacted too defensively to suggestions, they retreated and left him alone.

After reading a book called Military Brats, Joe learned that many military kids have problems connecting with people because they moved too often to ever really get close and stay close to others. After thinking about the number of people he knew and the fact that he kept feeling attacked, he realized the problem was mostly his. He sat down and thought about his Playbacks from Wayback and realized that if he didn't do something proactive and positive, he'd end up alone. He wanted friends and needed to learn how to make them. He needed his job and wanted to be able to enjoy it. He did a lot of journalizing about things he didn't like about his past and things he wanted for his present. He started paying attention to ways he could connect with people. He used affirmations, saying things such as "I'm not a kid anymore" and "I like to meet new people and learn new things." He started catching himself when he felt threatened and defensive, and he learned to react more optimistically at work. Despite his shyness, he attended every seminar, every party, and every event he heard about. He even joined the company bowling league! Bit by bit, Joe built a life filled with friends, activity, and connection. His lonely childhood was put to rest.

◆ REFOCUSING ON THE PRESENT

Being aware of negative thought patterns and committing to changing them is a terrific starting point for overcoming negative messages from the past. Inhibiting Thoughts are usually leftovers from childhood, and current situations may trigger responses from us that are based more on the past than on the present. When all the old, painful feelings flood over you, it's difficult to react with a present-based focus. When we find ourselves in situations reminiscent of old, unhappy events, we react to the overwhelming strength of the old event rather than to the relatively mild current event. It's almost as if a switch is thrown, turning on a tape from the past and blotting out what's happening in the Now. These Playbacks from Wayback are powerful and upsetting occurrences; after experiencing one, people may say things such as, "I felt like I was six years old again and trapped in the living room with all these people telling me to sing. It was horrible!"

You may recognize a Playback by the feeling of suddenly being younger, overwhelmed, or out of control, or the person you are with may suddenly remind you strongly of someone from your past. The situation may feel like a bad dream. Remember, Playbacks come from childhood, when we didn't have much say in what happened to us. Playbacks cause us to forget that we have more choices in adulthood than we did in childhood; in the midst of overpowering emotions, it's hard to think or to make rational decisions. We may feel like throwing a tantrum, or we may freeze in place.

If you find yourself caught in a Playback, the best thing to do is take a break from the current situation, get calmed down (by breathing, by replacing Inhibiting Thoughts with Healing ones, or by using Affirmations, which we will cover later in this book, in the "Step Four" chapter). When you have pulled yourself into the present again, you can tackle the situation that once so strongly reminded you of the past.

Your Body's Link to Playbacks

The first key to understanding your Playbacks is listening to your body. Often, when you are not consciously aware of a Playback, your body lets you know that something's wrong. Some people experience Playbacks in sudden physical symptoms such as headaches, neck or back problems, nervous tics, or tension in the stomach. You may discover that certain pains represent particular Playbacks. When you identify a physical symptom that occurs alongside a nagging feeling, you have spotted a Playback. When it happens, take a moment to wonder at the miraculous nature of your mind/body connection. What a smart body you have, one that can alert you to the subtle workings of your mind!

What we resist persists, and what we leave undone festers. When I have a headache, I relax and focus on it; I give it attention by zeroing in on the center of the pain. I clearly identify the center point. I identify its color, shape, and size and then ask the headache if it's satisfied with my attention. Most of the time it dissipates, satisfied that I have received its message.

Sometimes, when I am talking to someone, I feel a cold shiver or get a nose itch, an itchy eye, or an itchy spot on my body that needs to be scratched. I know my body is responding to subconscious thoughts and reacting defensively to the person or situation. The subconscious mind and body can often recognize a situation that is similar to a past experience. Listening and responding to our emotional responses and bodily reactions is a Life Mastery tool for keeping us in the present moment.

✦ WHEN THE BODY REBELS

Marty's father taught him well. Boys aren't supposed to cry, and when Marty was little, his father would shake him hard and roughhouse until the boy was in tears. Then he'd be punished for crying. Marty had an early memory of playing football as a kid. He got hit so hard that it knocked the wind out of him, and he lay on the ground trying to figure out which way was up. His father ran onto the field, ran over to his son, and screamed at him to get off the ground.

Marty grew up macho, and arrogance covered up how worthless he felt. He did okay at work but never really made a success of himself, which fueled his feelings of being a loser. No one knew his weaknesses because he didn't talk about them, not even when he started having strange muscular pains. He never told a soul, not even his wife.

Multiple sclerosis eventually caused him enough problems that he was forced to admit he needed help. As his body grew weaker and less reliable, his spirit strengthened. He learned to reject his father's evaluation of him as a weakling, and as he started to accept his unavoidable physical weakness, he watched his business start to take off. The failure that his father had created in his mind no longer held Marty down. He is sometimes in a wheelchair now, but he keeps his symptoms in check by controlling his negative Playbacks. In some ways, Marty has been terribly unlucky, but in others, he's luckier than many men. He no longer has to pretend to an importance he never felt: he is a worthy, significant person, and he knows it. So he's also luckier than his father ever was.

Deal with physical symptoms as soon as possible after they arise. Trying to "push through" a headache or strange joint pain because you have to complete a project usually ends up taking more time than ducking outside for five minutes to close your eyes, feel the sun on your face, and reconnect with Right Now. Whenever you possibly can, pay attention to your Play-backs—it'll save you time and energy in the long run.

Playbacks from Wayback tie up your present self, and accompanying In-hibiting Thoughts pull in the reins of your creativity and possible joy. That doesn't mean that anyone who has Playbacks from Wayback can't be happy! But to free yourself from Playbacks from Wayback requires a commitment to decrease Inhibiting Thoughts and change negative thought patterns that arise from your past. Creating synergy requires a present-moment focus, which means that the less history you relive, the freer you are to engage in and enjoy Right Now!

Other People's Playbacks

The second key to understanding Playbacks from Wayback involves your perceptions of others. Everyone has Playbacks; virtually no one is exempt. If you have problems relating to someone who seems to expect the worst from you or hold a grudge against you, who isn't hearing what you actually said or who is reacting with more emotion than the situation calls for, stop and realize that this person may be caught in the grip of a Playback. Rather than trying to reason with someone who's wrestling past demons, it might be bet-ter to take a break and come back to the discussion when everyone has calmed down. Sometimes there's not much another person can do about a Playback, so the most important thing you can do is to try to have compas-sion for the other person. If it's your Playback that is causing trouble, rec-ognize it, by all means, but also cut yourself a break. Again, apply the com-passion you would feel for a friend in a tight spot to yourself.

JOAN AND FRED'S STORY

Joan and Fred have been dating steadily for four months. They see each other once a week and are beginning to get close. The relation-ship feels nice, and Joan tells Fred that she wishes they could see each other twice a week. Now, although Fred actually has been thinking the same thing, he suddenly perceives that Joan is reciprocating his inter-est and acting on it before he's ready to act. However, he goes even farther than that; he now sees her as "chasing" him, and he feels frightened. Other women have tried to chase him, to "trap" him. She must want a commitment: his very way of life, his freedom, is threatened! He interprets Joan's request for a second date a week as her "desperation," so he withdraws. He doesn't even call her the next Friday (their usual date night).

Joan has been here before. She's dated men who disappeared into the sunset as soon as she expressed interest in them, and she doesn't intend to go through that experience again. She feels hurt and humiliated, not just about Fred but about Roger and Travis and Daniel and three or four other guys from her past (ranging back to junior high school). She doesn't stop to think about why Fred might be overreacting. She throws away all the little gifts he's given her, and when he does call (to apologize and make up) the following Friday, she doesn't answer the phone. He calls several times over the next week, but she ignores his messages. She never sees him again.

In this example, both people are caught in their Playbacks. Fred's experience of feeling "chased" or "trapped" coincides with his belief that the man should make the decisions about how fast and how far a relationship should proceed. It isn't Joan's idea but his own fear that causes him to avoid her until he finally realizes that his old Playback is interfering with his present and future happiness with an extremely nice woman.

Joan's reaction to her Playback prevents her from picking up the phone when Fred calls. Sure, he has acted like a jerk, and she has every reason to be upset with him. But she ends the relationship because she can't see beyond her past and into the present situation with Fred, who has not actually run away; he has just hidden out for a while.

This story could easily have a happy ending. When Fred calls back, Joan picks up the phone, listens to his apology, and reacts coolly (after all, Joan's only human, and he has ignored her for a solid week). But they start talking, and keeping in mind their own fears, they also start to understand each other's fears. Fred realizes he has overreacted and admits that he would like to see Joan more often, but that he has been freaked out about the idea of standing two-nights-a-week dates. Joan accepts that and ventures that she might be happy with a second weekly date on a more random basis. She also lets him know that she needs to hear from him by Wednesday if they are going out at all, and Fred promises to call on Wednesdays, come hell or high water.

By attending to their Playbacks but acting with a present-moment focus, Joan and Fred could negotiate themselves right into a better relationship, weather their first storm, and build a foundation for trusting each other.

Rewinding and Retaping to Prevent Playbacks

Have you ever ended a relationship that you now think might have been a good one to keep? Use this journalizing exercise to rethink it in terms of your Playbacks.

Who was the relationship with?

_____

How long had you known this person? How close were you to him/her?

_____

What happened to make you want to end it?

_____

How did you end it?

_____

What would you tell someone else was the reason that you ended it?

_____

What was the *actual* reason you ended it?

_____

What are some other choices you might have made?

_____

_____

If this situation arose now with someone else, how would you handle it differently?

_____

_____

_____

Sometimes we can't go back to relationships we ended with particular people, but life has an uncanny way of presenting us with new people in old scenarios. Recognizing your Playbacks and refusing to let them ruin your future relationships is a healthy way to connect with others and form better relationships throughout your life. Every time you choose a new response to an old and harmful tape, you increase your chances of participating in Right Now, connecting your responses to your present rather than to the past. Acknowledging the past keeps you from repeating old, harmful patterns of thought and behavior and helps you replace them with healthier, happier choices. Your conscious choice to participate fully in Right Now is the key to creating synergy in your present relationships.

Cleansing Your Inner Ecology

*Truly, the greatest gift you have to give is
that of your own self-transformation.*

LAO TZU

*If the mind is happy, not only the body, but
the whole world will be happy. So, one must find
out how to become happy oneself. Wanting to
reform the world without discovering one's true self
is like trying to cover the whole world with leather
to avoid the pain of walking on stones and thorns.
It is much simpler to wear shoes.*

RAMANA MAHARSHI

Your Personal Landscape

Take all the experiences of your life—your attitudes, wishes, and beliefs—and imagine yourself as a part of the physical world. Sit back and close your eyes, picturing what kind of landscape you would be. Are you a wind-swept desert with red-orange mesas under a burning blue sky? Or a lush forest filled with birds and monkeys and brightly colored flowers? Maybe you prefer to be a quiet, tree-lined street with peaceful, wide-porched homes and well-tended gardens. Take this moment to create in yourself a world that you find beautiful and compelling.

Once you've created this place, imagine how you would feel if someone trashed it, cut down the trees, littered the landscape with junk, and tore up the flowers. What would you do? Railing against injustice won't restore the environment. Turning away in anger or disgust will only leave you feeling helpless. You can't sue because there's no one here but you. The only thing to do is to clean it up! Plant new trees and build picnic tables out of the scraps of the old ones, or have a fabulous bonfire celebrating the night sky. Remove the trash, replace the flowers, and coax the monkeys down from the high tree branches where they've been crouched, silent with fear. You created this world, and it's your happy responsibility to care for it. As you work, you will discover that the joy you felt before the disaster is returning to you threefold, because you are re-creating beauty and working with hope and synergy.

Your Inner Ecology is just like this landscape: at first pure and perfect, it becomes littered with the refuse of everyday life. Negative feelings such as materialism, envy, jealousy, and guilt pile up in the inner landscape, obscuring the true self. Television inserts pictures of violence into our psyches, like hideous billboards along a rolling green plain. Pain and fear run rampant like weeds from a foreign world that devour the available resources and strangle indigenous wildlife. In the same way that you would clean up a park or a wilderness area with devotion and focused attention, your Inner Ecology can be cleansed, nurtured, and even rebuilt with time and the right tools.

Garbage on the Path

Most of the pollution in our Inner Ecology comes from comparisons: comparisons we were subjected to as children, and comparisons we learned to make for ourselves as adults. Expectations our parents had ("Why aren't you more like your brother?") grow into self-expectations ("Why does my coworker have a nicer house than I do?"), and we are tortured by the feeling of never having enough, never *being* enough. The things that trash your happiness are related to feeling a lack (notice that I don't say they're related to actually lacking something). Materialism tells us that we don't have enough stuff; jealousy cries that we are less loved than someone else; envy sneers that my life is insufficient compared to yours; and guilt pronounces us lacking in moral worth. We live with these obstacles and think them a normal part of life, but they distract us from what's important in life, and they act as trash strewn along a beautiful path. We are tripped up, twisted, and entangled by these ideas of inadequacy. Sometimes we are nearly suffocated by the garbage. But it's not something you have to live with—you can restore your path to its original purity, and a few simple maintenance skills can keep it cleared for life.

Think of synergy as fresh air. You need room for it to flow and circulate, and clear emotional spaces in which to honor and appreciate it when it comes into your life. Clearing the emotional path of harmful refuse leaves room for the needs of your true self, and room for the expansion of synergy.

✦ MATERIALISM

The most superficial comparisons to others result in materialism: we learn to buy things that proclaim our financial worth and make us feel superior to others. Since our economy is driven by consumerism and relies on producing shoppers, American culture values financial worth over everything else. Unfortunately, people who meet their basic needs and are satisfied with themselves tend not to care much about buying things, so the advertising industry creates "needs" that otherwise would not exist. In continuous and blatant fashion, we are told that we think slowly, make mistakes, are unappealing to others, look terrible, and smell bad. Once people have grown used to believing that their inner landscape is solely a reflection of their purchases, the switch from buying toothpaste and deodorant to buying big-ticket items such as SUVs and Vera Wang wardrobes is pretty simple.

Materialism makes everyone unhappy. For those who can afford the best toys, there's the initial high of buying something new, but the high wears off faster than the warranty, leaving them depressed and jaded. Those who can't afford more stuff but believe it's necessary for happiness are made miserable by their failure to acquire. Caught between luxury and poverty, many people spend their time and energy struggling for more and more money to feed our culture's addiction to material goods.

✦ JEALOUSY

Jealousy grows out of comparing relationships and believing that love, like all other precious commodities, is finite. In a way, jealousy is what happens when we apply our materialistic ideas about objects to people. If I consider your love a limited resource, I resent anyone else's claim on it, because that claim means less love for me. Small children feel jealous when a sibling is born because they can't conceive of love as being expansive. Many adults can't imagine it, either, especially if they come from families in which attention and approval were given out on a conditional basis or parents didn't have the emotional resources to adequately love their children.

In jealousy, the person we want becomes an object to be fought over rather than shared. But we rarely fight the contender; we fight the object! And through our fear and anger, we may end up driving away the person we want. Jealousy is like being a raccoon with one paw in a trap. The trap holds a shiny necklace glittering with beads. We grasp the necklace, but the trap, which was just big enough to reach into, is also just smaller than the circumference of a grasped fist. To get free, we have to drop the necklace. But in jealousy, the necklace is love, and we don't want to drop it, so we hold on tightly and are trapped by our own need.

Jealousy arises when we do not trust or do not know where we stand with another person. Distrust may be a Playback from Wayback, or it may be based on the fact that this person has let you down before. If your distrust is attached to a different relationship in another time, and you learn to recognize this fact, you can talk yourself through episodes of jealousy by reminding yourself that your feelings are a hangover from the past and irrelevant to this situation. If, on the other hand, you have a hard time trusting because this person has let you down before, you need to decide whether that disappointment was a one-time event or a pattern that will recur in this relationship. If you add up the evidence and decide that your jealousy is unwarranted (while realizing that you still feel jealous), then you will still want to pursue a healthy relationship. If the evidence looks bad and you realize that you don't trust this person because he or she can't be trusted, then you need to think about the reasons you're in this relationship.

✦ ENVY

Many people don't know the difference between jealousy and envy. They might say, "I'm so jealous of you!" when you get a great new job or terrific new hair-do, but they're actually talking about a mild envy that, within limits, is considered socially acceptable and might even make the other person feel good or special. Jealousy tends to be specifically about competing for the love and attention of another person, but envy is more insidious. Envy is competitive, a comparative process that constantly evaluates and measures what others have in life and what you don't.

A person who is inclined toward envy of others may have had a neglected childhood and goes through adult life with a Playback of unending need and resentment. She may present herself as a friend, vicariously experiencing the happy parts of others' lives, but she has a hidden need to see her friends feeling miserable. This is the friend or family member who arrives in the midst of your personal catastrophe and, while seeming helpful, actually manages to make you feel worse than you did before. Sitcoms are filled with such "friends," but they aren't funny in real life.

Envy is much more painful than it sounds because it represents emptiness of spirit. People who live with envy suffer endlessly, not only from the original feeling of internal emptiness but from the emptiness of their current relationships. When one person envies another, it is impossible to establish trust, so it's impossible to have a true friendship or a solid romance.

Even someone who started out with a happy, fulfilled childhood may end up envious—our culture promotes envy! Materialism is based on inspiring envy in others; although envy may be too deep an emotion to attach to wanting an automobile or washing machine, the idea behind advertising is that people obtain happiness and ongoing satisfaction through their purchasing power. The pictures of life presented by television may cause envy in people who don't have the kind of life imaginary TV people lead. It's hard to decide what's sadder: a nation of people envying each other, or a nation of people envying people who don't even truly exist.

Reducing normal envy may be as complicated as changing your entire spiritual base or as simple as unplugging that rotten TV. It really depends on how much you are affected by it and on how much pain it causes you.

We reduce feelings of envy by working on our relationship with ourselves. Caring for ourselves and understanding our own personal qualities shifts our sense of values: we begin to value competitiveness to inner growth. Envy is toxic not only to relationships but to you as a whole person. Constantly comparing yourself to others, constantly measuring what your life is against what you wish it would be, is exhausting emotional work. It is as if you have a companion who never leaves your side but spends all his time putting you down. The internal conversation sounds something like this:

> Gee, that SUV is so big I can't see around it. I won't be able to turn until she goes. Oh, look at that, she has an Irish setter with her. The setter's wearing a green bandanna around his neck, and he's holding a Frisbee in his mouth. I bet they're going to the beach. What a lucky dog. Dog, hell! Who is she that she gets to go to the beach on a Wednesday while I'm driving to work like a schmuck? She's either a dot-commer who made her million at twenty-four or she married one. What I'd give to have her life. Her life! I'd settle for her dog's life!

We've all had this conversation at one time or another, but like other negative thought patterns, the pattern of envy can become a seriously detrimental habit. If you have this sort of conversation with yourself every day, every day you are comparing yourself (your acquisitions, your lifestyle, and your perceived competence) to others and finding yourself lacking. Suppose I told you, "I'm going to fix you up with someone you get along with pretty well, and you're going to spend the rest of your life with this person. The only drawback is, this person will go everywhere with you and will criticize you every day. He (or she) will point out every person you run across who has more expensive possessions, will tell you all about the other person's happy and fulfilled life, and will generally remind you of everything you lack."

You'd probably tell me to stick it in my ear, right? Who wants to be with someone who makes you feel like a loser? Don't make yourself feel like a loser. Treat yourself as you would any friend for whom you want the best things in life. Remind yourself daily of what you have, not what you lack. Focus on the needs of your true self, the connection and present-moment happiness that come with being really alive, not the whims and desires of multimillion-dollar ad agencies. Notice that the times you're happiest tend to be simple moments of connection with other people, quiet times with yourself, or experiences with nature. Seek to increase those moments, and you will naturally stop worrying about what other people have.

CLAUDE'S STORY

Claude was a Haitian immigrant who came to New York to escape the grinding poverty of his family's home country. He couldn't speak English when he arrived, and he couldn't get a job, but one of his friends suggested an alternative career path, and Claude started selling drugs. He wasn't poor anymore, at least not financially, and he achieved his dream of owning a new Cadillac. But his ambition didn't stop there: he wanted his own territory. Maybe Claude moved too fast or wanted too much, because the people who held the territory he wanted for his own disagreed with his new career move. So they shot him.

The good news is, he lived! Claude decided New York was a little too harsh, so he moved to sunny California. But there he fell in love with a woman who was a drug user, and he started using drugs, too. I met him when he was in rehab, attending "A Day of Self-Esteem," a life-career program sponsored by Working Wardrobes. (This program helps people who've had problems with the law turn their lives around; it focuses not only on providing ideas and information on how to get a job and a new life but on how to put together a career-appropriate wardrobe so that they can dress for success.) Claude realized that his dream was no longer the Cadillac, but to put passion into his life. He wanted to help others, and now he works as a part-time speaker doing outreach at shelters and prisons.

Claude started out by trying to acquire a level of financial security, but he didn't know that money can do only so much for a person. He needed to find a focus that didn't jeopardize his physical security, and he needed to figure out that happiness can be found outside a large bank account. Once he reached that understanding, he became a happy, satisfied man and a positive contributor to the health and well-being of others.

✦ GUILT

Guilt is a two-edged sword: on the one hand, it is responsible for the misery of millions; on the other, it holds families together, keeps unbelievers in organized religions, and funds numerous charitable acts. How can something so damaging be so effective?

Okay, so I'm saying this a little tongue-in-cheek. Living with guilt is an unhappy existence and in many ways a false one, too, because it causes conflict between what you think you should do and what you actually do. Guilt is especially tough to deal with because we don't come by it naturally—there's no such thing as inborn guilt! We learn it at our parents' knees, we're taught it in our churches and schools, and if we don't break free of guilt, we pass it on to our own children because we just don't know any better.

Let's distinguish between guilt and conscience. A conscience is a useful and natural part of our mental makeup. If you've ever been around a two-year-old, you've realized that conscience is natural by the fact that the child knows when he's done something that's "wrong." When he does something wrong, he tries to cover it up or deny it, which proves that he knows it's wrong.

It's pretty much impossible to make a two-year-old feel guilty, on the other hand, because the beautiful thing about being two is that you don't hold with being manipulated. When you feel guilty, it's generally because someone has directly or indirectly *made* you feel guilty by telling you they are disappointed in you or will be disappointed in you unless you comply with their expectations. This process of learned guilt takes a little time, and two-year-olds don't listen very well, so they remain relatively guilt-free for a while. Guilt comes later in life, but not much later.

The main difference between guilt and conscience is that conscience is internal—it's dictated by what you know in your heart, by what your true self recognizes as right and wrong. When you act from your conscience, you feel right with the world, even if the world seems to be against you. Listening to your conscience is an important part of living the synergistic life, as your actions and daily activities express your spirit and intent.

Listening to guilt is quite another matter. Guilt is based on others' expectations and the demands that they place on you. It's not the voice of your conscience; it's the nagging voice of someone who wants something from you and uses your relationship to get you to do it, whether or not you necessarily should do it. Guilt is baggage handed to you by someone else, and you know what they say at the airports—don't take a bag that someone else has packed!

When you ignore or violate your conscience, it is an act of personal immorality and you feel ashamed. When you make choices that violate the wishes of someone else, you are "being selfish"—and you may feel guilty. But feeling guilty is different from feeling ashamed. Shame is a deeper, private feeling that is difficult to admit to, even to oneself. Shame is dark and internal and mysterious—Freud thought it came from our earliest toilet training and the disgust shown by our parents at the material expelled from our bodies. Abused children suffer terribly from shame, because it's impossible for them to understand that they didn't cause the abuse by being "bad." To some extent, we all have reserves of shame, some more vast and debilitating than others.

Guilt is painful and frustrating, but it's easier to cope with than shame. When you feel guilty, your true self nonetheless doesn't really recognize others' demands as a sufficient reason to feel bad, even though you may be socialized to feel bad on the surface. You might do something you're expected to do simply because, as a social creature, you don't enjoy the disapproval of others, not because you particularly think it's the right thing to do. In fact, guilt might even come from doing what the rest of the world says is "the right thing" when you know it's not right for you. During the Vietnam War, both conscientious objectors who went to jail and conscientious objectors who went to war were expressing their true selves, although some came home heroes and some came home felons. Society prefers heroes (even dead ones) to jailbirds, and surely some of these men felt guilty because they received messages from parents, society, and friends that their choices were wrong. But I doubt that they felt ashamed, because they were acting from their conscience. Guilt is a pervasive part of the human condition, but it's also as unique to each individual as our fingerprints. Guilt is thrust upon us, but we also make day-to-day choices about whether to accept the burdens of guilt. You can't stop others from trying to make you feel guilty, but you can decide how to react to their manipulative efforts.

Guilt can be challenged and dealt with, but too often you are told that you overcome guilt by confronting those who make you feel guilty. That doesn't work very well, for several reasons. First, the person who uses guilt to manipulate you probably has a history of successful manipulations through guilt. He has no motivation to change! Second, guilt is your response to someone else's demands, and changing your response is within your control—changing the other person is not. Third, guilt is a moral question for you and you alone. You have to decide whether to let someone else interpret your moral reality and whether you know your conscience well enough to take on the job yourself.

JANET'S STORY

Janet has an aged mother who lives alone in a large Chicago apartment. Her mother's health is frail from long years of smoking, but she has enough money and support from a local senior center that she can get access to home helpers and maid service. The problem is that she refuses to do it, saying she likes her apartment just the way it is. She rails at her daughters for not respecting her wishes when they offer to hire a housekeeper. Janet and her sister are stymied, as they live on the West Coast and can't keep an eye on their mother as much as they feel they should. If they could only feel assured that someone was watching out for her and that she was living in a tidy, clean place. But she is stubborn. Day after day, she sits alone in the dust and grime of her neglected apartment. Janet feels angry, stuck, and, above all, guilty. Her friends advise her to have the place cleaned top to bottom on her next visit, regardless of her mother's wishes. But if she does that, then she will be treating her mother like someone incapable of making her own choices. Her sister doesn't know what to do but says she'll help Janet if Janet will just make the decision. But it's a tough one: she can either let her mother live in filth or treat her like a stupid child.

Janet is up against a wall here. Two of her core values are in conflict—the value of cleanliness for health and the edict to honor her mother. The only decision she can make is the one she knows in her heart is best for her mother—nothing else will suffice, because if she chooses the wrong option, she will always know she didn't follow her conscience. In this case, Janet chooses to have the apartment cleaned. Here is her reasoning: "The easiest thing to do is to leave this whole thing alone. But it feels wrong. I am ashamed to let my mother live in dirt, and I think her reasoning in this matter is wrong.

"Cleaning the apartment will benefit Mom—her emphysema is worse in a dusty place. Also, no matter what she thinks now, I think it'll brighten her mood to have the apartment tidy and clean."

Janet also thinks about the possible outcome of her relationship with her mother.

"When I have the place cleaned, Mom will be angry with me, but it won't ruin our relationship. She's always wanted to be the boss, and with her aging, we'll surely fight other battles. She'll be mad for a couple of weeks, and then she'll probably get over it. At least in this case I'll know I did what felt right to me."

Thinking about it makes Janet realize that what she most fears is that her mother will be angry with her for disobeying her wishes. Once she looks carefully at her fear, however, she can see that it is out of proportion to what she can reasonably expect from her mother. She also realizes that loving her mother and pleasing her mother are two different things, and that while she values her mother's love, she can live with the idea of occasionally displeasing her. This understanding frees her to do what she thinks is right.

Religious Guilt

This kind of guilt is especially hard to handle because it arises from a combination of social and parental control. In Chaim Potok's *My Name Is Asher Lev*, a Hasidic boy wants to be an artist more than anything in the world, something that is not valued by his father or his culture. His father is a special emissary to the rebbe, their religious leader, and travels all over the world helping Jews escape persecution. In Asher's culture, art is viewed as frivolous, as it does not further the cause of saving his people from extermination. In desperation, this ten-year-old has a nervous breakdown, unable to reconcile the demands of his family, school, and religion with the talent and desire of his own heart.

When we are born into a faith, any faith, we grow up with a set of expectations that may not fit with the modern world or with who we are as individuals. If, as an adult, you choose a faith because it speaks to you and feels right to you, you have the opportunity to consider in advance whether your values will fit the values of your religion. As a child, your choices are not your own, which may result in great personal pain if you grow into someone whose values differ from the dictates of your faith. Even as an established member of a faith, you may find that your needs and wants create conflict, as in the case of Catholic nuns or priests who wish to marry and have children.

Religious guilt can cause much pain in families and in individuals who deviate from their family's religion, but it can be resolved, as with other forms of guilt, by doing what you believe is right. Organized religion can provide structure and assistance in times of need, but it can also force people into places they don't want to be. Many religions operate as big businesses, with gilded surfaces, imposing buildings, tithes, and strict rules that promote the growth of the membership. These same religions may save lives, help families, and give young people guidelines that help them throughout life. It's important to see the positive and negative aspects of your faith in order to understand your place in it, and it's important to realize that anything done by mankind will be flawed. When it comes to religion, you may want to take what works for you and discard the rest. If you feel guilty about your relationship to your religion, it's a good sign that something isn't fitting for you and that you need to make a decision about where you stand.

Religion may cause you guilt; God (or your Higher Power) does not. How could something that is perfect and all-loving want you to feel guilty? It is the people who benefit from your relationship with God who can cause you guilt. Never forget that you have direct access to your Higher Power. It doesn't need to be mediated by another human being, although it frequently might be. When you have an issue of religious guilt, ask yourself the following questions:

+ If I follow the rules in this case, who will benefit?

+ What does my conscience have to say about the issue?

+ When have I felt guilt like this before?

+ What are the consequences if I do what I want or do what is expected of me?

+ Who will I displease if I follow my own conscience?

+ Does my religion demand this, or does God (my Higher Power)?

✦ COCOONING—PROTECTION OR NUMBNESS?

When you were a kid, did you ever pack your backpack and tell your mom, "I'm running away and I'm never coming back"? Even if you didn't, there were probably times when you wanted to, either because life at home seemed to not be working out or because you wanted to punish your family by making them miss you. The sad thing about growing up is that we become unable to run away just as the world becomes colder, harder, and more complex. So, instead of packing our luggage, we find other ways to run away. We hide in our houses, in our hobbies and afflictions. We spin emotional cocoons that let us watch the horrors of the daily news without flinching, and we become inured to the suffering of others. The media and entertainment industry help us to take suffering less seriously as they flood the culture with gruesome images and unhappy scenarios. Muffled in our cocoons, we watch as if from a distance and feel we have no control over our world.

Cocooning is the most natural instinct in the world: when we are surrounded by ugliness, we try to burrow into something safe and hide our faces from it. But the drawback to cocooning is that you really do give up control. The cocoon feels safe, but it is constricting; we may feel secure and warm in there, but it is the warmth and numbness that people feel as they freeze to death in the snow. From a cocoon you cannot act, and there is the true problem: as we discussed earlier, action is the antidote to helplessness. When we are facing the miseries of the world, cocooning is just one step above utter hopelessness. We choose it above hopelessness, but it isn't a real solution. We use it to muffle guilt, but it doesn't work: guilt requires us to make conscious choices and decisions, but cocooning means that we are making the choice *not* to choose, not to decide.

People are not like butterflies. Butterflies grow cocoons as part of their life cycle; we grow them in preparation for death. Given a choice, who would choose to be blind rather than to hide their eyes from the bright sun? No one! But when you cut yourself off from emotional pain, you also cut yourself off from the possibility of joy. To experience synergy, you have to remain open to possibility, and that means the possibility of discomfort as well as pleasure.

MY SYNERGY JOURNAL | *Cocooning*

Do you cocoon? Follow this exercise to peel away the layers that suffocate you.

Write down the three things that bother you most in the world. They may be environmental concerns such as air or water pollution, social issues such as homelessness or domestic violence, or political situations such as injustice to a particular minority group. Don't censor yourself, and don't cocoon by saying, "Well, there's nothing I can do about this, so I'll pick something easier," or, worse, "Why bother?"

1._____

2._____

3._____

You've probably heard that the best (and only) way to eat a whale is one bite at a time. At this juncture, you are going to take just one bite. The only commitment I want you to make in this exercise is to do *one* small thing to target one of these important issues. You don't have to join Greenpeace or go to Africa to fight AIDS, but you must choose the most troubling item on your list of three and do something to address it. Write a check, volunteer to stuff envelopes for a couple of hours, serve soup, talk to an old person, make a care package. Adopt a cat. It doesn't matter what you do, as long as you do it. Do it this week. When you've done it, come back to this book and write in the following journal space any impressions, feelings, or ideas you got from this experience. How did you connect, and with whom? Often, when we volunteer, we encounter situations or people who seem hopeless, and we feel pain. Explore that feeling, but keep in mind that what you've just done is said "no" to cocooning and to helplessness. You did it for yourself and for the benefit of the world.

MY SYNERGY JOURNAL | *Volunteering*

✦ PAIN

No one in his right mind seeks out pain, and many of us go out of our way to avoid even the possibility of experiencing it. We cocoon to avoid pain, but closing off and shutting down our senses also numbs us to joy. Some of the greatest pain in the world is caused by our attempts to avoid another kind of pain. One way or another, you're going to hurt and be hurt in life. It's what you do with the hurt that determines whether you live a life of unhappiness or a life of joy.

It may sound crazy to say that it's possible to have pain in your life and still have a joyful life. But in a way, pain prepares us for joy. Kahlil Gibran likened pain to the fire that burns out the inside of a cup, leaving it hollow. Into the hollow is poured all the joy that you are now capable of containing. The more loss caused by pain, the more joy you can hold.

Pain is one of the miraculous facets of being alive. It serves an important purpose, for if our nerve endings did not send us messages every minute of every day, we would die quite young. Some people are born without the capacity to feel physical pain, and the world is an especially dangerous place for them. Diabetics sometimes end up having their feet or legs amputated because they lose feeling in those extremities and cannot tell when they have an ingrown toenail or another injury that doesn't heal and becomes infected. Pain keeps us alive!

Emotional pain also keeps us alive: alive to the possibilities of change and sensitive to the needs of others. Emotional pain holds you tight, breathes hot in your face until you say, "Okay, you are driving me crazy. I must do something!" In this way, pain is a teacher. If I know I'm unhappy in my work, I work to change it, and I use whatever resources I have to make sure the next situation is better, because I remember that pain and don't want to repeat it.

All that said, let's talk about how to deal with pain.

As I said earlier, our instinctual response to pain is to get the hell away from it. I'm not against that, not at all! But first, listen to pain. What is it telling you? What's it about? When you run from a wildfire, it's important to know what direction the wind is blowing so you won't run back into the flames.

Working Through the Pain—A Beginning

Sometimes pain can be paralyzing, and we cocoon and hide from it. We may feel numb, sleepy, or groggy. If you feel this way, the first thing I want you to do right now is to get down on the floor and do sit-ups. It sounds crazy and has nothing to do with what you're going through, but do it anyway. Do as many as you can—it might be three, it might be fifty. Do them until your stomach seizes up. Then, stretch your legs out straight, extend your hands over your head, and have a nice stretch for about a minute—no more than that. Then, do another set of sit-ups. If you can't do sit-ups, do leg-lifts or push-ups or run in place. Do three sets of whatever exercise you choose.

Now things are slightly different: you're probably sweating, your heart is beating faster, your face is red. Those are a few surface changes, but deep changes are going on in you, too. You have just given yourself the emotional equivalent of an ice-cream sundae. Your brain is releasing endorphins such as serotonin, the chemical responsible for lifting moods. Exercise is the number-one way to naturally increase serotonin; drinking more water also helps. After exercise, you will sleep better at night, and your digestion will improve. These few exercises will provide you with an example of what physical movement can do for you. When you're down, depressed, stressed, or angry, the best thing you can do for yourself is engage in a noncompetitive exercise. You are using your pain to decide how to use your body, and your body responds by creating the chemicals and processes that will eventually decrease your pain. Make no mistake: you're still a person who's hurting, and that pain should be acknowledged. But now you are also a person in motion, making choices to deal with pain in ways that benefit you. Rather than letting pain stop you in your tracks, you are making tracks—the first steps toward recovery.

MY SYNERGY JOURNAL | *A Pain Diary*

What was the event that started the pain? Who was involved in it?

_____

_____

_____

Does this pain reach far into your past? Is it connected with other hurtful events?

_____

_____

_____

Think back to the last time you felt this way. How long did it take for the pain to fade?

_____

_____

_____

If you could tell the pain to go away, when would you tell it to go?

_____

_____

_____

What do you wish would happen now? What is the likelihood that it will happen?

_____

_____

_____

How has this pain changed your life? What choices did you recently make that you might not have made if you weren't stuck with this pain?

_____

_____

_____

Imagine that the pain has gone. Now imagine an activity that you would do to celebrate the change in your life. What is it? Imagine it deeply and write about it in as much detail as you can.

_____

_____

_____

Sometimes our pain doesn't hold us; we hold it. Especially in times of loss, we grieve as though we believe that if we just wish hard enough, the universe will comply and bring our loved one back. Intellectually, we know that that can't happen, but emotionally, we call on our childhood belief in fairness and convince ourselves that if we're just unhappy enough for long enough, our prayers will be answered. We learned this faulty reasoning as children from the fairy tales we heard then. Sleeping Beauty fell into a long sleep until the prince blundered into her bedchamber. Cinderella went to the ball, then came right home and stayed put until the slipper brigade arrived. Cocooning works in fairy tales, but almost never works in real life. Letting grief cocoon you may keep you static for years, and if and when you do finally pull out of it, you will have more grieving to do over the time you've lost.

That isn't to say you shouldn't grieve. But it should be active grieving: time spent talking about your loss, thinking about who or what you've lost, and participating in established rituals that symbolize that loss. Removing yourself from the world (except in religiously prescribed mourning times) is not the answer. Resolve to live as fully as you can; use the synergy of pain and your determination to live despite that pain to re-create your life. If you can do nothing else, be physically active so you can simultaneously maintain your body's health and create the possibility of mental health.

If you feel depressed for more than two weeks, it's time to find a professional to help you. If you can pinpoint the mental or emotional reason behind the depression, you may want to speak with a mental-health counselor or a psychologist. If you can't think of a reason for your depression or anxiety (if, for example, you haven't had a recent break-up, bereavement, or other loss), you may want to start by visiting your physician. Problems such as low blood sugar, anemia, and other physical ailments can also cause depression and anxiety.

LOIS'S STORY

One morning Lois woke up feeling kind of tired, and the tiredness didn't go away. After a week or so, she found she was sleeping more, and she was feeling sad and blue. She was puzzled because she was generally a happy sort of person and nothing had happened to change the way she felt about her job, her husband, or her life in general. When the depression continued and she found herself bursting into tears, she got worried and made an appointment with Dr. Sayers.

"Well," said Dr. Sayers, after slowly reading the test reports, "You're not sick, but you may feel tired and moody for a while."

"What do you mean by that? Am I going crazy?" asked Lois, not knowing whether to be annoyed or alarmed.

"No, you're not going crazy. In fact, you're perfectly normal—for a woman who's pregnant," answered the doctor. "Congratulations."

Your Inner Ecology Toolkit

✦TOOL ONE: CHALLENGING FEAR

Fear is like pain in that it can save our lives or turn them into constant misery. Approaching fear from the Synergy Life Mastery viewpoint means embracing it as a lifesaver while firmly refusing to let it run your life.

Fear is a natural response to pain: we remember pain and want to avoid it. Fear is the memory of previous pain and the anticipation of future pain. It acts on a gut level to let you know when danger may be around.

The problem with fear is that it doesn't always discriminate between what's really harmful (the bus hurtling toward you as you prepare to jaywalk at a busy intersection) and what's possibly harmful (the leashed Pomeranian who seems mildly interested in your ankles).

Your fear is neatly packaged in your person, and it is owned by you and you alone. It may try to convince you that it's in charge of you, but, in fact, you are the powerful one in the relationship and can decide whether you want fear to live with you constantly or to chime in only when things get rough. You must make the choice, though, and because fear can't take a hint, you must be extremely assertive about deciding what part it plays in your life. Fear comes in many forms, and many of us own more than one kind of fear. I think of our fears as "Fear Buddies": a group of internal beings who go around with us and remind us of all there is to fear in the world.

When fear is out of control, we call it a phobia, and a phobia is usually focused on a particular situation or activity: heights, driving, flying, the outdoors, tight spaces, or one of a million other things. The best way to cure a phobia is systematic desensitization, a process in which you take gradually bigger steps to approach the fear in a controlled and planned way. If you have a phobia, find yourself a good behavioral psychologist or social worker and map out a plan to work on the phobia. Most phobias can be cured in a matter of weeks if you make your recovery a priority and work on it with all your heart.

Sometimes, our phobias act as cocoons, protecting us from other things in life we'd rather not face. Making the choice to rid yourself of a phobia may first mean taking an honest look at what it means to you.

For example: Sara left her highly conflicted and unhappy family in Ohio when she went to college in Southern California. Just before the Christmas holidays, she began to have recurring thoughts of plane crashes, and soon she couldn't stand the idea of flying. Just thinking about reserving her flight home made her break out in a sweat. Her heart pounded, and she felt dizzy and lightheaded. She canceled her plans to return home, telling her mother she had too much studying to do. Sara couldn't understand how someone who had flown all over Europe on a band tour could suddenly be terrified to fly. The college counselor she visited just before the winter break had another take on the matter: Sara's phobia gave her a guilt-free reason not to return to a home where she'd been unhappy for most of her life. It was actually keeping her safe! However, as Sara realized while talking to the counselor, fear of flying would also curtail most of her fun, as she planned to spend her junior year in France and wanted to travel while she was there as well. She resolved to work on and cure the phobia, and also to think about ways to handle her feelings and make healthy choices about how she wanted to interact with her family.

When you challenge fear, you are refusing to cocoon, and you are reaching out to life and choosing to act rather than to hide. Thinking synergistically, you are turning something hurtful into a learning experience and another opportunity to interact with your world. Fear is part of you, so there's no reason to hate it, but it is *only* part of you, so you have total control over it. You may need to learn particular skills to subdue unhealthy fear, but you are entirely capable of that!

Taking Fear by the Hand

Even when fear doesn't develop into a phobia, it may linger just outside your consciousness like an evil fairy, screwing you up while remaining invisible. Follow these steps to uncover and deal with your fear.

First, recognize it! Sometimes we are afraid to admit to fear. Remember when you were a kid and were sure there was a monster under the bed? But you didn't yell and scream for Mom because you knew that if you admitted the monster was there, he'd jump out at that moment. So you lay there, scared but not as scared as you would have been if you told someone that a monster was under the bed. In some ways, we don't grow up. I'm scared that if I admit that I'm afraid of something, it will become more real. So I try to ignore it, but my fear comes out anyway, in strangely twisted shapes from having been pushed down for so long. Sara was afraid to admit to herself how unpleasant her home life was and how glad she was to be out of there, so her fear mutated into a raging and noticeable phobia. Denying fear doesn't work. So if you're afraid, say so!

I once heard a great swami say, "Invite your fear to tea to discuss what it needs, and satisfy it by giving it the attention it is demanding from you. Then invite it to leave."

Psychological fear is a coward and a bully. Like all cowards and bullies, it leaves once we take a stand and have the confidence to confront it. You will be amazed at how quickly your mind and body respond once you develop the courage to face your fear.

MY SYNERGY JOURNAL | *My List of Fears*

I'm afraid of: _____

_____

_____

I'm afraid to: _____

because _____

_____

_____

Choose one fear and make a goal. Obviously, your ultimate goal is to get rid of your fear, but list some specific things that you would like to create. Be as detailed as you can. Sara's goal was to lose her fear of flying so she could enjoy her trip to France.

My goal is to: _____

_____

_____

Someone who can help me achieve my goal is:

_____

Now for the next step—this one is important, so don't skip it! Twice a day, for at least five minutes at a time, close your eyes. Visualize yourself succeeding at your goal. Picture where you'll be, what you'll be wearing, who will be with you. Be as specific and detailed as you can be, and visualize the whole process of doing what it will take to reach your goal and then celebrating your success afterward. You're using the synergy of your conscious will, your imagination, your goal-oriented mind, and your emotional desire to create your reality, so devote as much time as you can to this stage!

Work toward your goal. Use Step Four to keep you motivated, and find a helpful book, self-help group, or therapist to start moving yourself in the right direction. Affirm to yourself, "I am free of this fear," work on easing it, and chart your progress every day.

Finally, celebrate your goal! When you have reached your goal, do more than wipe your sweaty brow and move on to the next emotional challenge. Take the time to reward yourself, share your joy with the people who are important to you, or buy yourself a gift! Your achievement counts, and should be counted, as an important and happy moment in your life.

Although fear may feel overwhelming, you have the choice to suffer it, live with it, make peace with it, or completely subdue it. If you choose in favor of synergy, you will choose not to let fear constrain you, knowing that to live freely, creatively, and happily requires that you keep fear in its place. When you conquer a fear, you gain confidence and the strength to take on bigger challenges. You also become someone who can guide others in conquering their fears.

✦ TOOL TWO: HOW TO BE INSTANTLY HAPPIER— EUTHANIZE YOUR TELEVISION

Recognizing that we live in a country where materialism is practically a religion (*Webster's Collegiate Dictionary* defines *materialism* as "a doctrine that only the highest values or objectives lie in material well-being and in the furtherance of material progress"), what can we do to lessen its impact on our lives? Clearly, moving out to the woods and becoming totally self-sufficient are changes that only a few people would enjoy embracing. But there are a few strategies we can use to take control over materialism.

The most powerful and direct change you can make is to get rid of the television. Throw it out, lock it up, and say goodbye to many of your problems. Now, I know this seems tantamount to telling you to stop drinking water, but watching TV, relying on TV, is just a long-standing habit and is entirely open to change.

"But I'm Too Tired to Do Anything Else at Night!"

Believe it or not, you are more tired when you finish watching TV than when you started. Television seems restful because it enables us to plop down on the couch and stop blinking for six hours. Our bodies are at rest, our creativity is abandoned, but that's not the whole story. If you've ever attempted to download information from the Internet onto an older computer, you've probably experienced a similar situation. The download starts out fine, and the file tells you it'll be done in five minutes. After the first minute, it slows down considerably, and four minutes later you're staring at a message that proclaims your computer doesn't have the memory to complete the download. Watching TV is just a long download. I may be sitting there like an inert mineral, but I'm taking in visual and auditory information. I'm processing it, sending some to short-term memory and some into long-term memory. I'm making judgments about what I see and I'm interpreting my culture and my personal reality in light of this new pseudo-information. I'm reacting emotionally to what I see on the screen, the images sometimes flashing by my eyes faster than I can comprehend them. I see violence, rudeness, and things I can't afford. I see people being mean to each other, and I see a couple of gory murders (couched in the cachet of British mysteries) by bedtime. My attention is interrupted at twenty-minute intervals for commercials, and I watch six to twelve shows in one evening.

Television is seductive for so many reasons, but probably the most powerful is that has the ability to create and distribute fantasy. Sheer fantasy (negative or positive) is as compelling as any drug. It takes us away from our lives, places us in a different world, lets us feel like we are experiencing new things from the security of the living room. It seems so safe; we can always turn it off and leave the room.

But we don't, because the combination of fantasy and security is comfortable and numbing. As fantasy, it invites us to watch (and listen) uncritically. We don't ask if the evening news is true or complete—of course it is, because the newspeople say so. We don't ask if the most violent shows are real—they aren't, because they're on TV. When violence becomes real in our communities, we're shocked, but every night we invite it into our homes—we even pay for it! That box in the living room (and bedroom and kitchen) is as much a part of the household as the toilet, and most people can't conceive of life without one.

But suppose my television had exploded yesterday. I thought, Now what am I supposed to do? I complained for a while and wandered around the house. I looked at my checkbook and decided to wait a couple of weeks before replacing the Sony. I called my friends and asked what they were doing.

"Whatcha doing?"

"Watching TV."

"Wanna go out?"

"Nah, I'm too tired."

Finally, I grabbed a book I'd been meaning to read for the last four months and spent the rest of the night enjoying it. I got sleepy around 10:30 (I usually stayed up until midnight, when M.A.S.H. went off, even though my eyes were usually crossed by that late hour). I went to sleep thinking about the book I was reading and woke up before my alarm went off. I felt curiously refreshed!

Of course I felt refreshed! I was aware enough of my body to go to bed at the hour I needed to sleep rather than following my usual habit: staying in front of the TV until I passed out from exhaustion. I woke up early because I got enough sleep last night. What was this strange feeling that I'd forgotten? It was energy!

"But My Kids Will Never Speak to Me Again!"

Do they speak to you now? If they do, can you hear them? Granted, especially if you have teenagers, turning off the TV for even a night will start a huge conflict. Do it anyway. Here are some tips.

Take everyone out for a celebration, and don't tell them why. Go bowling (not to a movie), play miniature golf, take an evening hike, go to a planetarium, visit friends for a night of board games (not video games). Have a barbecue or dinner out, or cook hot dogs and marshmallows around a campfire. Keep the kids up a little late as part of the celebration, and when you get home, that's when you tell them. "The reason we're celebrating is that we spent the whole evening without one commercial, one stupid joke, one murder. Wasn't it fun?" After your stunning announcement, you might have a family talk about what's good and what's bad about TV.

Anyone who has successfully negotiated with kids can tell you: bribery works. Offer your kids an incentive to either ditch TV entirely or to abstain from it a few nights a week. You might take the money you save on cable each month and give it directly to the kids, or you might save up for a family treat. Replacing any habit takes some ingenuity (which is why we have habits in the first place!), but instituting Cookie-Baking Night or Finnish Sauna Night (complete with a steamed-up bathroom, smoked herring, and loud balalaika music) will stave off boredom. Take turns choosing what sort of entertainment will take place (remember, parents have veto power for reasons of safety, security, and finances, but don't abuse that power just because you don't want to hula in a homemade grass skirt!).

The extremely adventurous family may choose to have a weekly (or biweekly) reading night. It's important to choose a book everyone will like (the *Lord of the Rings* trilogy might be a good start) and to make sure any really young kids have lots of paper and crayons before the reading begins. Snacks are required!

Make a chart. Charting goals is intrinsically rewarding. It seems that no matter how old we get, we like to see checkmarks and gold stars next to our names. First, determine the number of hours your family watches TV each night. For every hour that a person usually watches TV but abstains, she earns a gold star. After ten gold stars, she earns an ice-cream sundae, a new book, or a watercolor set. Have each family member choose their intended prizes, and make them worth the work (for example, you wouldn't give your kid a new car for missing a hundred TV hours, but you might give him a day-long trip to a local amusement park).

For single people, it might be even harder to change the TV habit; after all, with no children to worry about and no one to watch over you, where's the incentive? But this is a great opportunity for you (no, really, it is!). This is the time to pick up that new hobby you've toyed with but never actually committed to. Take a sewing class, learn to fix your own car, start painting, refinish old furniture, join a book club, practice papermaking, learn French, sit and meditate, go swimming! Your energy will rise as you replace your old habits with fresh and inspiring ones. Your mental and psychological energy will be infused with your new experiences rather than drained away by constant exposure to negative messages from TV.

"There's No Way I'm Giving Up TV—It's Just Too Hard!"

Try it for a week: you can do almost anything for a week! But if this seems to be an impossible task, there's still something you can do to minimize television's damage to your spirit. You can use it like you would any other tool, without letting it use you. Television sells itself as a source of information, but, in fact, the evening news is often the government's interpretation of the day's events (and the government tells you only what it wants you to believe) or the press's spin on events (and the press is conscious of the sensationalism required to earn competitive ratings). It isn't necessarily your duty as a citizen to watch the news. It may, however, be your duty as a human being to protect not only your children but yourself from the crassness, violence, and ugliness of many television shows. How many of the shows you watch on a regular basis leave you feeling good rather than tired, overstimulated, paranoid, scared, worn out, or embittered? Isn't feeling good the purpose of entertainment? Would you pay me money each month to come to your house, violate your morals, make ugly remarks to your kids, and try to sell you stuff? No? Then why would you take that kind of treatment from a box?

You can keep your TV without being victimized by it. Seek out the shows that make you laugh (which increases endorphins, the body's natural painkillers, in your system). Find the educational shows: not gruesome and morbid forensic crime shows, but shows about polar bears and Egyptian

MY SYNERGY JOURNAL | *My Television Log*

Column 1	Column 2	Column 3
"Cops"	Fascinated, shocked. Kind of grossed out.	
"The Mary Tyler Moore Show"	I laughed, like the characters.	✓
1._____	_____	_____
2._____	_____	_____
3._____	_____	_____
4._____	_____	_____
5._____	_____	_____
6._____	_____	_____
7._____	_____	_____
8._____	_____	_____

(The format above is just a suggestion; create one of your own in your journal.)

pyramids and the solar system. Think as though you are planning entertainment for someone you want to protect and amuse, and refuse anything that doesn't come up to scratch.

In the table above, fill in the first column with the names of at least twenty shows you watch regularly. As you work, think about the reasons you watch each show, and then note each reason in the second column. Below I've listed some reasons we like particular shows, but you may have others.

It makes me laugh.

It scares me a little.

I like the characters.

It fascinates me.

There's nothing else on.

I like the subject.

I learn from it.

It helps my relationships.

Once you've written in the shows you watch most often, fill in the last column. Forget the other reasons you watch; instead, for each show, ask yourself the questions, "Does watching this show make me feel *good?* Does it energize, inspire, or teach me? Does it make me laugh?" Next to the name of each show for which you can answer "yes" to these questions, put a checkmark. I've done the first two for you as a sample.

How many checkmarks do you have? There's no scoring system here because *any* show without a checkmark is not good enough for you!

Now, get a *TV Guide* and look through it. Consider shows you may not have seen before, and choose the ones you think might fit the bill of making you feel good. Remember, changing your television habit is a perfect opportunity to increase your life choices in a highly specific and beneficial way. You don't have to eat that cheese sandwich day after day—you have the power to write your own menu!

Make a list of shows you want to try on a sheet of paper and stick it next to the TV.

Over the coming week, see how many shows from your list you watch, replacing the ones on your Television Log that don't make you feel good. Keep track of the shows you like, so you can watch them again. At the end of the week, consider continuing the experiment, and keep track of how you feel.

Taking control of television not only removes much of the garbage perpetuated by that medium, but it frees you up creatively. Things you'd never thought of wanting, such as clear mascara or beer made from icebergs, remain where they belong—in the minds of advertising gurus. Your needs are suddenly lessened, and just as suddenly, you have extra hours free in each day, an abundance most people can't even imagine. You can read a book, train your dog, study Spanish, make love all night, or just sit on the couch and daydream. Your life becomes richer and fuller, and you have the time and energy to appreciate the true wealth you've created—your true abundance.

✦TOOL THREE: ABUNDANCE

There is an old African story about a wealthy businessman who took a long vacation. He journeyed for many days until he came to the ocean on the east coast of Africa. Every day he walked along the docks and watched the fishermen. He noticed one particular man who brought home a great catch every day. This made the businessman think about the opportunities that the fisherman might be missing. So, one day he said to him: "You are a good fisherman. You could make a lot of money with your skills."

"Thank you, kind sir, but I'm completely content with my life. I work hard each day, I provide for my family with the fish that I catch, and I get to spend a lot of time with my best friend: my wife."

The businessman was adamant: "You don't understand. You could teach others to do what you do, and in that way you could buy many ships. You could export to many countries and become extremely wealthy."

"And then what would I do?" the fisherman asked.

"Well, then you could spend lots of time doing exactly what brings you great joy."

"Such as...?"

"Well, you could stay at home, look out at the ocean, fish as much as you want, and have a comfortable life."

"In that case, I am already wealthy—I do the things that you talk about every day!"

The fisherman knew about abundance because he lived it. His values were clear to him, his needs were met, and the things that mattered most to him were part of his daily life. The wealthy man couldn't see that because he was used to thinking of money as the most important element of happiness. Even when the fisherman told him, "I'm completely content," he just couldn't understand.

Abundance is the opposite side of the materialism coin. Materialism might say, "I want that," but abundance says, "I have that!" When I'm materialistic, I focus on acquiring possessions, so I notice what I don't have. Materialism, oddly enough, is based on a feeling of lack. It's especially strange that materialists have lots of stuff cluttering their lives, but they don't really see it because they're envisioning what should be there but isn't. Materialism is the mind's attempt to comfort an empty soul, but it's like saltwater to someone who's thirsty. Buying things can bring you a temporary high, but it doesn't assuage a true feeling of lack. The good news is that a feeling of lack can be soothed by spending time with people you care about, by walking your dog, by baking bread, or by doing something nice for someone else. That emptiness of soul is filled simply, but not easily, because it takes effort and energy to make life meaningful. It's worth it, though, for as you fulfill your essential self, your energy skyrockets.

People who feel they have abundance tend not to acquire much more stuff because they already have what matters. And what matters is the feeling of abundance! This feeling is the ultimate richness, and it isn't based on stuff.

Now, I've been talking as though the world is divided into materialists and nonmaterialists, but that's probably not true. We all have some materialism, and we all have the possibility of experiencing abundance. It takes money to fulfill materialistic urges, but experiencing abundance is free. Abundance is about opening your eyes to and actively appreciating what you already have. It's funny but true: when you feel grateful for your friends or books or the sunset or your lifestyle, the urge to shop greatly diminishes.

Some people eat compulsively when feelings other than hunger are raging and unsatisfied. They never feel full because they're filling the wrong space with the wrong things. Satisfy the true feelings, and that false hunger goes away. Other people shop when they're lonely or frustrated or sad or anxious, and their dilemma is the same: for a while it seems that they are taking action, but when it's over, there's more stuff in their houses but their lives still seem empty. Reaching out to abundance isn't something that's done at the mall; it's something you do in the quiet recesses of your mind.

Every day, take time to think about what you have. Even a geranium growing in an old coffee can has greatly comforted a poor woman when all around her was impoverished. Look for the small bits of beauty in your life, and if you can't find any, you have a duty to yourself to create them.

Create Beauty

Creating beauty can be an internal or external exercise: you can create beauty in the world, or you can learn, internally, to appreciate it. Any time you stop to appreciate something, that is a present-moment creation of beauty. The beauty in question might be extremely subtle, but it's no less wonderful for its subtlety.

I can give you an example without even leaving my desk. I have a calculator that I use mostly to balance my checkbook. It's one of those small, solar-powered jobs that does just the basics—adds, subtracts, multiplies, divides. It could give me a square root, if I ever need one. Nothing fancy. It's pale gray, and the buttons fit my hands just right—they're small enough to look neat and big enough that I rarely hit wrong numbers. The really amazing thing is, I've had this calculator since 1988, and it still works. A friend of mine gave it to me because I needed one; this one had cost him less than five dollars, and he had recently upgraded to a big Texas Instruments version that could calculate sines and cosines.

I appreciate the simplicity of my calculator, and its longevity. I'm surprised I haven't lost it in my travels. I like the smoothness of its shell and the brightness of its display, and I feel happy when I contemplate the friend who gave it to me. In short, I think my calculator is beautiful!

Creating beauty is also about using your energy and intention to clean, make art, write poetry, or even plan a party. Planting a garden, laying a walkway, clearing a streambed, painting a mural—these are all valid ways to create beauty. You don't have to design a fantastic skyscraper to be an artist—some of the greatest beauty is created (or uncovered) by window washers who remove dust and grime and let the sun stream through. Cleaning house can be an intentional act of beauty, as the serenity of a tidy home, the scent of freshly polished furniture, and the sight of fresh table linens restore many of us to a peaceful feeling, remote from the chaos of the outside world.

There is an artist in New York who seeks out the most degraded parts of the city—abandoned buildings, tenements, graffittied walls—and, with the utmost care and precision, paints a small, oval landscape onto the devastated place. She paints reproductions of "Old Masters" onto the crummiest buildings in the city, so that in the most neglected, the ugliest spots, there is a place of real beauty. Her painting is a gift to anyone who passes by and needs something beautiful. Sometimes, people who live in the area shout at her and complain, calling her a vandal, in which case she restores the wall to its original condition—right down to the awful words she might have just covered with art. She's attached not to the paintings, but to the process—if someone chases her away from one place, she just finds another and begins again.

Artistry is a byproduct of synergy. When you work at something with focus and will, you create synergy, and whatever you touch will be better for it.

Seek Joy

Freed from guilt, pain, and fear, we see the world much more easily, and we begin to live our true purpose as human beings: looking for joy. But many of us build habits that prevent us from looking for joy, such as looking for danger so constantly that we become caught in possible negatives and are unable to see the actual positives! Fortunately, seeing joy is as much a habit as anything else, so practicing it will make it a natural and, one day, maybe even an unconscious way of life.

There are many ways to seek joy. We can look for it in others, surrounding ourselves with people who have learned the knack of living a happy life. We can inspire it in others as well by giving the best of ourselves in friendship and love. We can notice and appreciate joy in ourselves by paying attention to the times that synergy works smoothly in our lives. And we can nurture joy in ourselves by doing what matters, being gentle with ourselves and others, connecting with nature, or communing with our Higher Power. Expressing your true self by using your talents is an excellent way to dip into joy, so make time to be your best. You may feel that you have to choose between mopping the floors or working on your painting tonight—you may feel inspired to paint but also that you "should" mop. Let the floors wait. Express your true self.

Create Compassion

You don't hear much about compassion in the modern world, and when you do it's often because someone is attempting to pry open your wallet. True compassion doesn't require a Visa card, although it may make you want to spend money to help someone else. We can use words such as *forgiveness, empathy,* and *caring* when we speak of compassion, but it might be clearer and more honest to say that compassion is the fine art of giving someone an even break.

Compassion is pity, but pity without condescension. It contains the realization that I could as easily be in your place, and it holds the heartfelt wish that things will go well for you. You may feel compassion for the sick, the hungry, the aged, or for the guy in the cubicle next to you who's suffering from indigestion brought on by beer and garlic fries at last night's ballgame. Compassion makes no distinction between calamity and the simple discouragements of being human; it embraces us all equally, the organized and the sloppy, the deserving and the undeserving, the fortunate and the chronically unlucky. Compassion can be as grand as the love of a mystic for all humanity or as simple as offering that poor guy in the next cubicle a Rolaids and a friendly grin.

Loss of compassion, even the smallest bit of it, is one of the world's great misfortunes. It's also a terrible waste, because losing compassion for others inevitably means losing compassion for the self. Why we lose compassion is not important—we could spend a lot of time talking about how the world's cruelties cause us to lose it—but regaining it *is* important. It isn't difficult to rediscover your compassion; in fact, many of the exercises you've already done are working in that direction anyway. Your true self holds as much compassion as anyone could ever have—but how do you access it?

You start with yourself. Do you worry yourself with things that you should do or things that you regret having done? Do you berate yourself for your looks, feelings, skills, or talents that you feel are inadequate? Do you condemn yourself for failures in relationships? What if a great and powerful being told you that it's quite all right to be far from perfect, that you are totally adequate and that you deserve happy, fulfilling relationships with others? If you could trust that this being was truthful, you'd probably break into tears of relief. What if it then told you that the finest, purest thing on earth that you can give, the contribution you are most suited to make and the one that the world needs most from you, is your compassion? That all you have to do is provide the people around you with acceptance and hope and the feeling that they're not totally flawed and alone?

Your children might or might not remember that you organized their closets and drove them to away games; but they do remember that you were kind to them, listened to their problems and their dreams, and tried to understand their points of view. Your friends might remember your way with soufflés and your fabulous wardrobe, but chances are, they more strongly recall the times that you talked all night on the phone about their love lives and how you encouraged them when they were down. Twenty years from now, your spouse might still think you're the sexiest thing in town, but he will probably value your tenderness above your physical charms.

To love, you must first know love. And to have compassion, you must feel it for yourself as well. It might not matter whether you start this process by feeling compassion for yourself or by practicing compassion for others. But in general, it's easier to live in the world if you start from a happy place inside yourself. In fact, if you want to gain access to the joy that flows around you every minute of your life, it's not a recommendation that you treat your-self with kindness and patience: it is an absolute imperative. Read the fol-lowing statements and see if they are true for you.

- ✦ I am kind to myself.

- ✦ I listen to my own needs.

- ✦ I encourage myself.

- ✦ I am gentle with myself.

- ✦ I take time to dream my own dreams.

- ✦ I make time for things that make me happy.

Chances are that if you could say, "Yes, I do that," to all these questions, you wouldn't be reading this book. So, beside each statement below, write one or two small but specific things you could do to make that statement truer for you. An example is written under each sentence to get you started.

I am kind to myself:

I make time to get plenty of exercise, which keeps me healthy and happy.

_____

I listen to my own needs:

I can say "No" to people who make demands on me.

_____

I encourage myself:

I say, "Nice work!" to myself when I've done something difficult.

_____

I am gentle with myself:

I don't beat myself up about not being able to do everything I want to do.

_____

I take time to dream my own dreams:

I spend time alone painting (or doing other creative things) or just staring out the window.

I make time for things that make me happy:

I always have a book that I'm excited about reading.

We cannot give away what we do not have. When you apply real patience and kindness to your relations with other people, people blossom and show you their true selves. The finest teachers and spiritual leaders embody compassion, working with people who initially don't understand even the basics of the lesson. Teaching is built on trust: the teacher's trust that the student wants to learn, and the student's trust that her teacher will be kind. Any time we reach out with compassion to another person, we attempt to learn what he is really about, and along the way we teach him what we are made of. Compassion isn't just a handout on a windy street corner—it's the divine expression of our true selves.

Making Authentic Choices

We do not choose the day of our birth nor
may we choose the day of our death, yet choice
is the sovereign faculty of the mind.

THORNTON WILDER

Choosing

Have you ever known someone who seemed to move smoothly through life, deciding early on a satisfying career, attending the right schools and taking the right internships, making enough money, meeting and marrying the love of their life, having happy children, and generally doing everything right? This person might have been blessed with early self-knowledge, a stable home, security, and a sizeable portion of luck. You've probably also known people who had all the advantages and managed to screw up their lives anyway. Why do some people float serenely on life's ocean while others tread water, flounder, or even drown? Some people come from nothing—they've had no love, no security, no role models—yet they manage to pull it together and create a happy, successful, and meaningful existence. Some come from nothing and spend their lives perpetuating their lack. What's the difference between these people?

The difference is choice. We have a certain amount of free will, and how we choose to exercise it determines the sort of life we lead. Sure, there are things beyond our control, and they definitely impact us, but how we respond to those things makes all the difference to our lives. Many of us are raised to believe that we have no choices, that our will is irrelevant, and that the universe does what it wills with us and we can like it or lump it. If you do have that feeling (and some of us are ashamed to admit to such a feeling), this is a good time to start thinking about the importance of faith in your life. If you do not have faith in any other person, religion or Higher Power, or yourself, pin your faith on this idea: you have choices, and they do count. If you don't really believe that at this point, then plan to act as if you do—once you see the way that your life changes when you begin exercising your will, you'll have a much easier time believing that your choices matter!

In creating a life of synergy, your choices make the difference in your success. At every moment, you can choose to do something: you can read and work through this book, talk about it to your friends, and think about it before you go to sleep. Or you can throw it in the trash. Your decision to have a cheeseburger for lunch could result in meeting the love of your life. If you choose pizza, you will travel in another direction and miss him (or her). So it's important to know what you care about, and fit your every choice to your overriding goals as much as possible. It's especially important to pay attention to the choices that clearly matter: what you study, how you take care of your body, how you relate to the people in your life, and how you work. Your choices should express who you are and what you need. Through your choices, you show what you believe and what matters to you. Don't let fatigue or world-weariness stop you from making your own choices, and don't let others make your decisions for you because you feel false indebtedness, gratitude, or guilt toward them.

I was recently at my local library, which offers free law consultations once a week. A harried mother was talking to a legal assistant about her child support and custody arrangements, but her six-year-old son was clearly bored.

"I want to go home," he announced. His mother tried to ignore him and continued talking to the legal assistant.

"I want to go home. I want to go home! I WANT TO GO HOME!" the child insisted. His mother sighed.

"I'm sorry," she apologized. "I'll have to come back another time. He just won't let me do it."

This is a perfect example of someone who has let another person make her decisions, which is a choice (although an ineffective one) in its own right. By not disciplining her child, by not insisting on a code of behavior for him while she was trying to conduct important family business, this woman created a situation in which her life choices were made by a child. Her choice of words, "He just won't let me do it," clearly stated that she saw her child as much more powerful in the relationship than any six-year-old should be, and indicated that she herself was victimized by him. Of course, the real victim is the child, who is given both a grandiose picture of his impact on the world and fare too much responsibility. Children whose parents don't set reasonable limits end up without a sense of their place in the world. They are either kings or dust particles, rulers of the universe or nothing at all. As adults, they have problems making good choices because they bump against social boundaries that they were not prepared to encounter. By abnegating her responsibility to make choices on behalf of herself and her child, the mother in this example set them both up for years of unhappiness.

MY SYNERGY JOURNAL | *Choices*

What choices did I automatically make today, without even thinking about them?

_____

_____

_____

What choices do I make because I feel I have to make them?

_____

_____

What choices do I want to make?

_____

_____

What choices do I avoid or shift to other people?

_____

_____

What choices do I make for other people that maybe I shouldn't make?

_____

_____

What could I choose to do differently, in ways that would enhance my life?

_____

_____

(If you can't come up with something for the last question, please write in the following sentence: "I could choose to see myself as a potential source of power. I could allow myself to dream.")

✦ CHOICES, RESPONSIBILITY, AND FREEDOM

Beginning in childhood, we careen wildly between demanding independence and refusing responsibility. We want to make our own decisions, but we aren't especially thrilled with the idea of living with the consequences. Also, some choices we make automatically rule out the possibility of choosing twice. As Jean-Paul Sartre pointed out, the problem with freedom is that it demands responsibility. If I have no free will, and thus I let you make all my decisions, whatever happens will be your fault. If I am at the utter mercy of an omnipotent God, anything I do is preordained and justified by Him. And if I make my own choices, the mistakes are all mine, too.

What We Sacrifice for Freedom

Because we are human, we hate the idea that making one choice precludes us from making other choices. If I choose a cheeseburger for lunch, then I can't have the pizza, too. If I marry my true love tomorrow, I won't be free to marry my other true love next week, so I don't want to commit. As Americans, we worship the concept of freedom above everything else in the world, and that's a problem for us, because we can be sold almost anything, even if that something contradicts what our hearts know to be right, if the word *freedom* is attached to the product. Listen to car commercials—the word *freedom* comes up a lot in them. The Gulf War was sold to us as necessary to "free" the Kuwaitis, so our sons and daughters went to war. Politicians tell us that despoiling the Arctic wilderness by drilling for oil there is directly related to our freedom—they want us to believe that we'll derive an inexhaustible source of cheap oil from ruining one of the last clean places on earth. It isn't true, of course: the price of oil has almost nothing to do with its current availability, but we aren't supposed to think of that, transfixed as we are by the possibility of being less than "free."

We allow the manufacture and purchase of assault weapons because we value our freedom to bear arms over our freedom not to be shot by someone with an assault rifle. Any child is free to download the most vicious pornography from the Internet, and in the name of freedom we protect hate speech, even though it clearly leads to violent acts against members of minority groups. So how, exactly, are we free?

We can be taken advantage of so easily through our worship of the word and ideal of *freedom!* We are in fact enslaved by our very desire for freedom. When we make choices, we have to do more than just choose whatever we're told to choose—that's copping out. Choosing requires research and reflection, the synergy of our heartfelt beliefs, logical capacities, and gut feelings. Ask yourself these questions when you're faced with an important decision.

✦ How important is my choice in this matter?

✦ Am I choosing for negative or positive reasons?

✦ What is my first reaction? What feels immediately right and immediately wrong?

✦ When I think it over, what logical conclusions do I reach?

✦ Who else is involved in this choice?

✦ How does this fit in with my values and my overall goals?

✦ How does my choice impact my family, my society, and my world?

✦ Who else has chosen as I want to? Do I respect those people?

Authentic Freedom

The more self-directed and personally organized we are, the freer we become. The more we listen to the needs of our true selves and follow our consciences, the less likely we are to become enslaved by ignorance, fear, or want. Personal growth invigorates the soul, the spirit, the physical mind, and the body, and authentic freedom is earned by focusing on achieving one's true and full potential.

In the next section, we'll talk about choices that make our lives healthier, happier, and more synergized than ever before.

Finding Strength and Potential in Others

When babies are still very young, you can see the different ways that they relate to other people. Some babies cuddle right into your arms when you hold them, but some "slow-to-warm-up" infants arch their backs away from you, won't look you in the eye, and at first are generally uncomfortable with being held. Not surprisingly, slow-to-warm-up babies are harder to love because their parents feel rejected by them and react by drawing away themselves. Mothers have a harder time nursing these children, and bonding may be negatively affected because mothers might think, "My baby doesn't like me!"

If you work with babies, you learn that some just take more time to get comfortable with you, and you give each infant the time and patience she needs to grow to like you. At some point, you realize that it's not personal, and you see the potential for love in that child. You can wait.

We're all slow to warm up sometimes, just as in some cases we're all slow learners. I might be a genius in one area and a real dunce in another. We all have our "off" days when we feel sleepier, dumber, meaner, and weaker than we usually are, and we've all made an awful first impression on someone just because we weren't on top of our game that day. An important part of practicing compassion is realizing that everyone is a jerk or a dope once in a while.

Some time ago, there was a debate in physics about whether light was made up of particles or of waves. Some physicists insisted that light was made up of billions of particles; others said just as strongly that light was made up of billions of waves. It seemed impossible that scientists could disagree on something so concrete, for particles are solid little things and waves take up space and move through time: they're nothing alike! The trouble was that both sides had proof. So at some point, and after some smartly done experiments, scientists determined that the construction of light depends on the person conducting the experiment. It seems that we find what we look for, and that light is magical enough to be both particle and wave.

Just as light has the properties of both particles and waves, people have the properties of both the base and the divine. Your true self is divine, but it may be masked by all the stuff the world heaps on you over time, which tends to impede more than to enhance your life. When you take the time and effort to understand that virtually everyone has a spark of divinity, you can challenge yourself to find that spark, in the same way that you hunt for seashells at the beach. And nature being what it is, what you hunt for, you will find. So if you decide that someone is a loser and has nothing to offer the world, what that person has to offer is lost to you forever. If you remember that everyone has a gift and set about searching for it, you find many gifts. Now, which strategy will make your life happier and richer? Which one will bring more joy into the world?

More than two decades ago, I read a *Reader's Digest* story about the effect of positive expectations on a person's life. The author of the story, an anthropologist, visited a village in the South Pacific to research marriage practices. Someone told him about a young man who had paid an exorbitant bride-price in order to marry the girl of his choice. It was a strange situation because the girl had had no other suitors, for she was shy and stooped and unbelievably homely in the bargain. But the young man had fallen in love with her for reasons no one else quite understood, and he had worked for two years to acquire the largest bride-price ever paid in the history of the village. The other men had laughed at him and counseled him to offer her father a small bride-price, since without his offer, the girl would certainly never marry. But the young man was stubborn and shook his head. At the end of two years, they were married.

"What happened?" asked the anthropologist, sensing that the story ended rather abruptly.

"Go see him and ask!" his informants answered laughingly, so he went to see this strange young man who paid too much for an ugly bride.

When he came to the door, he was greeted by a lovely woman who seated him next to his host and served them something cool and sweet to drink. The anthropologist tried to make polite conversation, craning his neck for a glimpse of the homely wife. The beautiful woman returned with a tray of food and sat beside the young man while they ate. They seemed to be very much in love, and finally the anthropologist could stand it no longer.

"Were you married before?" he asked. The young man shook his head and smiled. "No, this will be my only wife, for no one could replace her."

The anthropologist was confused. "I'm sorry," he muttered. "I heard you had paid a very large bride-price for..." And the young man and his wife started to laugh. The woman left the room to bring in more fruit, and the young man leaned over the table toward his guest.

"That is the bride I purchased for such a price. I worked and I waited for years to obtain her. My friends thought I was crazy, but I loved her so and knew she would become a wonderful wife to me. I wanted to pay a high bride-price so she would know how much she meant to me. If I had paid a lower price, she would have thought she was worthless."

"She's so beautiful."

"She was always beautiful. It's just that now she knows what she's worth."

When you look for the strengths of others, you find them. When people know you as someone who brings out their best, your own life is enriched by knowing them. Looking for the best in others is the most important trait a teacher can have and the greatest gift a parent can give a child, and it is also invaluable for employers seeking the best people to hire into their organizations and for people trying to build friendships. Like the man who saw potential in a shy, stooped girl, by seeking beauty in others, you actually create it.

Friendship and Strength

After my grandfather married my grandmother, he left Rhodesia and was gone for some years. He left his titled deeds to the farm with a friend, and as soon as he returned, she said: "I have your title deeds, and they are safe."

Not only did the woman keep my grandfather's important papers secure, she intuited before he could even ask that he might be concerned about them. This kind of friendship, which crosses miles and years, is one of life's perfect blessings.

Friends are the family we choose for ourselves, unencumbered by genetics and blessed by common values. A good way to judge the health of someone's life is by the richness and depth of her friendships. Healthy people are surrounded by other healthy people, and unhealthy people tend to draw people who are like themselves, or even needier.

If you've always thought of friendships as things that "just happen," you may not have the kind of friends you really want. Friendship doesn't just fall into your lap; it's a definite choice. If you allow friendships to be things that fall into your lap, you abdicate responsibility for an important life choice. Would you let your child be friends with just anyone who came along? No, you would want her friend to have certain values and behaviors, and you would have expectations of fairness, sharing, and enjoyment for the friendship. Expect at least this much for yourself, and wait until available friendships feel right to you.

If you don't like to be with someone, if you don't trust that person or feel there's some competition between you, you don't have to be friends, even if the other person seems to expect it. It's perfectly okay to choose not to be someone's friend, especially when you feel that a person wants something from you besides the pleasure of your company. If you don't feel the same way, friendship is impossible.

We choose our true friends through a process more subtle and mysterious than we choose our lovers, through a more soulful attraction. Like other matters of the soul, friendships are nurtured through conscious choices. Spending time with friends is important, even when you aren't doing anything in particular. Being there in times of trouble is important, but again, there is a protocol, a timeline for those things. Most people would agree that it's inappropriate to ask a new friend (say, someone you've known for less than three months) to help you to move apartments. It's probably asking too much to expect a birthday present from someone you've known less than a year, and it's certainly over the top to expect someone in the category of "pleasant acquaintance" (such as someone you've lunched with at work a few times) to hold your hand over a relationship gone wrong. True friendship can be as strong as the supports of a bridge, but in the early stages, it's more like a seedling. It can't stand rough treatment or extremes of heat and cold. It needs attention or it shrivels away, and it needs time to establish roots and grow. It makes sense that friendship takes a certain amount of planning and a delicate touch, because the ultimate payoffs are tremendous: a good friendship can last a lifetime.

As we grow older, it becomes more difficult to make friends, either because work doesn't allow the sort of interpersonal exploration we enjoyed in school or because there just doesn't seem to be enough time. It's not impossible to meet people and make friends in later life, but it takes more effort and organization than it did when we were kids.

I know a man who became a geographer because he loved to travel. His job took him all over the world, and he lived in exotic places such as Egypt and Iran. When we met, he was teaching at a small college in northern California. He'd been there a few short months, and he seemed to already know everybody in town. I asked him how he had accomplished that, and he told me that whenever he moves to a new town, he finds two or three places he likes and goes to them several times a week. He gets to know the bartenders and waitresses and strikes up conversations with the regulars, so soon it seems as if he's always been a regular himself. He accepts every invitation that sounds fun or interesting, so he goes to lots of parties and seminars after work. He writes thank-you notes and stays in touch through letters and email with people who live far away.

In short, this man enters every town like a friendly conqueror. He has a strategy and a timeline that takes him from total stranger to well-known figure in the shortest possible time. He's a planner, but he's also a warm, generous, and amusing person who has found a way to meet his needs for social contact despite a lifestyle that requires him to move around a lot. Because he meets many people and takes time to follow up with the ones he likes, he increases his opportunities to make friends. He has friends all over the world.

MY SYNERGY JOURNAL | *Friends*

Who are my best friends? What are they like?

_____

_____

_____

_____

_____

What qualities are important to me in a friend?

_____

_____

Am I a good friend? Why or why not?

_____

_____

How am I a friend to myself? Do I treat myself as well as I treat my friends?

_____

_____

Do I have enough friends?

_____

_____

If I sought out new friendships, how would I do it? (In the space below, brainstorm about where you might go to meet new people and how you would follow up with them later. When would you see them? What sort of activities would you share?)

_____

_____

_____

_____

_____

Many Kinds of Intelligence

My geographer friend is academically intelligent, but he is also socially intelligent. He knows what's important to other people, and he strives to make other people feel good when they're around him. This social intelligence has helped him build a career that spans the globe and a personal life that is rich and filled with meaning. There is more than one kind of intelligence, and an IQ test just isn't adequate to assess whether someone is really in touch with his creativity, or is a great athlete, or is especially good at training horses. It's particularly important for parents to understand that children as well as adults have different sorts of intelligences and that it's vital to help a child recognize what he's good at, even if it doesn't show up on a math test.

Our society is still into the outdated concept that academic ability and achievements equal wisdom, but I think that different situations in life require different approaches. An academically intelligent person can learn and retain information, but she might not have any social intelligence, and her poor social skills may inhibit her career and personal growth. Someone who has a real genius for leading business meetings may have the physical grace of a raging hippopotamus. Individuals have their own unique intelligences, and it's important that these particular gifts are discovered, accepted, and developed. It's possible to be intelligent in more than one way, and the more support you receive from others while developing your gifts, the more well-rounded and enjoyable your life will be.

Making authentic choices means knowing not only what you're good at and like to do, but also that there is a place for your unique brand of smarts. When choosing a career, some people let their parents tell them what they're going to be and never consider doing anything else, even though many people aren't perfectly fitted for their parents' career choices. In career-counseling circles, this is called *foreclosure,* because these people have opted out of their right to choose their own career paths. The choices that turn out to be good for you must be based on who you really are—the needs and talents of your true self. Even if your natural talents don't allow you to be a trial lawyer or a neurosurgeon, if you follow your natural strengths, you may be an excellent photographer or cabinetmaker or teacher instead. Here's a brief sketch of the different kinds of intelligence that people can possess.

> **Emotional intelligence** is an awareness of one's own emotional states and the ability to manage them in healthy ways. People with emotional intelligence are in touch with their feelings and able to intuit and empathize with the feelings of others.

> **Social intelligence** is the ability to communicate ideas, to interact with others, and to understand the needs of individuals and communities. Social intelligence incorporates things such as good manners and diplomacy as well as leadership ability.

Academic intelligence is the ability to assimilate, analyze, and learn certain facts, strategies, skills, and formulas and maintain that knowledge for later use—as in a preferred profession or occupation. Academic intelligence is highly prized in our culture, as our professional world relies on test scores and grades to certify its members.

Creative intelligence is the ability to conceptualize and build something within the framework of one's own mind; to express and create ideas, music, artforms, business formulas, paintings, songs, sculptures, computer programs, and so on. People with creative intelligence might not do well in school because of boredom or because they just do not fit in and do things differently than other students.

Logical intelligence is the ability to think in a clear and emotionally detached manner. People with logical intelligence can clearly calculate step-by-step processes and plans.

Physical intelligence means being in touch with one's body and knowing why it reacts in certain ways. It's knowing and loving the house that we all occupy. People with physical intelligence may be athletes or dancers or may work at trades in which they use their bodies.

Personal intelligence means that one clearly knows what's good and what's bad for oneself. Knowing one's likes and dislikes and having the ability to examine them and change whatever needs to be changed are important parts of living a fulfilling life. Personal intelligence is about making choices, having a purpose, and fulfilling one's dreams.

Spiritual intelligence is the knowledge that one is a part of something great and wonderful. One's priorities are to serve others and to contribute to the community. People with spiritual intelligence are grateful, and their inner strength is very real and visible. With spiritual intelligence, we feel powerful and joyful because we have synergized with nature and the universe.

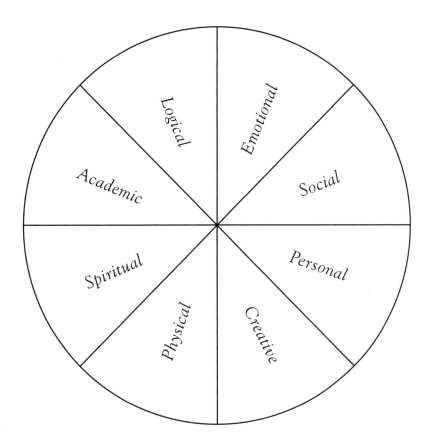

MY SYNERGY JOURNAL | *The Intelligence Wheel*

On the above illustration, with crayons or markers color in the amount of each triangle you feel represents the amount of intelligence you have in each area, and then ask yourself the following questions.

Which intelligences were praised in my family, and which were ignored or condemned?

_____

_____

Which intelligences are more impressive to me? How do I use my intelligence biases to judge others?

_____

_____

Which of my intelligences would I like to increase?

_____

_____

You can also make an Intelligence Wheel for your partner, parents, or children and compare their unique gifts to yours. Ask yourself what expectations you may have of one another based on those differences.

Some intelligences exist naturally but need encouragement to grow. Stretch yourself by trying these simple ways to increase your intelligences.

Social: Become part of a group (just as you would do when learning to experience group synergy). Pay attention to what effective and ineffective group leaders do. Listen to the way people talk to one another, and focus on positive interchanges with others. Practice good manners and notice how they can smooth the path to achieving goals. Notice things such as alliances and enmities that may harm the common causes of the group.

Academic: Half of academic intelligence is being organized and having a certain set of skills. Take a workshop on test-taking and study skills and learn to use a day planner. If you're currently in school or studying something, make sure that you know the important dates for tests, and practice exercises to improve your memory.

Creative: Buy yourself crayons or fingerpaints and some big paper. Don't plan, don't try for a certain effect; just start to put color on the paper any way you like. Put aside judgments or worries about making it "good." Creativity is all about the process, so don't worry about what you produce. Color and draw and scribble as long as you like. If you have a hard time relaxing into it, use your "wrong" hand (i.e., if you're right-handed, use your left; if you're left-handed, use your right). Not only must you abandon all thoughts of "getting it right" when you use your wrong hand, it's also very freeing.

Logical: Study algebra or even logic! Take a class that teaches you the notation and rules of mathematics or logic. Read and analyze mysteries or brainteasers. Start with simple problems, then increase their complexity as you learn the rules. Learn to play chess, which exercises your memory while helping you to plan.

Physical: Take up a sport, dancing, or an exercise class. Study yoga, lie in the sun, have a massage, or relax in a warm bath and pay attention to the way your skin, muscles, and joints feel.

Spiritual: Meditate and pray. Make time to do things that help you feel close to your god or the universe. Take a retreat, and read or listen to a spiritual leader you respect.

Personal and spiritual intelligence are enhanced by Synergy Life Mastery, and this book may stimulate social intelligence as well. Part of growing as a person means getting to know the good things about yourself and forgiving yourself for all the bad things you've said and thought about the person who is yourself. Exercise your personal intelligence by listening to the things you say to yourself, and don't berate yourself for not being good at everything. No one's good at everything! Love what you are, and give yourself a break from inner judgments and criticism.

The next section addresses the importance of getting past your past and moving into the warmth and reality of Right Now.

Learning from the Past and Letting Go

Life sometimes provides us with no resolution, no closure, and no way to get even with someone who has wronged us. Life may be unfair, but even accepting *that* fact is difficult, so trying to accept the particular unfairnesses of your own situation may feel impossible. It is a great grief to want what you cannot have and to watch the world spin merrily about anyway, despite your pain. Inside everyone is a two-year-old who sits down on Macy's marble floor and screams, "Nooo!" when he's told he can't take the life-size reindeer home.

As children, when we are faced with things we can't control, we try to console ourselves with the idea that when we're grown, our feelings will have more impact on the world. But when as adults we lose something that matters to us or lose relationships with people we love, we still feel helpless and enraged. When people are cruel to us in childhood, we don't forget it as adults, and we may not even accept it, trying again and again to reestablish relationships and make them work out right the next time. When women go from one abusive man to another, repeating the same relationship with different partners, it's often because they choose people who act in ways that are familiar to them. When your world includes violence, threats, and fear, you can't conceive of a world that's not dangerous, so you never even see that safer world. Repeating harmful relationships is a way of not accepting the first, damaging relationship by simply not recognizing any other possible way of life.

Fritz Perls, the founder of Gestalt Therapy, believed that we become poisoned if we don't release negative emotions and old resentments. Sometimes he even needled his patients to get them to express the anger they habitually suppressed (some people didn't like that strategy much, since Perls was an expert at annoying people). As much as we'd like to ignore our bad feelings and wait for them to go away, we have to be responsible for helping them to go away. Letting go is a painful process, and it doesn't happen overnight. That said, letting go is also simple: if you want to let go badly enough, it is possible.

We work through the letting-go process by identifying the problem, looking at its history (the events that created the problem), comparing the events of our present lives to one another, finding connections between them and the original event, and coming to accept what happened in the past while taking positive action to change what's happening now.

✦ IDENTIFYING THE PROBLEM

People often come to the therapist's office because it's so difficult to identify the real problem. Sometimes entire families show up, pointing to the "problem child" and screaming, "Fix him! He's driving us crazy!" A good therapist does more than take the family's word for it, though: too often, the "problem child" is a scapegoat and the real and ongoing problem lies elsewhere, often between the parents. I once knew a family whose adults had serious trouble: when the wife spoke of her husband, it was only to say, "When the girls are grown and I divorce Jake. . . ." The husband, who was Jewish, was decidedly Old World and had spent part of his early life in a concentration camp. The wife was a modern woman. Their love was gone, beaten to death by cruel words on both sides. And they had five-year-old twins.

The family was so conflicted that the husband and wife refused to eat the same food, and their children followed suit. Homecomings were terrible: the parents renewed their fighting as soon as the husband walked in the door. They didn't even hide it from their children, and they used the children against each other at every opportunity. The children—delightful, bright, pretty girls—naturally were affected. Things came to a head one day when, as their father entered the house and their mother went to meet him with an acid remark on her tongue, one of the children ran out into the yard and began stuffing mud into her mouth. Her parents were so shocked that they left off fighting to pull the little girl out of the dirt and yell at her for her bizarre behavior.

This "problem child" was not a crazy kid, but her parents' fighting was driving her crazy. So she found an ingenious way to distract them from their mutual hostility, if only for a minute or two. But I'm sure that if you asked her family at that time, they would have identified her as a problem and wouldn't even have recognized that it was the hatred her parents exhibited daily that had caused her to act out her pain.

We all have things from our past that still cause us pain. When we say someone "pushes our buttons," we are acknowledging the chinks in our armor. But it's also natural that some things are so hurtful to us that we don't want to drag them out of the closet to look at them again. Once was enough! But when we ignore the past, we find it difficult to recognize the reasons we have buttons to push, and we must defend ourselves daily against old hurts. It's exhausting to constantly defend and protect every tender place touched by time.

Often we pin our pain on someone else—the button pusher, for example. If you don't like someone but you're not really sure why, take the time to ask yourself which of their behaviors and attitudes push your buttons. Then ask yourself who they remind you of and at what point in your life you encountered that original person. The following journal questions will also help you identify the root causes of your discomfort with another person.

MY SYNERGY JOURNAL | *Identifying Problems*

What does this person do that I don't like?

_____

How do I interpret the way this person feels about me?

_____

_____

What other interpretations could there be?

_____

_____

Do other people have the same reaction to this person that I do?

_____

_____

How much of this situation is caused by my personal "stuff"?

_____

_____

How old do I feel when I'm around this person?

_____

_____

Who does this person remind me of?

_____

_____

Once you've established the source of your strong reactions, it is easier to identify the real issues. And identifying real issues, real problems, is the first step in letting go. When issues are complicated and difficult to understand or just too painful to face, you might find that a good therapist can help you work out your feelings and discover the original events that could have led to your current problems.

✦ AN EXAMPLE OF LETTING GO

The Problem: Fred's problem is that any time he's about to succeed at a job, he makes a tremendous mistake that invariably loses him the job.

The History: Fred grew up in his father's household, and his father always took the attitude that his son would never amount to anything. Fred's mother left when he was four, and he barely remembers her. He had a tough time in school, and his father beat him after every report card or failed test. Fred grew up determined to show his father that he could be a success. Fred had a wish that he never told anyone: that once he became successful, his father would love him.

The Comparison: Subconsciously, Fred realizes that when he was a kid, his father paid attention to him only when he'd done something wrong, and that his successes were totally ignored. Now when he fails, his father sends him a check along with a mean-spirited letter, but this is the only contact his father has with him. At some level, he has found that failing, the one thing his father can't tolerate, is the only way he can get his father's attention.

The Acceptance: It is agonizing for Fred to admit that if he allows himself to succeed, he will probably lose all contact with his father and any chance he thinks he has of gaining his father's love. He realizes that his father doesn't have enough self-esteem to let Fred be successful—his father is too envious and fearful for that. Although Fred can't readily accept what he knows to be the truth, he resolves to make some behavioral changes and wait for his feelings to change.

The Changes: Fred has always kept in touch with his father throughout his career changes, calling him when things go well (at which the old man grunts and finds an excuse to hang up) and when things go badly (when his father berates him for making stupid errors). Fred resolves not to discuss his work with his father, and he promises himself that he won't tell the old man the next time he loses his job. He isn't going to let his father bail him out financially while further undermining his confidence. This is especially tough because he knows his father won't call him about anything, and thus he is cutting off virtually all contact.

The Outcome: Fred is happy and amazed when he gets his next promotion! He so wants to call his father and share the happy news, but he resists the impulse, knowing he is still trying for approval he can never have. Once his father is out of Fred's career loop, he has no incentive to fail and every reason to succeed. Furthermore, he finds out that it feels good to succeed for himself, not just to get his father's attention. Fred has broken the chain of his failures and, over time, he comes to accept that his father doesn't have the emotional reserves to love anyone, even his own son.

MY SYNERGY JOURNAL | *Letting Go*

My problem (something that recurs in my life and causes me pain and trouble):

_____

_____

My history (what happened in the past that relates to my problem):

_____

_____

_____

My past/present comparison (what aspects of my current problem are familiar from my past?):

_____

_____

What I need to accept (even though it may take some time):

_____

_____

_____

Changes I can make starting right now (specific, different ways I can behave and different choices I can make):

_____

_____

_____

JODY' STORY

There is so much power in identifying the origin of negative program-ming. Once my friend Jody and I were discussing Inner Ecology and how we attract certain people into our lives. Jody had recently expe-rienced a devastating betrayal. She had worked with Mary for the past year, helping to arrange an accounting system for Mary's com-pany. Along the way, the two women had become close friends, and Jody had had every reason to believe that they would work together for some time. Unfortunately, Mary had become romantically involved with a man who took an interest in her company, enough interest that he had decided to work there himself. For reasons of his own, he had turned Mary against Jody. Tension had built until one day Jody came to work and was told she was fired. Her former friend just told her to "go." The man in question took over Jody's job.

Mary's rejection was such a painful experience that Jody had trouble coming to terms with it and letting it go. Her reaction seemed emo-tionally extreme for the situation, so I wondered if it had something to do with a Playback from Wayback. I asked Jody about her rela-tionship with her mother. Jody's eyes clouded over, and she stared at the floor for a long time. Her parents had divorced when she was four, and her mother had become bitter and neurotic as the affluent life they had known became one of poverty and uncertainty. Jody had taken the brunt of most of her mother's frustrations. One day her mother would be fun and loving, and the next day she would rage.

She had raved, ranted, and screamed at Jody, slapped and spanked her with coat hangers over trivial things. She had told her daughter that she would never amount to anything.

Jody's parents had taught her that she was unworthy of receiving love, affection, and support. The emotional abuse she had suffered as a child created low self-esteem and a victim mentality. As an adult, Jody thought she had dealt with most of her old baggage. She was not aware that, subconsciously, she was still allowing that young child to make her adult decisions. She still looked at the world through those young, hurt eyes.

Being fired by someone she thought was her friend had caught her completely off guard. She knew better than to keep asking herself why it had happened, but it was hard. During our conversation, Jody realized that she had a great deal of resentment and anger toward not only her friend but also her parents. Her feelings were so deeply buried that she had never realized them before. In the same way that her mother had scapegoated her after her parents' separation, she now had been scapegoated in Mary's relationship. History had repeated itself. The only possible way Jody could have anticipated the trouble was to notice clues about Mary's behavior: for example, that Mary placed her own priorities above her friendships. Jody might have been able to protect herself had she noticed her friend's callousness earlier in their relationship. But because she was busy re-creating the close relationship she never had had with her mother, she had failed to see the ways in which Mary resembled the worst aspects of her mother. The abandonment by Mary had re-created the pain and loss of Jody's early abandonment by her mother, and so it hurt Jody all the more.

In the weeks that followed our conversation, Jody began to release the hurts of the past and forgive her parents, even though they had both died many years before. Forgiveness is the absolute key to moving *beyond past hurts. Letting go of the past and the pain helped Jody grow and blossom. She started her own business, which became very successful. Meanwhile, Mary's business nearly went bankrupt under the influence of her boyfriend, who eventually left her for someone else.*

Living in the Present

Being stuck in the past or fantasizing about the future makes it impossible to live in a present-moment reality. But staying in the present moment is the beginning of awareness and the discovery and expression of our true selves! Schools don't teach present-moment awareness, as they tend to be future-oriented places. In school, under the best of circumstances, we learn good planning skills that will help us in later life. But under other circumstances, school teaches us to worry. We worry about tests, about how other kids treat us, about teachers who may be less than supportive. We worry about report cards and dances and French verbs. Our present-moment awareness is so consumed by things to worry about, it's a wonder we learn anything at all!

We worry as though it can protect us from harm. Our parents show us the value of worry by aggravating their own hearts and colons over the activities of their ungrateful children. Worry is a timesaver: we imagine the worst that can possibly happen, and we get the heart attack now rather than waiting!

If you're really good at worrying, you can worry entire hours away and wind up feeling upset and anxious. An added bonus is that when you're really worrying well, it's nearly impossible to do anything else properly. Worry actually steals your time while it saps your energy. It is the greatest obstacle between yourself and your present-moment awareness.

Living in the present is an excellent remedy for both "normal neurotics" (that's almost everyone!) and the seriously mentally ill. A few years ago, I designed and developed a program called "The Meaningful Life Course" for the John Henry Foundation, which helps people with mental illnesses lead happier, more productive lives. This course helps individuals with mental illnesses improve the quality of their lives by teaching them to practice present-moment awareness. I begin each course by taking a group to a local park and asking each person what they experience through their five senses. What do they smell? What do they hear? What do they see? What do they feel? I ask them to close their eyes and imagine that they are taking a bite of a lemon. Then I ask them this question: "While you were smelling, hearing, tasting, and feeling things, were you depressed?"

The answer is *always* "no." Depression happens when we dwell in the past or torture ourselves with unhappy thoughts about the future. With our senses engaged in the present, there's no room left for depression! Depression happens when we're not actively engaged in life, and it is dangerous because it slows us down further, gradually removing us from the present moment. Depressed people may feel sad and tired, then stop their usual activities, and then lose touch with friends and family. Someone who is severely depressed physically slows down, too—an experienced eye can spot depression by the way someone walks! Earlier in this book, we discussed the ways that exercise can provide a lift to help you work through emotional pain, and that prescription is good for depression as well.

Did You Know That…?

+ 40 percent of all our thoughts are If-Only Worries (past-oriented and focused on events that are impossible to change now).

+ 30 percent of all our thoughts are What-If Worries (future-oriented).

+ 12 percent are needless health worries.

+ 10 percent are daily frustrations and petty concerns that can be eliminated by our own action. These are the worries we can turn into goals!

+ 8 percent of all our thoughts are real and valid. *Of these, we can only control 4 percent.*

Imagine cutting down your worries by 96 percent!

A great alternative to worry is action. If you create doable goals designed to target areas that trouble you, you automatically reduce your worry, and you find that it takes much less emotional energy to get things done. Do it today, so you won't worry about it for the rest of the week! The major benefit of action (rather than agonizing) is that in the very process of taking action, you build your confidence and enthusiasm. It feels good to get things done! You become more effective, which builds self-esteem and empowers you to do more.

A corporate president once asked a management consultant to help him improve the performance of his top one hundred executives. The consultant didn't have to think twice. He said, "Ask them to make a Things-to-Do-Today list, and let them try to accomplish the six most important things on that list."

End of consultation.

Some months later, the president met with the consultant again and said to him, "You never sent me a bill for the last consultation; you know, the Things-to-Do-Today advice you gave me."

"Oh," said the consultant, "I just mentioned that in passing, but if it was helpful, you can drop a check in the mail in direct proportion to what you think it was worth to you."

Three weeks later, the consultant received a check for one hundred thousand dollars.

Question: If you did the six most important things in your life every day, would you get anything done? Of course you would. Would this be a formula for success? Of course it would. You would accomplish 1,440 *in-the-moment* life experiences per year.

For those of us who were taught to worry when we were young, worry can seem an impossible habit to break, but it really is just a habit and can be controlled with a few simple strategies. Living in the present is the simplest way to break the worry habit. Here are a few others:

✦ W.W.J.—WEEKLY WORRY JOURNAL

This is a notebook in which you write down your worries each week, much the same as you would do in a diary. Your scheduler/planner can become your W.W.J., if you like. Another good idea is to prepare a Things-to-Do-Today list and then use its goals as your "action list" for your W.W.J.: write your list on one page and write down your worries on another page (or even in a separate part of your notebook or planner). Use your weekly worry list to set your goals for the coming week.

Here's an example. Mindy's Weekly Worry Journal looks like this:

I worry that I'm gaining weight.

What if I don't meet that deadline at work?

I don't have anything to wear to the seminar Friday.

Did I pay the phone bill or just lose it?

After looking over her worries, she constructs her goals for the coming week. She plans to attend the new spin class at the gym on Wednesday in addition to her regular workouts, and writes a note to herself about having salad for dinner four times this week. These are small steps toward her weight-loss goal. For the deadline, she plans to review her progress on the project on Monday and seriously evaluate how close she is to achieving her project goal. (Because she's not sure how close she is, her insecurity is causing her to worry.) She plans to shop for a seminar outfit early in the week; if she can't find anything on the first try, she will still have time to look. And before she even writes down a goal for finding the phone bill, she calls the phone company and asks if they have received her payment.

Just making a solid plan to take care of something that troubles you can sometimes be enough to ease your mind.

✦ W.W.T.—WEEKLY WORRY TIME

This is the weekly time you schedule for letting go of things that trouble you. You do this by using your "Mental Workshop" process, which we will discuss soon (see "The Workshop of Your Mind," later in this chapter).

Besides using the Weekly Worry Time to focus on the issues that cause you to worry, it can also be used for thinking through and solving challenges and problematic situations, coming up with workable ideas, and calming yourself. Once you have allowed yourself a certain amount of Weekly Worry Time, you tell yourself, "Okay, that's it for the week!" When worries crop up during the week, make a note to cover them at your next worry session. Then get on with the important things in your life! If you insist on worrying, do it on a schedule, and do it *only* on that schedule. The rest of the time, consider yourself a free agent who doesn't need to obsess.

✦ W.W.C.—WEEKLY WORRY CHAIR

Your Weekly Worry Chair can be a comfortable friendly armchair, a desk chair, or even a park bench. It can be any chair that allows you to feel comfortable and secure while you list and work through your worries and concerns. Ideally, you sit in this chair only while you worry, so don't choose your favorite recliner!

Go to your Weekly Worry Chair when you plan to worry, but make a deal with yourself that you will worry only in that chair. When you catch yourself worrying in some other chair (or while standing in line or driving your car), remind yourself gently but firmly that this is not the time or the place to worry, and then turn your attention to the present.

✦ W.W.M.—WEEKLY WORRY MUSIC

I use music to motivate myself, and you might do the same thing. Moviemakers have always known that music can set a scene, so as you're finishing a worry session, you may want to put on something bouncy and happy to energize you. You may decide you like some background music while you worry, or you may start out with some super-heavy classical opera to remind yourself that worrying might be more about drama, and less about real life, than we sometimes believe!

✦ W.W.R.—WEEKLY WORRY REWARD

Each week, after you've accomplished your worrying in a relatively healthy way, select an uplifting, enjoyable activity, hobby, restaurant, or sport, and reward yourself with it. Another Weekly Worry Reward is to give the gift of love. Help someone, and don't expect anything in return. Do it once a week. Give flowers, a book, a card, a smile, a compliment, a hug to someone in need. People need love so much. We all need twelve hugs a day just to get by! Are you getting your quota?

◆ WORRY PREVENTION: CHOOSE TO HAVE A JOYFUL DAY

After you wake up each morning, have a great stretch, get out of bed, look at yourself in the mirror, and affirm, "I am unique. I am one of a kind, and today, I am going to have a wonderful day." If you're in a hurry, you can just say, "Ain't I cute?" You will start out smiling and in the present moment. If it sounds silly, think of it this way: what is more important than taking control of your day, being in the present moment, and channeling your thoughts into positive attitudes?

To have a good day, you need to do more than a wake-up affirmation, however: you may need to reaffirm your decision to have a good day after you've been cut off in traffic, spilled your coffee on your new white shirt, or forgotten an important meeting. Sometimes you have to stop a minute and adjust your attitude, just as someone might straighten his tie. Take a deep breath, let go of the frustration, smile once for yourself, and say, "Okay, but I'm still going to have a wonderful day." Stubbornly hold on to your right to enjoy your life!

◆ WORRY'S EVIL TWIN—ANXIETY

Anxiety may manifest itself as bodily aches and pains, such as TMJ (jaw pain associated with grinding your teeth), lumps in the throat or stomach, headache, backache, or any number of other somatic clues. Especially in people who aren't in close touch with their emotions, anxiety can appear as a sudden physical ailment that mysteriously appears and disappears when they're under particular stress. Anxiety attacks may make you feel that you have to escape, that you're suffocating or having a heart attack. Although they can be terrifying, they are totally treatable.

Five Strategies for Dealing with Anxiety

1. Go to a quiet place and breathe deeply and slowly. Breathing deeply fills your body with oxygen and helps your muscles to relax.

2. Talking to yourself is a great method to reduce anxiety. I talk to myself all the time. I talk to the TV and my car radio. I vent as much as I can. It's healthy. Another way to talk to yourself is to use affirmations. Affirmations can really reduce your anxiety level. Repeat the words "I feel calm.... Everything is all right...." and let your mind guide your body toward that calmness.

3. Music is a very powerful mood changer, and it is also very therapeutic. When you feel anxious, put on music you find soothing. If you're not in a place where you can get to music, just close your eyes and play something soothing in your mind. Hum it to yourself. If you have a hard time getting out of bed in the morning, choose music that uplifts you: put on something jazzy, and dance around while you get dressed. At the end of the day, use calming tunes to quiet your mind before bed.

4. Write your feelings in a journal. Sometimes it's also effective to write letters to other people or to yourself: you don't have to mail them; you're writing them as an exercise to get in closer touch with your feelings. It doesn't matter if you "can't write" (hardly anyone "can write"!), so don't judge your skill and don't worry about grammar. Just write and get it out. The journal exercises in this book are intended to help you do guided journalizing; you may decide to use writing in other parts of your life as well!

5. Get plenty of physical exercise. Run, walk, go to the gym, and burn off the stress. Cardiovascular exercise such as aerobics, swimming, or spinning improves your breathing and lung capacity, increases the amount of oxygen you absorb, makes your heart a more efficient pump, and improves circulation. The brain releases more endorphins, naturally brightening your mood and strengthening your immune system. If you sometimes feel like running for your life, just run!

Relax-Action

It is nearly impossible to envision where and what you want to be when your mind is cluttered with fragments of unfinished business, old hurts, trivial details, and the muck of everyday life. Fortunately, the mind-body connection works so perfectly that, when one system is relaxed, the other is, too. Relax-Action is a process that starts by relaxing the body, then lets the calm and purposeful mind bring you where you need to be: closer to your true self. Following the steps of Relax-Action is a process of synergy: you use your body and mind to access your spiritual self and its wishes. Listening to the desires of your true self creates visions and energy—the perfect way for synergy to work!

Relax-Action is a stress-reduction process that helps you to turn your wishes and dreams into reality. It can be used to calm anxiety and to prepare for new challenges in everyday life. You can do Relax-Action as a simple exercise to relax before or after work, when you're getting ready to go to sleep, or at any time you need to feel calmer and more focused. Relax-Action differs from ordinary relaxation: there is more than relaxation going on here. In fact, you are gearing up your mind and body for the ultimate action—the creation of synergy!

The Relax-Action procedure has four steps:

Step One. Breathe energy, release stress, and reenergize

Step Two. Release energy bottlenecks

Step Three. Visualize calm colors

Step Four. Go to deeper levels

Each step leads you closer to another essential Life Synergy tool, the Mental Workshop, which we'll discuss a bit later in the book. Relax-Action is a preparation for entering the Mental Workshop, where you learn to target very specific changes that you want to make and then imagine them as you want them to be. If you aren't relaxed, the Mental Workshop isn't totally effective; although a few hurried, harried moments of envisioning are better than nothing. To see results, it's important to start your personal-growth work with a focused relaxation period.

Relax-Action begins with quieting the body, so you'll need thirty undisturbed minutes each day to practice. Ideally, practice at the same time each day, seated in a comfortable, upright chair. Begin the process on your own, or use a prerecorded audiotape to take you through the steps (see the order form at the back of this book).

STEP ONE | *Breathe Energy, Release Stress, and Reenergize*

Sit upright in your chair and breathe in deeply though your nose. Your stomach should move in and out when you breathe—that means you're breathing deeply and optimally using your lungs. If your shoulders move, or if only your chest moves, concentrate on letting your stomach rise up and down with each inhalation and exhalation.

Breathe in through your nose and out through your mouth. As you breathe out, prolong your exhale, clearing your lungs completely. You should be able to hear yourself exhaling, even if you have to close your mouth slightly. Do this for about 1 minute. Then breathe in and hold your breath to the count of four, and then breathe out to the count of four. Do this for 1 minute.

STEP TWO | *Release Energy Bottlenecks*

1. As you breathe in, lift and tense your left leg, point your toe, and hold this position to the count of four. Breathe out through your mouth to the count of four, and then relax your leg. Repeat this procedure with the right leg, then repeat with both legs at the same time, and then relax.

   Say to yourself: "Relax—relax—relax."

2. Breathe in, then tighten the muscles of your stomach and hold to the count of four. Then release, breathe out through your mouth, and relax.

   Say to yourself: "Relax—relax—relax."

3. Breathe in and tense your arms as if you are picking up a heavy weight, and hold to the count of four. Then release, breathe out through your mouth, and relax.

    Say to yourself: "Relax—relax—relax."

4. Breathe in, lift your shoulders to touch your ears, and hold to the count of four. Then release, breathe out through your mouth, and relax.

    Say to yourself: "Relax—relax—relax."

5. Breathe in, slowly turn your head, look over your left shoulder, and then look behind yourself, slowly and carefully stretching the muscles in your neck. Hold to the count of four. Then release, breathe out through your mouth, and relax. Do this three times. Repeat the procedure looking over your right shoulder, then relax.

    Say to yourself: "Relax—relax—relax."

6. Sit in silence, just relaxing and allowing yourself to feel physical calmness. Drop your shoulders and imagine all your muscles relaxing, from head to toe.

STEP THREE | *Visualize Calm Colors*

Read the list of colors and their particular benefits below, then choose one or two on which to concentrate:

Red is physical. You visualize red to feel physically relaxed and energized.

Orange is emotional. Visualize orange when you want to calm your emotions.

Yellow is mental. Visualize yellow when you seek mental clarity.

Green is peaceful. Visualize green to feel calm and fresh.

Blue is aspiration. Visualize blue to inspire you with hope, focus, and energy.

Purple is spiritual. Visualize purple it to connect spiritually with your universe.

Violet is self-esteem. Visualize violet to center yourself, to let go of self-conscious thoughts, and to feel good.

White is purity. Visualize white to cleanse any negative ideas, experiences, or feelings.

Now, close your eyes, breathe evenly, and imagine the color you want to use. Beginning at the top of your head, let the color roll slowly and deliberately all the way down through your body and out through your toes. Imagine it all over your body: behind your ears, in the creases of your elbows, trickling into your hairline, and in the arches of your feet. Feel it warming your whole body like an herbal wrap. Pay attention to how each color feels to you, and to the way you feel after doing this part of your Relax-Action.

STEP FOUR | *Go to Deeper Levels*

This stage of Relax-Action is especially useful for clarifying your mind during confused times. Before you begin this stage, you'll want to choose a beautiful and calming scene from nature. It can be anything: a field, a beach, a forest, or the "personal landscape" that you envisioned at the start of Chapter 3. (Look ahead a few pages to the "Peaceful Scenes from Nature" section, which helps you choose and envision such a scene.)

Visualize a stairway leading downward. This stairway has twenty-one steps. At the bottom of the stairway is a door. On the other side of the door is a shower room. Here, before proceeding onward, you will cleanse yourself with a shower of white light. Beyond the shower room lies your peaceful scene from nature.

Now imagine that you are standing at the top of the stairs. You proceed downward from the top step (step twenty-one) to the bottom step (step one). Count down the steps. With each descending step, you feel yourself becoming deeply relaxed and in tune with yourself.

After reaching the last step, enter the shower room. Now imagine white light flowing and streaming down over your entire body. Feel it cleansing and removing all negativity. Now, step out of the shower and proceed to the peaceful natural scene that you've imagined. It is utterly clean and perfect. You are one with everything that you see. All your senses are captivated by the smells, sights, and sounds. You notice every single detail, and you are extremely relaxed and peaceful. You can stay here as long as you want.

When you decide to return, reverse the procedure. First, enter the shower room and let the white light cleanse you. Then step out of the shower door and see the stairway leading upward. Count from one to twenty-one. On each ascending number, you feel more energized, relaxed, and in tune with life. Come up through a rainbow of calming colors: violet, purple, blue, green, yellow, orange, and red. Open your eyes, stretch, and breathe deeply.

That concludes a simple Relax-Action stress-reduction procedure. Next, you are ready to enter the Mental Workshop, where you uncover your dreams, address your troubles, and plan for success—all by using the power and strength of your imagination.

The Workshop of Your Mind

Your ability to create pictures in your mind—images of your desires, which are supported by a driving sense of purpose and a clear set of goals—can transform your life into one of fulfillment and validation. You lessen stress, learn to relax, and, along the way, the future becomes clearer and more definite. Now that you've learned how to visualize through Relax-Action, you're ready to learn how to use the visualization tools found in the Workshop of the Mind.

Imagine that you are in a movie theater and that you can choose whatever you want to see on the screen. You are the producer, the director, and the main character in your movie. You can bring it all to life because you are the designer of your life. How will your story unfold? Will the hero win or lose? Will the hero be admired and seen as a person of honor? Will the poor boy, the underprivileged girl, the abused child overcome life's challenges and rise to the occasion? Will your heart be full of joy and your spirit sing at the images of the great accomplishments you create? In the Mental Workshop, you use your dreams to create your present.

Creating your own big picture is the most powerful ability you possess. Using your imagination and your ability to visualize, you can liberate yourself from fear, motivate yourself to make your dreams into reality, and inspire yourself to dream often—and dream big.

You use the Mental Workshop to rebuild life from the inside out. The Workshop helps you deal with personal truths and your perceived failures and also helps you envision the future and build your character. In the Mental Workshop, you can practice being the person you want to be, plan for the future, and let go of the past.

Your Mental Workshop is a room that you design yourself. You set it up inside your mind as though you are actually redecorating a den or study where you will do important work in a comfortable atmosphere. Put your favorite pictures on the wall, include furniture that feels welcoming, and see that the room includes the colors, plants, books, and personal mementos that make you feel safe and happy.

In addition, some basic equipment should be included in all Mental Workshops: a computer, a control chair, a "Truth Booth," and a corner shower that emits white, purifying light. Here's an explanation of each item.

First, you have a powerful, user-friendly computer that has the complete history of your life, starting at your birth. You can access any year and anything that has happened at any given time. Your computer can also project these images onto a movie screen, television screen, and a "mental mirror," all of which you'll want to arrange around your Workshop (explanations of how to use each of these special tools are given below). This ability to project images will help you accomplish your current goals.

You also have a control chair. It's a comfortable chair that fits your body like it was built for it (it was!). Position it so that you can easily turn on the television or movie screen.

In one corner of the room is the Truth Booth. The Truth Booth is used to come to terms with the real you, your true feelings and submerged angers and resentments.

The white-light shower is just like the one that you used during the Relax-Action procedure. Position it just outside your Mental Workshop's door. Then work through the Relax-Action as it's described above, but rather than entering your peaceful scene from nature after you've showered, enter the Workshop and set to work on improving what area, or areas, of your life that you want to change.

Here's an explanation of how to use each special tool that you've now set up inside your Workshop.

✦ MENTAL MIRRORS

Your mental mirror is used to transform your self-image. In your mental mirror, you envision yourself the way you want to be. You may have physical goals such as losing or gaining weight or getting stronger, or you may have emotional goals, such as becoming happier and calmer. Mental mirrors are useful for envisioning a slimmer body or for imagining what it's like to go through life smiling.

Once you've entered your Workshop, stand in front of the mirror and picture yourself the way you are now, the image you'd like to change. You might say something such as, "This isn't what I have in mind." Then replace the current image with the one you want to see. When you envision your new image, be as detailed as you can, right down to your clothes and the expression on your face. If you want to be more successful at work, you might picture yourself in just the right outfit for your career, holding your briefcase (or the tiger you're training) and smiling broadly because your job makes you so happy. If you're interested in strengthening your body, add your "mental mirror" visualization process to your regular physical workouts and picture yourself fit, toned, and strong.

Mental mirrors can even be used to change your feelings! When something makes you angry, go to your mental mirror and see yourself angry. Then say, "This isn't how I want to be! This isn't how I need to be! How do I want to be?" Watch your face change as you re-imagine yourself as calm. Visualize your face growing smoother as those cranky wrinkles ease up. See your eyes opening wider as you stop frowning. Once your face looks

Your Mental Workshop

pleasant again, just hold it there for a minute and enjoy the sight of yourself in a serene state. Use your serene face to let go of anger.

When I diet, I use affirmations along with my mental mirrors to keep myself motivated and to synergize my intentions with my actions. I see myself as I am (almost but not quite perfect), then I visualize myself the way I want to be (closer to perfection than ever before). My affirmations go something like this: "I'm too sexy to be pudgy" (although a more serious man might say, "I'm too handsome not to look good"). Visualizing myself slim also helps me remember the goals I'm striving to reach when I choose between a bacon cheeseburger and a nutritious salad. When I use my mental mirror, I usually find that I crave the salad.

The mental mirror is a great tool—the hardest thing about it is remembering to use it! When you're pursuing a goal, use your mental mirror every day to help yourself achieve what you want. Visualize yourself successful, healthy, happy, and confident, and you'll be surprised at the strength of your images and the way that they follow you into your ordinary life, transforming it so that it becomes as you want it to be!

✦ MENTAL MOVIE SCREENS

Mental movie screens are used to envision the future. On the screen, you use the power of your mind to create your future by imagining what you want to have, to be, and to do. Again, be as detailed as you can, and always give your movie a happy ending. If you're not yet sure of what you want, use the mental movie screen to fantasize about the things that make you happy. Imagine yourself in situations that you enjoy and around people whom you like. Use these daydreams as a starting point for the creation of new, life-enhancing goals. Maybe you've been contemplating a change such as taking up singing or acting, or a new career move such as becoming a real estate agent. Picture yourself singing on stage and being wildly successful. Imagine yourself acting out a scene in front of a spellbound audience. Or visualize yourself selling a fantastic house with the ease of an old pro. Your mental movie screen is a great tool when you're setting goals and planning your success. Envisioning your desires helps you to access the synergy of your mind to bring them into reality.

✦TELEVISION SCREENS

Mental television screens are used for interpersonal conflict resolution. Upon them, you can "rewind" situations that were uncomfortable and review them like videotapes from the safe comfort of your chair. As you review the situation, you can watch for things you might have missed the first time around. Sometimes conflict arises through misunderstanding, and it helps to step back and look for missed cues. As I review a tape, I can ask myself if I had any negative input into an argument, whether I came into it with a competitive agenda, a prejudice, or an axe to grind. I can review my choices and the way that I dealt with the other person in the "scene" and consider ways I could have behaved differently. Finally, after carefully looking over the scene, I can re-create the scene in the way I would like it to be, and then resolve to play such scenes differently next time they occur in reality. The mental television screen is terrific for teaching us to be honest with ourselves and to make changes in the way we react to unpleasant events or arguments.

✦PEACEFUL SCENES FROM NATURE

These imaginary scenes are used to calm yourself and open your mind to new ideas. In the process, they can teach you about self-love and help you to release toxic relationships and Playbacks from Wayback.

It doesn't matter what scene you envision, as long as it makes you feel peaceful, hopeful, and content. The place you choose might be the beach, the mountains, the desert, or a meadow. Relaxation happens easiest in these imaginary places, where you can take a minivacation from stress. These minivacations are unlike "real" vacations in that you may be tempted to cheat on the time you spend in your imaginary scene, but they're also better than real vacations: every ten minutes you spend visualizing your peaceful scene is like a whole day in the real place, and there's no airfare or customs officials to interfere with your enjoyment. If you give yourself the time to truly relax in your imaginary scene, it will pay off for you in better health, increased creativity and energy, and a happier attitude.

◆ THE TRUTH BOOTH

When you step into the Truth Booth, you take time to discard your ego-related defenses and the excuses you offer to others that you know, deep down, aren't true. The Truth Booth is useful for teaching yourself to say, "Okay, I haven't been facing this, but now I'm going to do just that."

Linda used the Truth Booth to decide to leave her job of ten years. She had been working at a community health center, and although she was good at her job, she had always found the paperwork tedious. She was organized, reliable, and efficient, so she was quite successful and soon rose to a management position. But the more she was promoted, the more she sat at her desk and the less she interacted with people. Suffering from mild depression, she attended my Life Mastery Seminar, intending to bring back ideas to her health center to use in staff training. After the seminar, she went home, tried the Relax-Action, and built her Mental Workshop. Here's what she told me about the experience.

> I used the Mental Workshop for a couple of weeks, with my focus being finding more joy in my work—the kind of pleasure I used to take in working with people to help them solve their problems. But I kept hitting a wall, because my job was no longer about helping people as much as it was about documentation and higher-level reports. After a couple of weeks, it occurred to me that I was ignoring the Truth Booth, and I wondered what else I was avoiding.
>
> I was afraid of the Truth Booth because I didn't want to face the fact that my job no longer excited me. I didn't want to make a change at that time in my life, and I think a lot of my old Playbacks about security, about being a reliable, career-oriented person, were getting in my way. In the Truth Booth, I recognized that no matter how hard I tried, I couldn't just accept my job the way it was. So I had to make a change—in the job.

When Linda fantasized about the kind of work she wanted to do, she realized she wanted to return to hands-on work with patients. Rather than just searching for a new job, she went to her boss and explained that she missed doing occupational therapy and wanted to leave her administrative position for something more fulfilling. After hiring and training her replacement, Linda returned to working directly with clients, but because of her expertise, she also became the intern supervisor of the training program. The health center retained an enthusiastic and experienced counselor, and Linda created her dream job.

I have used the Mental Workshop as a primary tool for patients at mental hospitals. Some people fear that giving mentally ill people imagination exercises will exacerbate their symptoms, but I have found the opposite to be true. It is as if giving patients the permission and the skills they need to use their imaginations also gives them control over a part of their lives that they once felt controlled them. We teach them to visualize lives of hope and dignity and help them set goals and take steps toward independence, and that is an empowering process. It's a beautiful thing to see someone who started out looking like a scared rabbit take on the glow and joy of a person who finds meaning and purpose in life.

Imagination: The Playground of Potential

The recognized five senses are touch, taste, sight, smell, and hearing. Some people believe in a sixth sense, extrasensory perception (ESP). Probably, senses exist that we don't even have names for—can you believe that people are truly capable of sensing things in only five ways? What about the feeling you have when you walk into a room and can tell people were just talking about you? What about when you get a really good or really bad feeling about someone you've just met? Which of the five ordinary senses do such experiences fall under?

The senses we don't name still exist. One of our strongest senses—one that can be used to drastically improve our quality of life—is the imagination. Imagination is a tool that we use to spark the flames of directed passion and thus manifest our hopes and dreams in reality. It is your personal playground. It also contains your Mental Workshop, where you connect your hopes and dreams through purposeful planning. The imagination is the power switch for all potential; it's the source of possibility and the foundation of probability.

The most effective way to make deep changes is to use the imagination to clearly envision your goals and then support those goals with physical action. Using your imagination lets you reveal your true and full potential, change your consciousness, release hate, fear, and prejudice, and replace them with spiritual love and harmony.

GEORGE'S STORY:
THE POWER OF THE IMAGINATION

George was a highly successful businessman. He had everything his heart could desire: a happy marriage, a beautiful home, and a thriving business. George personified the American dream: a driven and ambitious overachiever. He prided himself on being a self-made man and was proud of how hard he had worked to achieve his goals.

I first met George at one of my seminars for small-businesspeople. He stood at the back, and I was particularly moved when I noticed his tearful response to a story I told about achieving success. In the next seminar, I was dumbfounded when I saw George literally sobbing as he listened to my talk. At the time, I didn't know that his emotional volatility was a symptom of Lou Gehrig's disease, amyotrophic lateral sclerosis (ALS). ALS destroys the muscles, rendering a person unable to move. Mentally and spiritually, sufferers remain very much alive for a time, but their bodies deteriorate in this relentless and eventually fatal illness.

As ALS took hold, George could no longer work at his usual hectic pace. When the disease progressed, he asked that I come to his home and help him. The only thing I knew how to do in the situation was to teach George how to meditate, to quiet his mind and visualize his body becoming healthier. George used meditation and visualization— the foundation of Relax-Action—every morning upon waking and every night before going to sleep. After each session, his family noticed an improvement in his skin tone and mobility. By using the Relax-Action techniques, George was able to reduce his pain, improve his sleep, and experience a peace he had never known before. As the disease progressed even further, he was grateful that he could improve his quality of life under the worst of circumstances.

Even when George's body was no longer under his control, he used the power of his mind to effect changes in his health and well-being. It seems too good to be true that we can change our body's response to pain and illness by just thinking, but for the last thirty years, research has shown again and again that our mind can and does control our bodily processes. Cancer patients are now taught to visualize their cancers being chewed up by chemicals, their tumors shrinking out of sight. A sizable number of those who use visualization to fight illness do manage to shrink tumors, go into remission, or noticeably decrease pain—just by thinking.

✦ ENVISIONING

We come from stolid, "show-me" stock. Fantasizing never got the field plowed, and we don't trust what we can't see. Our highly imaginative children are labeled as "daydreamers" and scolded for coloring outside the lines or not paying attention in class. By the time we finish our education, we have had little training in using our minds to create our realities and have still less time to do so. But it's never too late to start! The toughest part about using your imagination is setting aside the time (a few minutes twice a day) to sit down, close your eyes, and dream. Much of this book is about making commitments: to yourself, your family, and your community. The ongoing challenge is to take care of yourself in such a way that you can make time to learn new strategies and skills. Although the results of imagining and envisioning may be miraculous, the process is straightforward, so commit to donating a few daily TV commercials' worth of time to making miracles happen!

The word *vision* has several meanings, but, interestingly, we as a culture consider two of them direct opposites. Vision is the physical process of sight—the way rods and cones and lens and fovea work together to create a representation of the "real" world. Although vision is a miracle in itself, we tend to take it for granted as a normal, mechanical function. A vision, on the other hand, is something one sees while in a spiritual ecstasy or trance. If I say, "I saw the end of the world," you will respond much differently than you would had I said, "I saw a blue jay in that tree." *Vision*—it's one word with two wildly different meanings. In the first, it is a normal process that most of us can understand because we experience it daily. In the second, it is an abstract process that most of us may not understand—probably we even distrust it. Visions are had by saints, mystics, and lunatics, not by normal working folk like you and me.

In making this conceptual distinction between normal sight and what some might call second sight, we deprive ourselves of one of the most powerful and universal gifts—the power to create a new reality. In fact, we all have visions every day—the new mother sees her baby grown and with children of her own; little kids with toy trucks entirely destroy, then rebuild civilizations; a young man at work dreams of owning the company. These are all visions, fleeting, unexpressed, even suppressed because we think it's silly to daydream.

But daydreams are the fiber of reality. Envisioning a different reality is the first step toward changing the current one, and a practiced, conscious, aware method of envisioning is necessary to reach your goals and express the passion of the true self.

Rose is five-foot-four and once weighed upward of three hundred pounds. She attended one of my Synergy Life Mastery weekend retreats. There she learned to set goals, practiced envisioning, and spent time writing out affirmations. This thirty-five-year-old mom decided to lose weight. She made an audiotape of her affirmations and listened to it every day while she drove to work. By the time I wrote this book, she had lost one hundred pounds and was on her way to losing still more. Through simple imagination and affirmations, she has changed her whole life!

Creativity

Rose is a terrific example of using creativity to achieve your goals. She used her commuting "down time," when she might have listened to the radio news, to re-envision herself. Creativity is not always elaborate; it is what works, often in ways others wouldn't think of trying. Creative visualization is a powerful tool to get what you want, and a side benefit is the fact that visualization opens up other aspects of your creativity. For example, you may find that when you use daydreaming to envision your success, success shows up in your nighttime dreams, too. Like Linda, in the Truth Booth example, you may start with one set of goals and discover that your visions and night-time dreams refuse to cooperate and lead you in a new direction, one you want so deeply that you can no longer ignore it. In this case, your goals may need revision. Maybe they're old goals that you no longer truly value, or maybe they were imposed by someone else and aren't truly part of you. Pay attention to your daydreams and nighttime dreams—write them down, draw pictures of them, discuss them with trusted friends.

If you feel that you don't have time to use your creativity, that may also be a clue to things that you need to change. When you have trouble committing to the time needed for visualizations in your Mental Workshop or for affirmations, don't bewail your heavy schedule, but look for the internal brakes that keep you from your desires.

Why Is Change So Hard?

A body at rest tends to stay at rest, which is what keeps us from falling out of bed at night. And a mind at rest is something we all strive for—a sense of peace. Sometimes we might feel that our sense of internal peace is threatened when we realize that we need to make changes. We all are childishly wishful when change is needed: we want the world to change around us or we want the people in our lives to change. People rarely say, "I want to change"; they say, "I want *a* change"—a change of scenery, change of partner, change of career.

Change is difficult because it takes effort and because there's no guarantee it will be an improvement in the end. We don't really know what to expect once we've made the effort, and it's that fear that causes indecisiveness and entropy. I used to commute with a woman who was a nurse, and after we'd ridden together a few times, she confided to me that her husband had been beating her and that she was planning to take the children and leave him as soon as she had enough money. "How long has this been going on?" I asked, thinking I should try to help her get out right away.

"Twelve years," she answered.

Since her wedding day, this woman had been smacked around, threatened, and humiliated. She started nursing school as part of a long-term plan to leave her husband, and she had worked as a nurse's aide while she got her education. I couldn't decide whether to be impressed by her ability to withstand trauma and still plan for her children's future or to be saddened and upset by the fact that she had waited so long for her life to begin. And now I wonder if she ever left him.

Trying to change can feel like wading hip-deep in a bog, or like slogging through the first few days of a stop-smoking program: it's easy to want to lie down and give it all up. Using the Mental Workshop is a great help when you're making changes because it can help you to rehearse and envision new behaviors, such as saying, "No, thanks" when someone offers you a cigar at a party.

Affirmations

Affirmations are the link between your dreams and action: they state your intention to make things go a certain way. If I say to you, "After work, I'm going to walk for at least twenty minutes today," there's a better chance that I will actually take that walk, simply because I announced my intention to you. Part of it is pride—I want you to think of me as someone who does what he says he'll do. But another part of it is that, by stating my intention to walk, I have strengthened that very intention. I have made an affirmation, and it has changed my behavior.

Words have great power, for both good and evil. "Sticks and stones may break my bones, but words can never hurt me." We've all said or heard that, usually after we've been devastated by someone's verbal cruelty. But it's not true. Of course words can hurt! And words can heal, soothe, make us feel loved and safe and hopeful. Our most powerful ceremonies center on the words we say: "ashes to ashes," "what do you name this child?" and "I do" are a few of the words we use to bring shape and substance to important times in our lives. In rituals, as in prayer, we affirm our feelings and intentions by attaching words to them and sending them winging into the universe. And the universe replies.

Positive affirmations can replace negative ones in the same way that healing thoughts can replace inhibiting ones. Saying affirmations aloud makes them even more powerful.

Here are some examples of positive affirmations, and what they may be used for:

+ I,_____ [your name], *am strong, flexible, and lithe* (countering arthritis or other joint problems).

+ *I work with enjoyment and energy that helps me succeed* (motivation for work).

+ *I have fun with my children and participate fully in their lives* (enjoying family).

+ *I feel confident when meeting and talking with new people* (overcoming shyness).

+ *I am going to ace that algebra test Friday* (nervousness about upcoming tasks).

The mind is a sophisticated and calculating organism. Do not wish for something that you do not have, because you are then affirming that you do not have it now. If you say, "I wish I were happier," it affirms that you're actually unhappy now. Say what you want, not what you don't want! What if you asked me, "What do you want for dinner?" and I said, "Well, I surely don't want chicken!" That wouldn't help you much in your choice of menu, would it? Remember that the universe is a grand buffet—only take what you want.

Clearly state your wish as though you already have it. Say, "I'm happy and fulfilled," not "I want to be happy and fulfilled."

The magic of affirmations lies in their repetition. If you've ever trained a dog, you know it takes hours of dedicated practice, scheduled at regular times, to effect a change in behavior. The human mind is more sophisticated than a dog's, but as we discussed earlier, we don't especially like to change, either. Use affirmations every day, not only to state your goals but when you feel down and something has made you feel negative. At least twice a day, speak your affirmations out loud; a good time to practice is when you're driving.

And in addition to speaking your affirmations, write them down—don't underestimate the power of written affirmations. Instead of doodling while talking on the phone, write down your affirmations. A student who attended one of my classes improved her attitude this way. She usually drew little pictures as she spoke on the phone, but now she wrote the words "I will, I can, I will, I can, I will, I can, I will, I can." These words were her mantra, and she found that she felt more capable, more purposeful, and more effective in her schoolwork. Affirmations spoken aloud, spoken within the mind, and written down are all an extremely powerful force for growth.

MY SYNERGY JOURNAL | *Affirmations*

Write ten affirmations that you intend to practice twice a day for the next month. (I've done the first one for you!) Keep track of any changes you notice—you may find that after a while, you no longer need certain affirmations because they've been fulfilled by the universe. When that happens, give thanks and write new ones!

My Affirmations

1. I,_____[your name], *feel energetic and filled with life.*

2. _____

_____

3. _____

_____

4. _____

_____

5. _____

_____

6. _____

_____

7. _____

_____

8. _____

_____

9. _____

_____

10. _____

_____

Synergy in Choice

I have always had a dread of becoming
a passenger in life.

PRINCESS MARGRETHE OF DENMARK

Using Your Thoughts and Your Feelings

When we talked about the different kinds of intelligence in Step Four of this book, I mentioned that many people have more than one kind. In addition to the fact that everyone possesses different kinds and levels of intelligence, people also possess different levels of logic and emotion. Yet we're taught that logic and emotion are opposites of each other. Sometimes this expresses itself through gender stereotypes—the stereotypical male is logical and unemotional, and the stereotypical female is illogical and emotional—but in real life, we are all mixtures of logic and emotion. In fact, the most persuasive speakers, the finest legal minds, and the most respected spiritual leaders tend to be logical and emotional at the same time. Emotion can fuel a speech with passion and create sympathy in the listener, and logic explains the reasons behind the argument. Martin Luther King, Jr., was a perfect example of the logical and emotional at work together. His "I Have a Dream" speech explained through sheer poetry the deep need for racial harmony. It was one of the defining oratories of American history, based on clear thought and his deep desire to connect with his audience.

So, it's not necessary to choose between being logical and being emotional. One of the most freeing things in life is the realization that you are so much more than you've been told! You can break the habits of a lifetime and the expectations of those around you by making a deliberate choice to use more than one aspect of your being to accomplish your goals. Essential to making that choice is awareness—I have to realize that I have social skills and physical skills and logical skills, and that I'm not just "the pretty one." After awareness comes choice itself, the choice to be more than you've been told you can be. This might be hard for many, especially women, who have been told it's impolite to make choices that contradict social convention and may unconsciously limit themselves by trying to be what the world tells them they should be. Choosing to be everything that you truly are is revolutionary, but you owe it to yourself to access and use everything you have—everything you are to create the reality of your choice.

When you choose to be "purely" logical or entirely emotional, you use only part of your available resources. When you're being wholly emotional and feelings overwhelm you, it's important to stop and use logic to take a look at what's happening inside. Feelings, especially negative ones, are signals that you need to slow down and then try to think straight. On the other hand, insisting that only rational thought counts is a mistake, too, and if you find yourself doing this, ask yourself whether you're using logic as a cocoon to protect yourself against some sort of pain.

You achieve synergy by using all your available resources, by turning your physical, spiritual, mental, and emotional attention to the task at hand. Synergy requires using every part of your personality to accomplish the things that matter in life. If you're a "Star Trek" fan, you remember that a large part of Mr. Spock's charm was due to the fact that, although he was supremely logical, he had deep and abiding ties to Captain Kirk—evidence of an important emotional connection. Mr. Spock may not have expressed his emotionality, but his values clearly included more than the esteemed Vulcan trait of pure logic.

Compartmentalizing the parts of your true self, ignoring your intelligences or even your reprehensible desires, hinders you from reaching your goals, as the shut-off parts aren't allowed to join in the pursuit of the goal.

As James Hillman once said, when talking about the importance of paying attention to the "shadow" side of the personality, honoring even the marginal parts of your personality, the biker babe behind the bank manager, the seal-hunter in the strict vegetarian, is vastly important in learning to live with the entire self. When we submerge parts of ourselves that we consider weak or dangerous or useless, we also chain ourselves to a lesser expression of our true selves. Left out, our shadow sides not only cannot contribute to our well-being, but also they clamor loudly behind the scenes and can even sabotage our success. The bank manager needs that hidden biker babe to come to her defense when her boss passes her over for promotion or sexually harasses her.

This is not to say that people should run around expressing every part of themselves all the time—that would be insane. But it's important to recognize that every part of your true self may serve a useful purpose when life presents you with new and often unexpected challenges. Actions require balance: don't be ruled by any single part of yourself, but do let them all work together whenever possible.

DAVE'S STORY

Dave, a civil engineer with his own firm, thought of himself as a highly rational man, and his sharp, clear mind impressed everyone else as well. But when his wife had their first baby, Dave's logical mind was of very little help. The baby was colicky, his wife drained and exhausted, so Dave rearranged his work schedule to help with his daughter. His wife tried every possible medicine, but nothing seemed to help. His mother-in-law, an old woman from Appalachia, suggested that they boil an onion in water and give the baby the cooled juice to drink. Dave checked in with the pediatrician, who laughed and said, "Well, it won't help, but it won't hurt, either."

Based on the doctor's feedback, Dave reasoned that his mother-in-law's suggestion was just an "old wives' tale," so he ignored her advice. Meanwhile, the baby screamed half the night and vomited up the little food they could get her to eat. One evening, as he held the wailing infant, Dave admitted defeat. He boiled the onion, cooled the liquid in the freezer until it felt barely warm on his wrist, then gave the baby the bottle. At first she fussed, but then she drank a little of the juice, then a little more. Her cries stopped, and she went to sleep on her father's lap.

"The rational side of me said there's no way something so simple could work," he admitted later. "But once I started feeling desperate enough, I didn't care if I had to use a magic wand and chant 'abracadabra'— I just wanted Daphne's colic to go away. Maybe I'm not the purely logical creature I thought I was."

In this case, his daughter's distress (and his own helplessness) helped Dave find a part of himself that he had long denied—the part that believed in more than what can be proved. He made a choice to listen to the part of himself that pleaded, "Don't ask why it should work, just try it!" and his choice paid off. It's a lucky thing that he chose to express more than one side of himself, for with a new child in his life, Dave found many uses for every intelligence he possessed!

(A word about "old wives' tales." The term is often used to mean something silly, fallacious, or superstitious, but in many cultures, the old wives are the most revered people in the entire village. Before modern medical associations killed off the "witches" and midwives of Colonial America, these women cured pain and illness, brought babies into the world, saved lives, and buried the dead for people who had no understanding of how the body worked. Much of modern medicine is based on quantifying and laying claim to medicines derived from herbs and other ingredients that were once gathered and preserved by "old wives." The *Foxfire Books* (see the Bibliography) are a marvelous collection of backwoods wisdom and contain information on how to do everything from making soap to curing foods to building a house, based on interviews with elderly people who live in the mountains and have a deep comprehension of what it means to live independently. Like Eliot Wigginton, the high school teacher who created the *Foxfire Books*, we should treasure our old folks and preserve and respect their knowledge.)

Using Your Mind, Body, and Spirit

Because we live in a culture that values material goods, we tend to see ourselves and each other as materials as well. How often have you looked in the mirror and felt bad about yourself—not just the bad hair day or the pimple on the end of your nose, but your entire self? What do people say when they're trying to set up a guy with a girl who's not considered physically attractive? They say, "She has a great personality." It's understood that if she has a terrific body and a fabulous face, those would be mentioned first. In fact, if she's good-looking enough, people might not even notice her great personality.

As for the spirit, we hardly ever comment on people's soulfulness, their depth of understanding and wisdom. We have hardly any language to describe manifestations of spirituality in ways that don't sound naïve or pretentious. That could be because we live in a childish culture that focuses on the external, or—more optimistically—that could be because we recognize the intricacy of spiritual matters to the extent that we don't talk about them in polite society.

Loving someone else gives us the opportunity to look deeply at another's spirit while our own responds to loving by growing larger and deeper. Certainly, personality figures into the relationships we choose: we find some people charming and others repugnant based on the ways they act, their foibles, and their idiosyncrasies. We may initially be drawn to someone by the way they look, but we keep on loving them because of who they truly are. Loving ourselves, too, is about so much more than just approval of tight bodies and pretty faces, for while our outsides invariably age, what's inside tends to become smoother and perfected by time.

Many people join health clubs and spend a few days each week working on their bodies, which is great for their physical well-being and positively impacts their mental health as well. But it's also important to spend spiritual "workout" time—to express the finest parts of your personality and to increase the spiritual aspects of your life. In order to act as a whole individual, to access synergy and thereby attain joy, remember that you are more than a body, a mind, a spirit. When all three aspects of yourself are at their best and act in concert, you are as free as a person can be.

Of course, perfect self-expression of body, mind, and spirit is not possible or even especially desirable, because the quest for perfection is a hollow one. But we all tend to favor one aspect of ourselves above the others. Take a few minutes to think about how much of your attention goes toward the physical, the mental, and the spiritual in your life. Are you an outdoorsy athlete? A bookworm? Do you search for meaning through seminars, workshops, or meditations? Which parts of yourself could you strengthen in order to achieve a happier life?

I am a busy person, and I like it that way. I give workshops on weekends and run my business during the week, and I love my work because it is my purpose and the best expression of my true self. But I travel a lot and eat in restaurants instead of at home, and I don't get enough exercise. So, to keep my heart healthy and my cholesterol low, I eat salads when I travel, and I walk four days a week. I don't have to be Tom Cruise to fulfill my purpose—only Tom Cruise needs that! But if my body breaks down, if I get too tired from poor nutrition and lack of exercise, my immune system may develop some chinks in its armor. I love my work and my family, and I want to be energized and fully able to participate in anything I want to do, so I pay extra attention to my physical well-being, which enhances my life. In fact, because my mind and body are tied to each other, and because I need them both to express my purpose (which in turn is tied to my spirit), I realize that anything that strengthens my body also positively impacts all the rest of my being.

Remember George, discussed in Step Four of this book, who had ALS? His body was in such a state that there was little he could physically do, so he used mental exercises to strengthen his spirit. He had fewer choices than most of us, but he effectively used the resources he did have to express his purpose. Mental exercise soothed his spirit, and it also calmed his body so that his pain and other symptoms noticeably diminished.

Balance is important. When you neglect one aspect of yourself, it sends you messages, although they may not always be direct messages! I know a woman who had a job she disliked and a boss she couldn't stand. Rather than quitting immediately, she held on for six months until she found another job that paid her as well as the one she was leaving. In that six months, she developed arthritic pain in her hips and knees and painful boils in uncomfortable places. She had nightmares and always felt tired because her mind rebelled against her imprisonment. But within a month of starting her new job, her physical symptoms disappeared, the nightmares stopped, and a dimple in her cheek that had been totally erased reappeared as if by magic. Surely good jobs don't directly cause dimples, just as bad jobs don't cause boils, but when the mind is tormented, it drags the body into its torment. A person who does not listen to his distressed mind may have to take more notice when his whole body is covered with hives! The equation works in the opposite direction, too: your body may protest your neglect of it by affecting your mind. Depression and fatigue are common side effects of many physical illnesses, so that if these symptoms descend on you without any psychological cause that you can see, it's a good idea to visit your M.D. for a physical.

Spiritual neglect is probably the most common type of self-neglect today, and the main reason I wrote *Creating Extraordinary Joy* was to remedy that neglect. Synergy and joy are all about the expression of your spirit and your true self and purpose. Looking for opportunities to multiply your happiness, to draw closer to other people, to learn to love and accept yourself, and to replace harmful habits with helpful ones are the keys to living a spiritually enriched life. Reaching out to others is a vital component of expressing yourself as a spiritual being, and that is what we will discuss next.

Communication and Conflict

Our society does not teach us about synergy because our economy is based primarily on competition. It does not teach us about peace, either: a people who cannot conceive of cooperative social arrangements are incapable of resolving conflicts through peaceful cooperation.

Civilization is a collective agreement among people that certain standards, principles, and morals will guide us toward a less primitive way of life. These civil standards and rules are theoretically created for the comfort and protection of all, and although they are always in flux, we should neither adhere to them once they have outgrown their usefulness and meaning in our world nor casually abandon them entirely. Changes in civil standards often create conflict, sadly: it's a tremendous waste that people are willing to murder one another over shifting social rules, changing boundary lines, and threatened natural resources. As an individual, I may not be able to single-handedly stop a war, but I can prevent wars in my own backyard by choosing to communicate respectfully, by being open to compromise and change, and by actively creating synergy in communication with others. Creating synergy in communication is in some ways more difficult than bullying or dictating because it requires tact, empathy, and dedication. Great diplomats have excellent manners and the tenacity of a bulldog. If we must be stubborn, let's stubbornly hold on to the idea that everyone can and should win, and that forcing a win-lose situation means that we have simply chickened out.

✦ WHEN TRICKY COMMUNICATION HAPPENS TO GOOD PEOPLE

Suddenly, the air mushroomed with tension. He stared at me for a solid minute and then abruptly swung his chair around. He stared at the wall for what seemed like an eternity and didn't say a word. All I could see was the back of his neck, flushed crimson with anger, just above his shirt collar.

I had just told this brilliant business genius that he was the biggest problem in his company. That was not an easy thing to do, because he had hired me to help him improve staff morale.

"What do you mean, I'm the problem?" he growled as he slowly turned and faced me once again.

"Eric, your employees are frightened of you."

"Fear is good. It keeps them on their toes."

"Fear motivation does work to some extent. But not very well. It doesn't last long, so you have to continually threaten and scare people into doing their jobs."

"I don't do that!" Eric shouted.

"Not deliberately, but there are some things you do that cause fear."

"Oh, yeah? Like what?"

"Like micromanaging."

"Chris, my business is not big enough to absorb costly mistakes. I have to make sure that everything is okay."

"Eric, micromanaging limits your growth and makes your job boring. It also teaches people not to think."

What I love most about the entrepreneurial spirit is its creative ability to problem-solve, and Eric had that true spirit. He immediately shifted his ego aside. WOW!

"Okay, what needs to be done, and what do I have to do?"

"Great! First, we must get a very clear idea of where you want to be with this business in the next ten years."

"I know where I want to be!"

"Have you written it down?"

"No."

"We know you haven't shared your ideas with your people, so let's begin by clearly defining your vision, your values, and your goals."

Many organizations find themselves in the same situation as Eric was. They began with a great idea. In the early days of the new business, the growth was phenomenal, the excitement and energy were almost beyond containment, and that was what customers bought. Customers want to support an organization that exudes enthusiasm and creativity.

In this case, enthusiasm and creativity were stifled by the heavy-handed communication style of the CEO. Notice, in the example above, how he resisted what I had to say to him by denying, shouting, and arguing. This is not a bad man; in fact, he's a very good man! But he had a classically authoritarian style of communication that frightened his employees so badly that he had to hire outside help to get the truth he so badly needed.

One fascinating aspect of my work is that, in times when clients become overwhelmed with intimidation or irritation, it's my job to barrel through their defenses and help them see what stops them in their pursuit of excellence. When your personal goal is to get through to someone rather than to win an argument, it's much easier to be empathetic, to keep your temper, and to tell them what they need to hear in a way that they can hear it.

✦ TRIPLE WIN: A RECIPE FOR COMMUNICATION

Communication is the soul food of personal relationships, families, cities, and nations. Two or more minds, when they're connected together, are a powerful opportunity for each participant to trust, understand, and accept other points of view. The entire premise of synergy is that connection creates something greater than the sum of its separate parts, and synergy in communication creates greater solutions and understandings.

I use the term "triple win" to describe the fact that synergistic communication results in all participants getting what they want. Each person wins, and the greater whole—the two of them—also wins. In a very real sense, the triple win is about applied ethics—really living your belief that everyone deserves to be heard and to have his needs met. Triple-win communicators are secure in themselves. They know what they want and are willing to get it, and they base their goals on two important ethical principles:

1. Everyone should win.

2. There is a way, through respectful caring and communication, for all to win.

If it were easy for everyone to win, communication would be a breeze! It takes creativity and ingenuity to come up with solutions that please everyone at the table, but 99 percent of the time, this is a completely achievable goal. The most important basis for achieving the triple win is the commitment of the people involved to the belief that a triple win is not only possible, but entirely probable. In the way that one plus one can equal three, the triple win is an example of synergy in communication—and it often leads to better results than could have been predicted by any one member of the group.

It's important to remember, when you're trying to achieve synergy in communication, that communication is not only about the words we use. Words can be misconstrued, misunderstood, and not heard at all. Words travel on positive or negative energy and can be enhanced or overridden by body language: in fact, more than 80 percent of communication consists of body language, not our spoken words! So communication is about our true intention, the positive energy we project, and the kind of people we are deep inside.

Synergy in communication is an excellent way to work with others. Focus on looking for solutions, new ideas, and new ways to solve problems. Try to discover completely new and even better ways to build relationships, too.

Resentment, Resistance, and Revenge

All of us have to deal with life's lessons at one time or another. We have all experienced emotional batterings from a problematic job, a hard relationship, or one of many other difficulties. We have all been knocked down at one time or another. What's important is how we deal with it, how we roll with the punches, how proactive we are in the face of such difficulties. Sadly, in the face of these challenges, some people give up and give in to what I call the "Three Rs Syndrome"—feelings of resentment, resistance, and revenge.

BILL'S STORY

Bill Martin was employed by a company in New York called Magic Products, and because he did such a fine job, he was promoted from national sales manager to sales director.

Because Magic Products had a policy of promoting from within, Bill needed to find someone to fill his old position. So, Bill met with Bryan Adams in Los Angeles and said, "Bryan, I have been promoted to sales director. I believe you have the qualities needed to take over my old position, national sales manager. George Abrams also has all the qualities to fill the position. This is very difficult for me because you both have been with me since we started this division. So, I have decided to give the position to the person who achieves the highest sales between now and the beginning of the financial year, six months from now."

Bryan exclaimed, "George Abrams does not stand a chance! I'm going to give you no alternative but to appoint me as the national sales manager. I have been waiting and working for this opportunity since I joined this company."

Bryan was excited as he drove home. He pictured himself in the new position. His excitement continued as he shared the events of his afternoon with his wife and children. That same evening, he contacted all his field managers and instructed them to be in the office at 7:30 a.m. the next day. He told his salespeople exactly what Bill Martin had told him, and he pointed out to them that if they performed well, there was the likelihood of a promotion for them as well.

Immediately, sales began to increase. July was a record month. August was even better, and September was outstanding. October, November, and December were also great months, and Bryan Adams was delighted.

In January, Bryan Adams received a phone call from the head office, requesting that he attend a special meeting in New York to announce the appointment of the new national sales manager.

"This is it—this is it!! They're going to announce me as the new national sales manager. There is no way that it can't be me. I looked at the figures on Friday at lunchtime, and we were ahead of George Abrams. Great!!"

He boarded the airplane and was the epitome of enthusiasm, talking to everyone and generally enjoying himself and life. When he arrived at JFK, a company car was waiting to whisk him away to the head office. In the lobby, the receptionist told him that Bill Martin wanted to see him before the meeting.

Bryan thought, "Well, of course, Bill wants to see me. He wants to congratulate me and go over things before the meeting. He is a real gentleman."

With a confident stride, Bryan entered Bill's plush office, "Hello, Bill, how are you?"

Bill handed him a folder and said, "Bryan, I wanted to see you before the meeting because there is something really important that you should know."

Bryan opened the folder, which contained both his and George Abrams's sales figures in large colored graphs across the page. To Bryan's dismay, he saw that George had put in a huge order on the closing afternoon.

"Are you trying to tell me something, Bill?" Bryan asked.

Bill responded, "Now, Bryan, you know what the deal was."

During the meeting, Bryan switched off his awareness and felt numb all over. He went through the motions, doing his best not to reveal how angry he was. At the end of the meeting, Bill announced George Abrams as the new national sales manager. Everybody wished him well, except Bryan. He felt an overwhelming sense of betrayal, anger, and resentment and immediately left for the airport.

As he got off the plane in Los Angeles, his wife detected from forty yards away that Bryan had not gotten the job.

As they walked toward their car, she asked, "You didn't get it, did you?"

Bryan looked at her and said in a sarcastic tone, "Do me a favor, I don't want to discuss it!"

She felt hurt. A dark cloud hung over their drive home.

Once home, Bryan fell into a depression. He didn't feel like doing anything or seeing anyone, including the children.

At work, Bryan kept to himself. During the following months, his attitude pervaded his work group, and sales, attitudes, and motiva-

tion became progressively worse. Bryan secretly felt satisfaction, almost a sense of revenge achieved. He became more and more cynical and unmotivated.

Two months later, George Abrams, the new national sales manager, flew to Los Angeles to fire Bryan Adams.

What happened to Bryan...?

He fell into one of life's lesson plans. Bryan couldn't or wouldn't take the punches. Mentally and emotionally, he gave up. He became reactive. He was bitter and clearly succumbed to the Three Rs Syndrome.

✦ RESENTMENT

When our expectations aren't fulfilled, we resent it, whether our expectations were valid or not. In Bryan's case, the expectations were valid, and his disappointment was very real. But just when he suffered his loss, Brian needed to exercise choice before he reacted negatively. He resented not getting the job, and his pride was hurt when overheard his colleagues expressing pity for him. He felt empty and betrayed. He wondered why he should try so hard. The resentment he felt acted as a poison, causing him to act childishly by not congratulating his opponent. Then it followed him home, where he hurt his wife's feelings and ignored his kids.

In our culture, our most important needs are recognition and acceptance, and the most painful things are rejection and isolation. When Bryan didn't get the job, he felt rejected by his company. His reaction was to draw away, further isolating himself from his coworkers and his family and thus increasing his unhappiness. In fact, if an unbalanced person—someone who has been rejected and isolated throughout life—faced a situation like Bryan's, violence could be the result. But as it stood, Bryan lost face at work, lost any enthusiasm he once had had for his job, and lost a precious hunk of his self-esteem.

✦ RESISTANCE

Resistance and closing down are ways to psychologically run away from a problem. They're also an expression of anger when we can find no other outlet. In Bryan's case, resistance manifested itself as a sort of industrial sabotage. Bryan stopped caring about his work and endeavored to get his work group to stop caring as well.

Resistance as a nonviolent opposition strategy works wonderfully well, used successfully by the followers of Gandhi and Martin Luther King, Jr. People who practice purposeful or passive resistance become physically difficult to move, extra-heavy, and floppy, which is very useful in some situations. But unplanned psychological resistance is rarely useful because it lacks a direct focus and tends to boomerang on the person who's resisting. Although the resisting person probably wants action very much, he becomes stuck in his wanting and can't effectively make the very change he needs. When Bryan was resisting accepting that he had lost the job of his dreams, he could have been making a new plan and coming up with creative choices. One of those choices might have been to find a new job as soon as he could, and that choice would have also entailed keeping his sales high. He could have negotiated a bigger bonus for himself and his group based on the last six months' sales. But instead he got lost in grief over the job he didn't get, and that hurt him much more than it hurt the large company he worked for.

Bryan's internal monologue reflected what was tormenting him. It was full of revenge: in his head he was saying, "I'll get you back for this" and "If you can't treat me well, I won't even try." Sure, he was talking in his mind to Bill and George and everyone he imagined had had something to do with his loss, but he was talking *only* inside his head, and so the only person who heard him was him. A part of Bryan was punishing himself, because his subconscious was listening to his angry pronouncements and helping to perpetuate his feelings.

Sometimes we get into the Three Rs because we're scared to stand up for ourselves. Passive-aggressive behavior arises directly from an inability to be open about anger. For example, your partner does something stupid and thoughtless, but instead of saying, "Hey! You hurt my feelings, you big oaf!"

you bite your lips because nice women aren't supposed to get angry (an interesting idea passed down by men and by generations of furiously contained women). But a single lip-bite won't do, because the original hurt starts to fester, and soon there are a dozen more small but irritating issues. You start to think vengeful thoughts, and then the passive-aggressive stuff starts, maybe with the silent treatment.

If you're mad at someone, it's much easier to tell them why and wait for an apology. State your case. Say no when you want to say no. Feel free to disagree, and if you were taught as a child that it's bad to disagree, it's time to let go of that mistaken idea.

✦ REVENGE

Bryan tried to get even with Bill Martin by not maintaining the terrific growth of his branch. He did not attend meetings. He closed his door and was slow to return calls. He was generally defensive and rude. But his greatest revenge of all was against himself. His feelings of failure about himself generated a self-fulfilling prophecy and an outward attitude that was intolerable to others. Bryan was fired, and it was a wake-up call for him. He reassessed his life, his purpose, and his goals. He made changes in the way he thought and acted. Today, Bryan is very successful at another company.

Awareness, Attitude, and Action

The Three Rs can be counteracted by the Three As. Replace resentment, resistance, and revenge with awareness, attitude, and action for a successful answer to life's challenges.

✦ AWARENESS

Awareness is the first step out of the cycle of the Three Rs. Think about how people describe their angry feelings: "I just blew up"; "I lost it." It's important to be aware of how you feel before you get angry. Usually hurt, fear, and shame precede anger, either one at a time or all at once. Anger is the follow-up feeling that distracts you from the others, which are more painful. Awareness of feelings underlying anger helps actually tone down anger and lets you focus on getting what you really need from the situation.

✦ ATTITUDE

Attitude is everything! It's hard to stay positive when you've had a major disappointment, but the payoffs make it worthwhile. Take time to digest unpleasant events, and plan ways to make the best of them. Ask yourself what you can learn from your experience. Use visualization techniques such as the mental movie screen, described in Step Four, to project happy outcomes. Have faith that you can and will find positive choices in your situation. Be gracious to others when at all possible, and be very kind to yourself.

✦ ACTION

Awareness of self and a great attitude naturally lead to correct behavior and actions. What are correct actions? Grounded in the best intentions, correct actions are designed to improve the quality of our lives and the lives of those we love.

The concept of damage control has moved beyond the shipping industry, where it originated, and into the speech of commerce, politics, and everyday life. Damage control can be a necessary action when you're trying to avoid the three Rs, too: it may include actions such as congratulating business competitors, apologizing, or explaining. After the fires are all out, it's time to take charge of the situation. Action of some positive sort is necessary to prevent moping or negative ruminations. Action may relate directly to the situation at hand, or it may take the form of distracting yourself from the situation in life-enhancing ways.

Interpersonal Conflict Resolution Steps

Conflict is unavoidable, but the right attitude can make all the difference in whether you see it as an occasional challenge to your creativity or as a terrifying threat to your very being. There are a number of techniques you can use in order to minimize interpersonal conflict.

STEP ONE | *Be Proactive, Objective, and Diplomatic*

The first step in managing interpersonal conflicts is to be as proactive and objective as possible. Be honest with yourself as you think about what the real problem, the real source of the conflict, may be. Recognize that sometimes a problem represents something bigger, something that is more threatening to talk about. Once you locate the real problem, you can think about the right solutions.

This is an important time to use both your logic and your emotions in problem-solving. Pay attention to your feelings expressly for the purpose of avoiding more conflict generated by hurt feelings or wounded egos. In an emotionally charged situation, the first temptations are to look for competitive solutions (in which one person wins and the other loses) or to go off on defensive tangents about who is "right." Arguing about who is right only delays a solution. What's important is not *who* is right, but *what* is right.

When we try to resolve conflict through power struggles, we use win-lose thinking, which is exactly the opposite of synergistic thinking. Win-lose thinking causes wars, although a war may start out as something as small and manageable as a trade disagreement. The triple-win solution requires win-win thinking, which makes for true conflict resolution. The triple win requires more thought and more creativity at the outset, but in the end the energy it saves is tremendous because it tends to create positive relationships and more long-term benefits for everyone in the conflict.

In conflict resolution, the focus cannot be on blame or judgment, but on resolution. Choosing the correct focus invites proactive responses. Find and focus on the positive connections between you and the other person, not on the areas where you might differ. Out of respect for yourself, take time to care when engaged in conflict. Speak respectfully, keep your dignity, and phrase things as carefully as you can. If you feel things are worsening or you just can't seem to get through, consider taking a break and returning when things (and people) are calmer.

You can be both diplomatic and honest, and that's the best way to work through conflicts. I was once asked to consult with a CEO of a large company that should have been successful but wasn't. It seemed there was a communication problem in the company, and my challenge was the fact that it stemmed directly from the man who had hired me!

My first clue came soon after we met. Dean was a big guy—over six feet tall—and he had a booming voice and a big stomach. Just talking, he was an intimidating man, but as an added bonus, he was a physically demonstrative man as well. At our first meeting, he picked me right up off the ground, nearly crushing me to pieces. He did it with friendly intent, but it was a double message: it told me clearly that he was big, strong, and unafraid to use his strength. Another disconcerting trick of his was to bump people with his stomach. The first time he did it to me, he shoved me entirely across the room. Dean didn't know it, but he was bullying people without even saying a word. His employees feared and mistrusted him. People avoided him, as his communication skills were like his physical being—too direct, too pointed. He routinely trampled people's feelings without knowing what he did. He was a nice man, but he had the sensitivity of a grizzly bear. And it was my job to tell him that.

There was definitely a motivation and communication problem at his organization, and it stemmed from the Chief Executive Officer himself. Sometimes the work I do leads to confronting difficult problems head-on, and this was one of those occasions that usually makes me feel uncertain and scared. I assumed he would blow up at me; however, after I explained how his style was affecting the business, he surprised me with his maturity and strength of character. Although he was still slightly defensive, he admitted that he needed help with certain aspects of his communication skills.

I told him the first thing he could do was to stop harshly barking out orders. I told him he needed to phrase his orders as polite requests, which would thereby lead his staff to respond more positively to his requests. "That is going to be difficult," he said. I told him that I understood that habits are hard to break and that the process would be difficult but not impossible. He agreed to give it his best shot.

I structured a series of executive coaching meetings to assist him with his problem. In one follow-up meeting, Dean really began to open up and even revealed that he grew up in a large family and learned to survive by using his size to get what he wanted. After that disclosure, he seemed to relax, and his whole demeanor became less threatening and more receptive to suggestions and ideas.

Dean practiced what I taught him, and over time, the organizational culture changed. People work better when they are happy and unafraid, and removing communication problems with the CEO was all it took to turn the company around and create success.

It took guts for me to tell Dean what he needed to hear, but it took more guts for him to hear it and respond maturely to the challenge. A lesser man would have punched me in the nose or perhaps listened politely, then declined to change. The fact that Dean had the courage to change his behavior as a boss for the betterment of his company says a lot about his personal inner strength and determination to succeed.

If we believe in synergy, if we believe in peace, if we believe that our minds and bodies are healthier if we can reduce tension and stress, then we can reconcile our differences.

STEP TWO | *Project Loving Energy*

Our words travel on waves of positive or negative energy that is created by our attitudes. It is important that our attitudes remain positive. Body language—a certain look, a roll of the eyes, or what I call the Elvis lip—can all create barriers to relationship growth. Negative attitudes create invisible energy barriers that can be felt by almost anyone.

Communication is clearer, quicker, and more effective when our attitudes are right. Some years ago, Lyall Watson, in his book *Super Nature*, demonstrated the damaging effects of negative energy on the environment, including plant life. He proved, through various electronic measures, that plants were affected positively or negatively when a person entered a controlled room. If the person was hostile and angry, the plant registered erratic activity on the electronic gauges. When cheery, laughing persons entered the same room, the gauges recorded a more stable, less volatile response. If even plants can tell when someone's in a bad mood, think of the effect of a grouchy supervisor on his employees!

If this research is taken to its logical scientific conclusion, it suggests that present-moment energy affects the environment in which we live. If this is true, it means that we affect and are responsible for the collective peace and personality of our towns, cities, and nations. Hostile, negative energy creates a hostile environment; positive energy creates a welcoming one. It is vitally important that we understand that projecting loving energy is not only an individual choice, but also a collective responsibility.

STEP THREE | *Listening—The Key to Great Relationship Building*

Listening is the great forgotten communication secret. It takes work to listen, but it's worth it, because when you listen to your children, to your lover, and to your coworkers, you give them a rare gift. Listening to someone is one of the highest compliments you can pay them, since it sends messages such as, "You're interesting" and "You're important. What you say matters to me." Listening can cure loneliness, both for the one who talks and the one who listens, because when you listen, you truly connect, without competition, and you give yourself to the speaker through your attention and empathy.

We're busy people, and the world demands much of us. Much of the time we only partially listen, just following along enough to interrupt and get a chance to talk. Some people pretend to listen until an opening occurs, and then they jump in. Sometimes we all practice selective listening, in which we hear only the part of the message we want to hear. We might listen only to the words themselves, not their subtext: when a man asks, "How was your day?" and his wife mutters, "Fine," with a bleak look on her face, he might choose to hear just the word and offer a dumb response, such as "That's good."

Active listening means listening to another person without judging what he says. It means paying attention to body language, voice inflection, eye movements, and energy level. Maintain eye contact and nod your head or say "mm-hmm" to let the other person know you're listening. When the other person stops talking, you might even summarize what he said. So let's replay the short conversation above with active rather than selective listening.

Husband: How was your day?

Wife: (*Looking bleak*) Fine.

Husband: You don't look like you feel fine. Do you want to tell me about it?

Wife: I backed my car into the redwood tree by the driveway, and I had to get a tow truck out to pull the fender out of the tree. The tow truck driver was laughing so hard he could hardly stand up. All the neighbors came out to watch. It took him almost an hour. I felt like a total idiot.

Husband: That must have been pretty embarrassing for you. I'm glad you weren't hurt.

Wife: (*Still cranky*) The repair shop said it'll cost six hundred dollars, and I won't have my car for a week.

Husband: You poor thing, you really did have a rotten day! First the accident, then the tow truck scene, and then the cost! I'll be your personal chauffeur next week. In the meantime, can I make you dinner or rub your feet to help take your mind off it?

Wife: (*Starting to smile*) Thanks. I feel better already.

Synergy in Loving

We are the dupes of myth when we upbraid
ourselves because we love; for we are made for
loving: all the seeds of living are for
those that love. Be joyful, unafraid!

THE RUBAIYAT OF OMAR KHAYYAM

The Three Types of Love

The first spiritual expression of human life is love. Love is our greatest need, yet it is the most misunderstood. The ancient Greek philosophers categorized love into different types of love: *philos, eros,* and *agape.* We can use these types to explore what love truly is.

Philos is brotherly and sisterly love. This is the love that we feel for a family member. It is a caring, understanding love but is not romantic. It is what brings us together for Thanksgiving even when it's a tremendous hassle and what makes us worry about people we used to try to beat up when we were kids. Not all brothers and sisters feel this kind of love for each other, but those who do have a rich and special connection all their lives.

Eros is erotic love, the feeling of sexual attraction to another person. Erotic love is only in part romantic, however: it may not stand the test of time once the physical features that drew two people together begin to droop with age. *Eros* is an infatuation with the physical and erotic aspects of love, without a deeper, more emotional and spiritual sense of belonging to each other.

179

Agape is unconditional love. It means that you love someone completely, without conditions or special wishes and without hope that they will change or be different from who they are. You don't want that person to change in any way. *Agape* is free of judgment, criticism, and the need to satisfy an idealization or fantasy. We experience *agape* when we're secure enough to be vulnerable and when we synergize with another.

Our culture is highly focused on romantic love—something many cultures perceive as practically aberrant. Traditionally, marriage was a matter of economics and social connection: it was about adding to a family's wealth and connecting families to one another through the exchange of women. It wasn't until the Victorian era that most British and American people, at least, started marrying based on romantic attraction. In a traditional marriage, by contrast, people might not have been in love when they married but might have begun to love each other after some years of getting to know each other. Maybe in reaction to that, Americans focus on romantic love as the be-all and end-all. We tend to ignore the different kinds of love that exist, so when we marry, we may let friendships lapse or may move away emotionally from our families. When we throw away everything for romance, we end up cheating ourselves out of the very relationships that help romance endure—friends to confide in and enjoy, family members to advise us. Putting all your eggs into the basket of romantic love stresses that love—no one can be all things to a partner without buckling under the strain.

The great thing about realizing that there are several kinds of love is that it shows us that we have several times as many ways to care about other people, which expands the number of people we have the opportunity to love. It also helps us sort out our feelings when we love someone but want to love someone else. How many people have been faced with the choice of staying with one partner or trading them in for someone new and, by that definition alone, more exciting?

Women who have affairs with married men discover the men almost always stay with their wives in the end, and that makes sense. When you go to all the trouble of marrying someone and living with them for years on end, you have the opportunity to form more than one kind of love and many other connections with that person. A mistress or girlfriend, on the other hand, is someone with whom you have an erotic relationship, a relationship that might not last long enough, or command enough of both people's attention, to deepen into something more. It's sad for the "other woman" because she gets some of the fun and romance, enough to make her want more, but little or none of the thing that makes relationships truly great— the spiritual intimacy that arises from really knowing someone. She waits and waits for a day that almost never comes.

When two people make an equal commitment to each other, and then multiply that commitment by the joy of experiencing synergy or "flow" together, they achieve the profound euphoric feelings of love. When a person loves another person, she's filled with a sense of satisfaction, and in many cases this can lead to the discovery and surfacing of latent, hidden talents, talents that she may never have known she possessed. Loving someone can be like creating a work of art.

Falling in love with another person may be the most creative, exciting, and challenging endeavor we ever undertake. But love is powerful even when we don't fall in love with a person, but with an idea or concept. That, too, can call forth unique talents. A special calling or mission in our lives gives us a sense of purpose and can change a shy, withdrawn person into a driven dynamo.

The Intimate Relationship

Everyone wants to be loved, but more people want to be loved than there are people willing to give love. As one young woman once said, "I was involved in a love triangle; he and I were both in love with him."

We all want the security of a permanent, enduring, intimate relationship. Being cared for and truly loved is a profoundly spiritual experience. A desire both men and women dream of fulfilling is that of finding their true soulmate.

The depth of a relationship depends on the openness, sincerity, and candor expressed by each person in building the relationship. Intimate relationships are based on reality as well as hopes and dreams for the future, so honesty is of paramount importance. However, avoid tactless honesty or honesty at all costs, such as revealing the intimate details of past relationships. Sensitivity to your partner's feelings is essential.

The foundation of an enduring and deep relationship is true love, and true love is expressed through our spirit: each partner must agree to embrace and admire the couple's collective spirituality. Individually, one's spirit is pure, authentic, and beautiful. But the uniqueness of the spirit may scare some people—they get so caught up in looking for differences and flaws in other that they cheat themselves out of the opportunity of finding things in common with others. We should focus on connection, rather than being afraid of differences. There is so much to discover at a deeper level; our differences should be celebrated.

A couple's combined sense of purpose in creating, and growing in, a love relationship is the strongest predictor of the relationship's success. When both people want to be close, are excited about experiencing life together, and are willing to encounter changes and obstacles as a team, they will look beyond pettiness and win-lose ideas. They share a common goal of making their relationship happy and strong. When the relationship comes first, problems that would break up other couples are overcome in the service of the greater goal, because the goal itself acts as a sort of emotional glue during times of uncertainty.

You've probably heard that to have a friend, you have to be a friend. This is also true of having a lover! Give yourself to your lover: be the first to apologize, and take the initiative to resolve conflict. Serve each other, but one person should not act as another's slave. Take turns, and serve each other in small and large ways. Bring her an iced tea on a summer night when she's tired. Write his mother a friendly note, and sign it from both of you. The little courtesies and pleasures we give each other nurture and strengthen the relationship in the same way that spring rains bring out the flowers.

Be kind and gentle. Caressing each other is healing and crucial to intimacy. Hug each other and say "I love you" every day. Say it with words, flowers, cards, compliments, loving eyes, and moments of your undivided attention.

Serve each other breakfast in bed. Find something funny to say; entertain your partner. Sing in the shower together, and laugh a lot together.

Snuggle and cuddle while watching favorite movies. Take vacations often. Never storm off in a fit of anger or go to bed without resolving conflicts. Sleep cuddled up; take naps together. Be a good sounding board for each other, and avoid negative criticism. Build something together: a garden, a house, a town. Look good for your partner. Give each other space and respect each other. Be helpful. Be romantic.

To have a lover, be a lover.

Building Loving Relationships

The greatest opportunity we have for creating synergy and joy is our intimate relationships. In intimate connection with someone else, we can have the most satisfying human experience possible. When romance first blossoms, it seems that synergy is natural and unique to just this person, just this relationship, but eventually we realize that the initial connection was primarily chemical and thus bound to change over time. If the relationship grows beyond the initial phase of romantic attraction, new opportunities emerge to synergize with your partner at home and at play.

A smoothly running household may use synergy to effect the most ordinary changes in an extraordinary way. Especially in households where both partners work, both are tired at the end of the day, but there is still dinner to be made, dishes to be washed, laundry to be done. If you've ever had the chance to observe a long-partnered pair, you may see that they have developed a system for doing chores together, so they both have more time to do the things they enjoy doing. Cooperating, communicating, and finding creative solutions together do more than get dinner on the table; they set the stage for making big decisions together at other times. Every successful interaction with your partner builds something else into your relationship: more understanding, more trust.

Statistics software can sort through data sets to pull out the numbers that relate most strongly to one another. Every time the program pulls out a set of numbers, the rest of the data set is affected by the change, so the program runs through it again, pulling out the next-strongest related numbers and then the next. Each pass through the data set is called an iteration, and the program runs until the remaining data is so random that it has no significance or relationship. In a way, relationships of all sorts are like this statistical program, for every occurrence in the relationship adds, in effect, new data to the set, where it will be either incorporated as relevant or abandoned as useless. The more positive experiences you have together, the greater the likelihood that your relationship will continue to be relevant and useful over time. In other words, the ways that you and your partner choose to approach the small challenges of life will not only influence how you approach the big challenges together, but also will determine the relationship's ultimate success or failure.

When the creative aspects of a relationship become dormant, people start to take each other for granted. If both partners do this simultaneously, it might not matter much, because neither will notice it! But, unfortunately, when one person takes the other for granted, the other usually feels it keenly and may react with tears, anger, or accusations. However, the other partner can make simpler, more enjoyable choice: he can react creatively by reaching out rather than withdrawing, by drawing his partner back to him with good humor and grace rather than drama and pain.

I was walking in the mall the other day behind an elderly couple. The old man stopped and sat down.

I heard the woman say, "Frank, you know what's wrong with you?"

He said, "No, Martha. I don't know what's wrong with me."

She looked him straight in the eye and said, "Frank, you don't walk with enthusiasm anymore. You don't have any enthusiasm for me or for anything around you. Just get up, Frank, and walk with enthusiasm."

Her words stopped me in my tracks, and I said to myself, "Look at this woman. They're both the same age, yet she is living life to the fullest, with excitement, with energy, and with enthusiasm."

Martha got her point across and let her husband know she wasn't thrilled with his behavior. She didn't stage a teary scene; she used humor to get her husband back on track. She must have had a lot of years of practice to learn to talk to him with just the right mixture of challenge and honesty. Well, she lit his fire, all right. He got right up. He wanted to show her that he hadn't lost his enthusiasm!

Notice that Martha didn't engage in a lot of "feelings talk" to get Frank's attention. She knew her audience: an old, cranky man who was feeling less than energetic. She chose to talk to him in a way that he understood, so she acted a little tough, a little teasing, and a lot straightforward. Couples don't always have to have deep, emotional exchanges in order to get what they want—sometimes all you have to do is ask!

✦ THE LOVING FIGHT

The most important thing in your relationship is the respect you have for each other. Even in fights, it's possible to maintain a respectful manner toward each other. Obviously, someone who hits, threatens, or tries to intimidate another is not only disrespectful but abusive. Staying in an abusive relationship is pointless because abusive people rarely care to change their ways: they'd rather just find someone else who will take their bullying. Luckily, most people are not abusive and can learn to fight fairly. Here are some useful rules and strategies for the "loving fight."

1. **Remember that the goal is to achieve a triple-win solution:** If both people remember this rule, fighting becomes obsolete as you join together to solve the problem. It's not a fight if there's no loser! So, when problems arise, think of them as opportunities to synergize, and start out by talking over ways you can both get what you want.

2. **Listen:** Sometimes we fear that if we listen, we will never be heard. Maybe this fear is a Playback from family or school situations in which there wasn't enough attention to go around and the quiet kids were ignored. Make an agreement that when problems come up, you will take turns really listening to each other.

3. **Speak his (or her) language:** When diplomats serve in another country, they study the language and customs out of respect for the people of that country as well as for the practical reason of being able to communicate more clearly. When you meet your partner, especially in conflict, go out of your way to speak in a way he or she can understand. If you're the type who tends to give orders and ignore the

emotional aspects of things, soften it up a bit. Imagine how your partner may feel, and tell her your feelings, too. You may find that the disagreement evaporates when she finds out more about your reasons for the stand you are taking.

If you are a teacher or a social worker, you may be used to talking about feelings, and you may find your partner isn't the same way. Meet him or her halfway by focusing on practicality and reason.

4. **Let the past go:** Present-moment thinking is extremely important in a conflict. Leave unresolved issues for some other time, and approach each new problem as though it is the first time you've discussed the matter. Don't fall into old patterns of arguing, and don't bring up old fights.

5. **Don't burn your bridges:** It's tempting to pull out all the stops just to win a fight, but in winning the battle, you lose the war. Don't say things that hurt, and don't ridicule your partner. Hurtful words may rankle in someone's memory longer than the reason for the argument, so restrain yourself from causing your partner pain.

6. **Keep at it:** If you have to take a break to think over things or to calm yourself, do so, but make resolving the conflict a priority. Use whatever creative means are at your disposal to achieve the triple-win goal, and work together to create the best solution.

7. **Celebrate:** When you have a solution you can both live with, share a nice meal to celebrate your achievement and the continual building of a strong relationship.

✦ SYNERGY AND SEX

Great sex consists of more than just two people hitting the sheets; physical attraction is necessary, sure, but so much more is possible! Anyone is capable of connecting physically, but really great sex happens when your souls are connected. When you just fall into bed with someone, it feels good (often very good) on one level, but there are many more levels to explore.

When you are infatuated, when you genuinely like and enjoy the other person, when you're in love, you're doing more than "making it," because all those other aspects of your relationship come together in your lovemaking. When we make love, we meet in a field of unity, and it's a whole new world. We disappear into that different place and stay much longer than we do when a simply physical spasm is all we're after. No matter what *Playboy* says, you can't reach that state of euphoria when you're just screwing.

Sex starts between the ears, as the synergy of ideas and feelings blends with your vision of your lover at his or her best. When sex starts that way for both people, you have the basis for sexual synergy. Synergized sex is extraordinary—the altered state of consciousness it creates can last for more than an hour and may be best known to lovers as "afterglow." In harried and hurried times, we may neglect to take the time to truly connect with our partners and rob ourselves of the long-lasting pleasures of sex. Some people may not even be aware of the possibilities, seeing sex in only one way; others may feel that something is missing but aren't sure what. Follow the suggestions below for creating synergy in sex!

Step One: Reconnect with your partner. Work, traffic, and the demands of family life take their toll on people. It's not practical to expect to squeeze something as big as sex into a short period of time between other duties, and it's really impractical to expect each other to be in a constant state of readiness. After the daily rush, get your minds in sync by arranging to spend a decent amount of time together just being close. You might go to dinner and flirt outrageously, cuddle up on the couch in front of a movie, or take a long walk together. Do anything you like as long as it relaxes you and reminds you of your attraction to each other. Prevent distractions by turning off the phones. Talk to each other, look at each other, and laugh together.

Step Two: Don't skip foreplay! In step one, you've connected romantically with your partner. Step two is about taking the romantic into the sexual, and it's an important step. To make an awfully practical comparison, you wouldn't do a heavy workout at the gym without a decent warmup, and foreplay is an essential part of the warmup for sex. Some people find it the most delicious and memorable part of sex, as it's when the games, the teasing, and the playful aspects of sex happen. Think about it—when you look back on satisfying sexual experiences, is it the actual "doing it" that made it into your long-term memory, or the fun and surprises that led up to it?

Foreplay comes naturally when we first fall in love, but after a while it may seem that the creativity is running low. Later in the chapter, we'll talk about communicating with your loved ones, but for now it may be enough to suggest that if things have become a little routine, step into the Workshop of Your Mind and make a movie detailing things you'd like to try. Then get down to the store and buy the whipped cream, cling-wrap, and block and tackle, and have some fun tonight!

Step Three: Doing it. This is not a book about sexual technique, but there are plenty out there! In creating synergy in sex, the groundwork is laid (pardon the expression) well before you get to this stage. Ideally, both partners are in flow and communication is open. Ideally, orgasm is not the only goal—that's a lot of pressure to be under! In this step, you're concerned with making your partner feel good and feeling good yourself.

Step Four: Afterplay. Some people claim this is the greatest part of sex, when the tumult is over and both people are drowsy and calm. Men who've really been in love understand how great it is to cuddle, although the stereotypical guy rolls over to snore. Cuddling and pillow talk hardly ever make it into the movies these days, but they're important components of intimacy. Even men who aren't cuddlers by nature need to understand the value of holding their partners after making love, as it may very well affect how soon and how often they will make love again. If nothing else, think of cuddling as a bank account in which affection builds equity. In a way, everything you do after sex could be considered a down payment on reconnection for the next time.

In talking to men who have cheated on their wives, I have discovered that they have no idea what synergistic sex is. Their wives also say that sex with their husbands isn't all that great. These men look for a thrill that they don't know how to get at home, and they don't even realize that they could create it themselves! It's not that their partners are dull or inhibited, but that they have yet to explore the entire course of sex. If your relationship is basically good, there's no reason that sex has to suffer. Connection is mandatory! Communication needs to take place in one way or another, even if you're so shy that you have to write each other notes about what you do and don't like in bed.

The problem with synergistic sex is that it's an addictive process. Like other relationship experiences, each of your sexual experiences together builds on the last, so that great sex is never the same thing twice. Our complexity guarantees that. It's like a dance to which you keep adding new steps. The dance is different every time it's danced, and even when the steps are simple, the entire dance is deeper and richer than it was the time before. Each time we make love we change the process of lovemaking, and the lovemaking process changes us—you cannot be the same person after making wholehearted love to someone, because it alters your entire psyche.

Synergistic sex: you can never get enough of it! But it sure is wonderful to try. There are few things as important as totally loving someone. When you can, drop everything for it. If you have to choose between cooking an elaborate meal and some really hot, synergized sex, order a pizza, turn off the phone, and get down to what matters.

✦ TALKING WITH THE ONE YOU LOVE

The finest thing you can do for another human being is to really listen when he or she talks. Listening lovingly to your spouse or partner is crucial in creating and maintaining a connection and in building your relationship. Good parents find out right away that children pit their parents against each other by playing the role of a "faulty translator" who distorts communication. Parents need to remember that aside from the usual relationship talk, they have to check in with each other daily to see what crimes against truth the children are committing. It's also really important for the health of the whole family that children are not entrusted with messages they can't handle. A prime example of this is when a fighting couple uses children to send messages to each other or when one parent confides in a child about a parent-to-parent argument. This is totally inappropriate behavior, as it places an emotional burden on the child that he doesn't have the power to carry. In family life, it is the parents' responsibility to establish clear communication between themselves and to give children a complete understanding of family rules.

We've already discussed how to fight, but how do we communicate lovingly? Much of communication isn't about the words we use but about the intention behind those words. Some couples meet at the end of each day with a kiss, and although the embrace may become automatic, it's an excellent way to refocus and project your loving energy squarely onto your partner. Take time not only to ask, "How was your day?" but also to evaluate the response. Maybe your partner isn't the type who wants to talk about an unpleasant day, and that's okay, but it never hurts to notice—by a facial expression or slumping shoulders—when your partner is unhappy and to offer a warm hug or an extra scoop of ice cream with dessert.

Communication is paramount in relationships, but sometimes it can be too much of a good thing. Perfect honesty isn't helpful when it causes pain, and sometimes it's a good thing to wait until anger has faded before addressing conflicts. Sometimes people use the excuse of "honesty" to hurt each other; other times, people are just too blunt. White lies about new hairdos probably don't hurt the basic relationship, and sharing fantasies about sleeping with your personal trainer is totally unnecessary.

One place where communication is vital is the bedroom, where people are often too shy to talk about what they really want, what feels good, and what doesn't. If you have a hard time talking to your lover while in the midst of making love, you do have options. At a time when you're not romantically engaged, have a discussion about bedroom codes and agree upon body language you'll use to communicate your wishes: a gesture may say something such as "Don't stop," "That feels great," or "It was your ex who liked having her toes licked, but I'd really rather you didn't." Especially for people who use a lot of fantasy play, it's important to create a signal that says when one person wants to stop the game.

Letters, notes, and email are also useful: not only can they clear up communication about sex, but they can also add a definite spice to it. (But do be careful about using your work email to send naughty notes—your system administrator may read it!)

✦ COMMUNICATION AND SILENCE

There are times when words can't help. But as a culture, we tend to be afraid of silence. We use TV, radio, and cellphones to fill up as much silence as possible. We live with so much noise pollution that some people are actually nervous in the countryside or the woods because, as they say, "It's too quiet." Silence is almost an alien word in our noisy society.

When we learn the value of silence, we add a new dimension to our lives. The true self and spirit cannot be expressed if they can't be heard, and it is in silence that your true self rises. You just have to pay a little attention to it. When our five senses are engaged in receiving and assimilating information, it is very difficult for the mind to be quiet and relaxed; thus silence is an essential tool for discovering your true self.

It takes only twenty to thirty minutes of me-time to begin the process. At first, it's very difficult. Thirty minutes may not sound like an eternity, but sitting alone and stopping the thoughts that usually career around the mind takes practice. You're not actually doing nothing when you sit silently—it takes great energy and concentration to bring real silence into your mind.

Many people haven't learned to enjoy their own company and so are afraid to sit alone. They are afraid of the unknown areas of their minds, and of what might emerge. So, they keep running away from themselves, on a treadmill to nowhere, like a hamster on a wheel. It seems safer to keep busy, but it's not. It's more dangerous. it is just another way of cocooning and shutting out the world. Learning to be silent is learning to be with yourself. Take time to practice being silent until all the noise in your head has subsided. You may find that family members, friends, and those who have not learned the value of silence may not understand or appreciate the time you need, but time and practice are essential and will make you feel clearer, calmer, and happier.

Silence is as important in relationships with others as it is in your relationship with yourself. When you are with your partner, you don't always have to talk to share. You can just be together, working on different projects or collaborating, reading your books, gardening, or cooking. When children play alongside each other without necessarily playing *with* each other, it's called parallel play, and it seems to be a natural need. We don't always want to be right up against another person—just having her or him around is enough. Don't let talk shows and pop psychology books fool you into thinking that you must be constantly verbal. If it feels good to be quiet together sometimes, then be quiet.

✳ *Ten Things Couples Can Do Together in Silence*

1. Take a long walk in the rain, then towel each other dry.

2. Sit in a darkened room with one lit candle, holding hands.

3. Give each other a neck massage, foot massage, or hand massage.

4. Prepare and consume a special meal together in the kitchen.

5. Write each other a note on some special topic. Exchange the notes and read them.

6. Spend a relaxed hour together in a room without music, TV, phones, or computer, just doing nothing.

7. Find a temple or church that sponsors silent weekend retreats and attend one together.

8. Choose your favorite clothes for your partner and dress each other up.

9. Drive to a nearby hilltop and look at the stars.

10. Spread a blanket on the grass and sit and listen to the sounds of nature.

Synergy in Family and Community

Two are better off than one, because together
they can work more effectively. If one of them falls
down, the other can help him up. But if someone is
alone and falls, it's just too bad, because there is
no one to help him. If it is cold, two can sleep
together and stay warm, but how can you keep
warm by yourself? Two men can resist an attack
that would defeat one man alone. A rope made of
three cords is hard to break.

ECCLESIASTES 4:9–12 *GOOD NEWS BIBLE*—TODAY'S ENGLISH VERSION

Your First Community: Your Family

Celebrating life together is not as common as we would like to believe. Albert Schweitzer said, "We are so much together in crowds, yet all of us are dying of loneliness."

Probably the saddest thing in the world is an unhappy family. With half of all new marriages ending in divorce, families are barely established before they fly apart, centrifuged by the pressures of modern times. Many people have discovered that it's much easier to be happy as half of a family than to keep an unhappy marriage going for the sake of children who would just need therapy eventually anyway!

Families come in many different forms, but as long as unity prevails, it doesn't matter who's in the family. The traditional family structure of Mom and Dad and 2.5 kids has changed dramatically, and people have formed families with good friends, sharing parenting and rent and other responsibilities. There are lots of single-parent families, and that's just fine, too. Families are the most interesting sorts of organizations, combining as they do *eros, philos,* and *agape.* The erotic component, the love between intimate partners, often begins families, and ideally it lasts as long as the family does. *Philos* is the ideal love between siblings (although in early years, there may be a lot more yelling and screaming than *philos*), but *philos* can also exist at times between partners, as the original erotic attraction mellows into a calmer, steadier sort of love. *Agape,* which Aristotle described as the finest, purest form of love, is also found in families. The love of true friendship, *agape* asks for nothing but to fulfill its own agenda—to experience the wonder of someone else.

Families aren't necessarily biological: we can choose our brothers and sisters from among our truest and best friends. It's not the traditional structure that we need to focus on; it's the relationship that's all-important. Family makes sense—that's why lions and elephants live in groups. Any group provides more protection than is available to individuals: there are more to hunt and gather, more to sound the alarm, and more protection for everyone against predators.

Consider a group of elephants, moving slowly across the South African desert. It is a large family group, with mothers and youngsters, an old bull and a young one. They walk in a line, trunk to tail, until a young elephant decides to forge his own trail. He takes a few steps to the side but is immediately approached by the young bull elephant, who nudges him back into line. The family group is protected from marauding cheetahs and the young elephant has learned a family rule because the bull elephant has taken responsibility for the behavior of his offspring.

In human families, the structure of the family is also determined by the adults. Children don't have the intellectual capability to see the family as a unit—it's practically their whole world. Adults make the rules, decide what's right and wrong, provide the food and shelter, and teach their young. Strong, healthy adults create strong, healthy children, and loving adults teach children how to be loving as well. When parents abdicate their responsibilities out of a sense that children should have "equal rights" in the family, it is a mistake. Little people who have equal rights but unequal access to resources or unequal emotional or intellectual experience should not have to make decisions that are too big for them. Modern parents may fall into the trap of confusing respect for their children as human beings with respect for their children as equally socially powerful people. Children don't have the social rights or the intellectual capacity that adults do, and it's unfair to expect them to know how to make all their own decisions.

MARSHA'S STORY

Marsha wanted to be a good mother, but when she divorced her abusive husband, she felt guilty of depriving her son, Jeremy, of a full-time father. She tried to make it up to Jeremy by allowing her ex-husband to control visiting days, changing them when he needed to or sometimes ignoring them altogether. He kept the boy on weekends, and the five-year-old would return to his mother hollow-eyed, constipated, and hypercaffeinated after playing video games, eating pizza, and drinking Coke all weekend. Her ex-husband seemed to delight in making sure Jeremy came home in a screaming frenzy. He hurled epithets at Marsha whenever she dropped the boy off or picked him up, and she felt humiliated and powerless. But her feelings of guilt prevented her from seeking a custody arrangement that would keep the boy away from his father, reasoning that even a bad father was better than no father. Her child had frequent nightmares, wet the bed at night, and threw a tantrum every time he left his father's house, insisting that he wanted to live with his dad. Marsha knew her son loved her and that living with her was much healthier for him, but she felt unloved and resentful. What could she do?

The first thing Marsha needed to do was to see how the connection between her ex-husband and her son harmed the boy. The man used the boy in an ongoing game to control Marsha, and she played into it by allowing a half-custody agreement even when her ex was severely depressed and refused to even bathe, much less take care of Jeremy, who continued to visit him. She told herself that she was doing what the boy wanted, but she didn't let herself realize what the boy needed. The unhealthy ego needs of his father still came first, even after the divorce.

The second thing Marsha could have done was to set limits with her son. He was not old enough to understand the dynamics of the process between his parents, but she could have told him, "When you scream and cry at the end of your visits with Dad, it hurts my feelings. You don't have to act that way—I know you love Dad, and I know you love me. It's hard for you to leave him to come home with me, and I know that. But we're not going away, and you don't have to get upset about it. You'll have another visit. Okay?" Any parent who's held a screaming five-year-old knows that the best time to have this talk is not in the middle of the tantrum but at a time when both are calm and feeling close. Marsha could have asked Jeremy to try to put a happy ending on his next visit to Dad, and Jeremy might just have agreed.

The third thing Marsha needed to do was to give herself permission to take charge of her son's life. Her love for her child may have blinded her to the fact that he relied upon her to set the rules and to maintain order in their family. All children subconsciously want that from their parents and caregivers, even though they rail against the "unfairness" of it. The successful family lets a child know that she is connected, even though sometimes that means reining her in. When rules are fair, consistent, and logical, children are given the tools for understanding and moving successfully in their world. Rules also make kids feel safe, in the same way that the bars over our shoulders make us feel safe on a rollercoaster ride. In a way, living in the world is a twisting ride into the unknown: the one security your child has is the containing field of love and attention that you place around him.

The family's primary function is to give children a way to understand the world while growing in a safe and reasonably protected environment.

Families are like little game preserves, and parents are the game wardens. Children are the animals (and I mean that in the nicest way!) whom the wardens protect.

✦ COURTESY

The rules for loving communication, discussed in the previous chapter, apply to parents and children just as they do to romantic partners. Even when families face conflict, it is possible and preferable for people to respect one another's feelings (and their toys, too!). As soon as your children are old enough to understand you—at about age three, and don't let anyone tell you that it's much later than that—start teaching them the basics of tact: saying "please" and "thank you" and sharing.

✦ PARENTAL PLAYBACKS

The families we create are often images of the families we grew up in, with just enough distortion here and there to keep us mystified. New parents swear that they won't make the mistakes their parents did, but then find themselves either acting exactly like their parents or acting in ways so reactive and based on the past that they have little relevance or positive effect in the present. The ultimate irony is seeing your parents' own craziness in your children and realizing you've been acting like your grandparents did with their kids and perpetuating the very family history you wanted to erase. Resolve to keep the good things your parents did for you and throw out the bad ones. Don't be afraid to try new things, but don't succumb to fads. If some child-rearing strategy that's trendy at Mommy and Me doesn't feel right to you, ignore it.

MY SYNERGY JOURNAL | *Family Playbacks*

What were the major problems in my family?

_____

_____

How did my parents act as parents? Did one do more parenting than the other did?

_____

_____

Was one a disciplinarian and one the "good" parent?

_____

_____

Did they talk to each other about their kids, or could we get away with telling each parent a different story?

_____

_____

Was one of my parents missing (due to death, divorce, or just being too busy to be around)? If so, what effect did that have on me?

_____

_____

What do I believe are the most important parts of parenting?

_____

_____

If I already have kids, do they know that I love them? Do I tell them often?

_____

_____

What are my responsibilities to my kids?

_____

_____

Do any of my children remind me of someone else in my family? If so, is that a good or a bad thing? How might that resemblance blind me to my child's true self?

_____

_____

Were my parents abusive? If so, how can I keep from hurting my kids?

_____

_____

What is the happiest childhood that I can imagine? How can I give that to my kids?

_____

_____

When am I afraid to control my children?

_____

_____

What sort of punishments work best with my kids? What kinds of distractions work for them? What would my kids say is the best way to bribe them into good behavior?

_____

_____

In a way, creating a family is the sole chance many of us have to build our own world in the way we think it should be. Clearly, a family is affected by the whole world, and children are sometimes so different from their parents that it's as though strangers have been forced to live together by some greater power. But one of the finest goals people can have is to make a happy family. It takes a lot of courage and a lot of nerve, but people do attain it. Family life is a continuous process of letting go as well as building: letting go of preconceptions, old tapes, and control issues, and finally even letting go of your family as your children move out into the world to create their own lives. Entering family life with the knowledge that you're taking a deliberate step to better the world and provide for your loved ones is a bold endeavor, and it's one of the most satisfying things you can do.

What Is Your Community?

The culture of the Rhodesian village where I grew up was extremely helpful and caring. There were some problems—for example, racial prejudice was an issue and some colonial families didn't treat the native people with respect or consideration—but not everyone believed that skin color mattered. My family's religion taught that everyone is the same in God's eyes, and my parents didn't care who my friends were as long as they were good kids. I was really lucky to grow up not only with the children of other settlers, but also with children whose heritage in that place reached back thousands of years. Children who are taught the value of equality and who experience cultures other than their own tend to grow up to be citizens of the world—happy to accept, interact with, and love people with different backgrounds, ideas, languages, and skin colors. I'm glad that my parents weren't isolationists—my whole life would have been the poorer for it.

The families who settled in Rhodesia looked out for one another in much the same way that early settlers in American helped one another. Village life in Rhodesia was a kind of an extended family environment. My mother was always sending me to our neighbors with gifts of food or flowers—little things that mean so much. When a woman of the house was away, the neighbors joined in to make sure that there was food for the men and children and that all the chores were done (there was still a sexual division of labor in those days and many men couldn't cook—except over a campfire!).

Adults had the authority to discipline naughty children, even if the children weren't their own. People trusted one another to take care of such things.

During harvest, farmers gathered together and combined their efforts to complete the work at one farm at a time, just as American Quakers built houses for one another. Synergy has always been an important part of getting the job done fast: twelve people can cut the work of three months down to two days. Social benefits are an important reason for working as a community to achieve goals—building something of wood and nails or mud and rock also builds such things as trust, respect, and understanding among people.

✦ FINDING YOUR SPOT

In grade school, children start searching for their natural place, outside of their families. Some kids race around on the playground; others stay back near the fence. Some excel in reading or math; others struggle with the basics of learning. Teachers may label students as "bright," "slow," or "not living up to potential," and the children may either accept the labels or reject them furiously. By the time kids reach high school, an order has been established, and kids know the "spot" where they have been placed. There are the popular kids and the nerds, the brains and the dopers. Kids hang out with people similar to themselves, and they continue to do that through college.

But when kids reach adulthood, things change. The problem with the working world is that when we enter it, we tend to lose our community. With some effort and commitment, we can start to find friends through hobbies, shared interests, or religion. A lucky few find community in such a seamless group that it's possible for them to drop in and out without feeling either submerged or alienated.

Community feels optional today, but it hasn't always been that way. Traditional farming community activities once included barn-raisings and dances in which the dancers trod on dried grain, threshing it with their feet. Such rituals existed for good reasons: the work of building a new barn could take a single family months and was fraught with danger, as there weren't enough participants to safeguard one another (there might not be someone free to hold a ladder in place while someone else climbed it). But a dozen families might take just one long day to raise a barn, and the whole community pitched in to make sure the work got done well and safely. Some people worked on the building, while others prepared a magnificent feast to feed everyone. By combining time and resources and rotating the activities among different properties, the work was greatly diminished and social harmony was increased. The community had chosen a common goal, and just as common goals help couples achieve synergy, the same is true in communities. Aside from the new barn itself, weary homesteaders got the chance to talk to one another, a rarity in times when neighbors might be separated by miles and there was no telephone. Children worked and played together, young couples flirted, and romantic matches were made at these events, which drew the community still closer together.

Our survival seems to no longer depend on the presence of community—indeed, independence is a highly valued quality in this culture. Even though we may not need our neighbors to help thresh the wheat or build a barn, we need them for other, less tangible things. For example, in some big cities people live in buildings whose outside doors stay locked. In the lobbies and elevators of these buildings are signs reminding people not to let strangers into the building, for reasons of security. Clearly, if you know someone lives in your building, you will not stand at your mailbox and watch her dropping groceries while she hunts for her keys—you will go over to the door and let her in. One day you'll be standing on the stoop without your keys, and one of your neighbors will recognize you and return the favor. So even in the big city, even in the age of telecommunication, knowing your neighbors can be a boon. Neighbors are the people who look out the window and yell at the neighborhood bully who's got your kid cornered. Neighbors give you things such as aspirin when you have the flu and can't go out to get it yourself, and some of them might even bring you soup. Neighbors occasionally put your wash in the dryer, invite you to parties, and commiserate with you over everything from taxes to divorce. In exchange, you might water their plants when they're on vacation or tutor their kids in algebra. People who don't get to know the people they live near miss out on the pleasure and security of being part of a small community of people who watch out for one another.

There are so many kinds of community, so many different kinds of "spots," that it's hard to describe them all. People may organize themselves into cohesive groups based on shared labor, experience, or need. Victor Frankl talked about people in concentration camps who shared their meager food with others and cheered up their comrades while staring down death day after day. The horrors of the concentration camp brought out something fine and brave and heroic in people who had every reason to be terrified and helpless. Hopefully, none of us will ever be tested in that way, but if we were, what a wonderful thing it would be to find our highest purpose in comforting others! Being part of a community is really about serving others and getting satisfaction not from what we have but from what we can do.

JOANNA'S STORY

Joanna lost her community and found it again through a personal trial. She was a speaker and trainer for a large retail organization, but at twenty-nine, she started to feel tired all the time. It was hard to get up in the morning, she was losing weight, and she didn't feel much like eating. Her most disturbing symptom wasn't physical, though; she worried because she no longer laughed. She had lost her enthusiasm, and her laugh had gone with it.

She went to the doctor and was diagnosed with leukemia. She started using daily meditation, visualization, and prayer to deal with the pain and to become still and quiet. She also did one other thing every day: she laughed. Through these practices, she found that she had regained something else that she had lost without even realizing it— her sense of compassion. She had once worked with children and loved it, but she had acquired a high-paying, high-powered job. After her realization, she gave up the job and went back to working with children, which was an authentic passion and the best expression of her true self. Joanna came to visit me some months later and told me she had been maintaining her leukemia—it had not worsened since her diagnosis.

Joanna's community was the children with whom she worked. It was there that she felt connected, secure, and needed. When people find their perfect community—their "spot"—they blossom, and the community thrives on their joy. An important if indirect benefit of focusing upon your true self is that when you do, your needs lead you to where you truly belong.

✦ WHAT IS YOUR PLACE?

So, where do you belong?

You may say to yourself, "Nowhere. There's no place on earth where I fit in." Would it surprise you to discover that most people feel that way? Would you believe upward of 95 percent of people feel left out, like there's a big party someplace that they can't get invited to? So if you feel you don't belong, you're already in a large group! The truth is, you *do* belong. It may be an invisible mystery to you just now, but somewhere out there is a book club, an orchestra, an environmental movement, a religion, a homeless shelter, or a doggie park made just for you. There is at least one place where you belong and can make a difference, and you will find it if you don't give up searching. Way back in Chapter 1, we discussed group synergy, which is an important part of finding and contributing to your community. When you're in the right place, synergy comes naturally.

It makes sense that people feel disconnected from things that matter to them. The world is complicated, and we cocoon to protect ourselves from its demands. When your phone rings at dinnertime, how often is it a sales call or your local charity requesting money? When you walk down the street and make eye contact with someone, how often does that person ask you for a handout? Walkathons, causes, clean-ups—there are too many requests to even consider, so we screen them all out. And out of fear, we screen ourselves right out of the chance to be happier, because doing things for a worthy cause can bring you a unique kind of joy. Nothing feels as good as being needed and being able to fill that need.

If that doesn't sound familiar, try this test: go to the nearest coffeehouse or candy machine and buy something for a coworker. It can be a sixty-cent candy bar or a cup of coffee. Bring it to your coworker and watch her face light up. Doesn't that feel good? Now multiply that feeling by ten, and you'll be close to how it feels to meet a need. You feel good not just because you met someone's need but because your need to be appreciated, to contribute something of yourself in your community, was also met. The emptiness that many people feel is the emptiness of being useless to others. The only reason for our emptiness is that we're unaware of how necessary it is to give.

The old saying is that charity begins at home, but in homes that are increasingly made up of just one person, charity needs to begin someplace else. We have a spiritual need to contribute something, and neglecting that need leaves us dissatisfied and empty inside. Taking your contributions into the larger community is a way to build a family in the best sense of the word—a group of people who depend on one another, share common goals, and help one another. A single person can energize a situation with passion and purpose. Passion is contagious, and it can ignite a whole group.

The things that extended families once did naturally may now take place outside our homes, but they are still vitally important to the health of our communities. We are bound together in a web of need and potential: I may have what you need, and you may have something I need. Healthy communities tap the potential of all their members. Among the greatest gifts children can receive from their elders is the understanding that they have something to contribute—for example, eight-year-old boys who think they can't do anything important can clean up lakes or teach littler kids to play baseball or run errands for older folks who can't get around by themselves. Older folks also need to know that they have something worthwhile to do, even if it's only giving a stray cat a home, staying with little kids while moms are out shopping, or just watching out the window to see that the children playing outside are safe. Nearly everyone has the potential to do something good for others!

✦ SYNERGY AND COMMUNITY HEALTH

In some communities, the town government and schools work together to provide a safe, clean, healthy environment. In some places, neighborhood groups take on these local challenges. No town is perfect, but when the leadership is good, quality of life improves for all citizens. As individuals, we may not all be Abraham Lincoln, but we can choose to put our energies into things that we feel strongly about, and we can make things happen. When people are involved and committed to reaching civic goals, synergy takes hold and propels their activities to success.

The answer to apathy is action. To make civic synergy a reality, the only thing you have to do is join something and bring your whole heart to the process.

All beings tremble before violence. All fear death.
All love life. See yourself in others. Then whom can
you hurt? What harm can you do? He who seeks
happiness by hurting those who seek happiness
will never find happiness. For your brother is like
you. He wants to be happy. Never harm him, and
when you leave this life, you too will find happiness.

GAUTAMA BUDDHA

Expressing Your True Self and Your Higher Purpose

The only true joy on earth is to escape from
the prison of our own false self, and enter
by love into union with the Life Who dwells
and sings within the essence of every creature
and in the core of our own soul.

THOMAS MERTON

The Eagle's Story

A collection of sharp familiar smells filled the farmer's nostrils and rays from the sun warmed his face. This, he thought, is what makes South Africa so beautiful. The mountains, the forests, the sea. He was on his way to purchase supplies at a nearby village. As he ambled through the forest through streams of sunlight, he saw, lying on the ground, a baby eagle.

"I wonder what this little king is doing lying on the ground," he thought. "No, I must not pick it up. Its mother may be near, and female eagles protecting their young can be ferocious."

It would be better, he reasoned, to go on his way. If, on his return, the baby eagle was still lying on the ground, he would pick it up and take it home. So he trudged on toward the village, the image of the eagle never leaving his mind.

"This eagle," he thought to himself, "is a good-luck omen. If it's still there when I come back, the gods will have surely blessed me."

Upon his return the baby eagle was in the same spot. It almost seemed to be waiting for him. He picked it up and tenderly cradled it all the way home, thinking as he went, "My family will indeed be blessed."

"Look," he said to his wife, "this baby eagle was lying alone in the forest. This is the king of the birds. Where shall we put it?"

"We'll put it in with the chickens. That's the place for a bird," said his wife.

"But this is the king of the birds, woman."

"I don't care! He's a dirty bird, and he can't come into my house."

And so in the eagle went with the chickens. He slept with the chickens, ate with the chickens, and lived with the chickens for the next year, and he grew into a majestic eagle.

One day a forest ranger, a naturalist whose first love was birds, passed the chicken farm. In the yard, to his amazement, he saw the eagle, a young male in all his glory, pecking the ground for grubs alongside the chickens.

Astonished and hardly able to contain himself, he asked the farmer, "What is this eagle doing in there with the chickens?"

With embarrassment, the farmer replied that the eagle didn't know anything different. "He's been living with the chickens for a year already, and he thinks he is a chicken."

The ranger asked if he could take the eagle and try to bring forth his talents, to help the eagle fly and return to nature, where it belonged.

The farmer answered, "You'll never succeed with that. This eagle now believes he is a chicken. He will never catch the wind with his wings like a true eagle."

The ranger offered to buy the eagle, but the farmer didn't want his money. He knew the forest, he knew the lay of the land and all the creatures of the forest, and he was convinced that the ranger would not be able to make this eagle a real eagle again. But he gave his permission for the ranger to take the bird.

The next day, the ranger took the eagle to a nearby hill, grasped him just above the talons, and held him up, saying, "Fly, eagle! You are an eagle! You must fly! Come on, eagle, fly!!"

But the eagle just looked at him and looked at the ground. The ranger, disappointed, took him back to the chicken house. Discouraged and upset, this lover of birds wondered what he could do to make this eagle fly.

Days later, the ranger returned and took the eagle out to a higher hill.

Again, he held the eagle up and said, "Fly, eagle! You are an eagle. You must fly. Come on, eagle, fly!"

The eagle just looked at the ranger. There was no fire in its eyes. Then the eagle looked down into the valley where the chickens made their home.

The ranger, not knowing what to do, went home and read about eagles. He talked to experts, but no one could help him.

At dawn the next day, the ranger took the eagle to the South Coast, where there were extremely high cliffs. He held the eagle over the cliff and shouted passionately, "Fly, eagle! Fly! You are an eagle! You must fly! Come on, eagle, fly!!"

He threw the eagle over the cliff. Down the eagle went, tumbling and falling like a stone. But just before he smashed onto the rocks below, those magnificent wings opened. As the wind caught its wings, the eagle swooped over the waves with magnificent splendor.

In some ways, we are all eagles. We don't know what we're made of, and we often live in environments that don't teach us what we need to know in order to soar. It might take disasters or a feeling of despair as we feel ourselves tumbling over the cliff to awaken us to possibility. Awakening to your purpose can happen in an instant, but you never know when that instant will come. Or you can choose awakening in a deliberate way, choose to live your life on purpose. Your purpose is inside you; your true self is always there, waiting to be expressed.

I think I've always known my true purpose, and I think it came from the harmony I felt when I spent time with the farmworkers of my childhood, and from the contrast between my father's unhappiness and my passionate love of and respect for nature. I always knew that I wanted to bring people closer together, and I knew that connection is the most important thing in the world and the secret to real happiness. I discovered synergy long before I ever heard the word, and maybe my whole life has become a quest to rekindle synergy wherever I find it missing.

When I was a kid, I would gather my friends to create theatrical plays or tell stories. My imagination has always been incredibly vivid. If my friends were not interested in listening to a story, then I would tell it to the farmworkers or to my dog, Rusty, or to Jaco the baboon. I was always sharing information. Sometimes I created imaginary stories, and then I'd get into trouble for "lying." My parents and the culture in which I grew up believed that kids should be seen and not heard and that imagination was most certainly an undesirable trait. It was only once I was grown that I discovered that the ability to create and share an idea through verbal communication is a blessing.

From childhood onward, I have never been afraid of the unknown. In fact, I was such a wanderer that I got the nickname Christopher Columbus, which was later shortened to Columbus. My mother would stand on the back stoop and call, "Columbus, where are you?" And wherever I was, swimming in the river or playing by the kraals or in the native village, I could hear her. I don't know how, because sometimes I was miles away. Maybe in the way that new mothers can hear their babies cry from some distance away, children can hear their mothers calling, too!

I find life exciting and exhilarating and cannot wait for new things to happen. I believe I have my grandfather's adventurous spirit in my genes, and I love it. I love to travel, I love to teach, and if there is one small thing that I can share with others and will bring them joy, then that's my mission in life. To me, sharing ideas is what it's all about. I always knew I would be a teacher or an entertainer of some kind. Now I am an entertaining teacher!

Finding and discovering who you are and what talents you possess are so important to the essence of living. Don't be the poet who wants to write but never does. Don't sell out to fear. Don't be the singer who loves to sing and sings with love but never passes that love to someone who's ready and waiting for it. Share your talents with those who need them. Share your real self with the world. Bare your soul, be vulnerable, and let God take care of the rest. It can never fail. Nothing loving, spiritual, and divine ever fails.

> *Pursue some path, however narrow and crooked, in*
> *which you can walk with love and reverence.*
>
> HENRY DAVID THOREAU,
> JOURNAL, 18 OCTOBER 1855

Know Your Values

In days gone by, schools taught children what they should believe, and the lessons were reinforced at home. These days, schools do a lot less in imparting values to children, and parents work much more and don't have the time and access to their kids that parents once had.

As the 1960s came and went, people started to realize that concepts they had taken for granted—such as marriage, family, and patriotism—were no longer necessarily relevant to them. We started forming new alliances and alternative families, and we came to understand that patriotism can be corrupted by such things as racism and greed. Like children do when they discover their parents' imperfections, Americans rebelled, and our cultural values became more permissive and more relative.

Some of the changes that took place were necessary and good—it was high time Americans looked hard at racism and sexism, for example, but in some ways we threw the baby out with the bathwater. Many people, in rejecting everything, ended up with nothing. And that is a problem, because not knowing what matters to you erases your ability to do what's right.

How old are we when we realize what we really value? I suspect that our values change as we grow. We start out caring about only what directly affects us, and we are taught values by our parents and culture. At some point, we start thinking for ourselves and facing situations that require us to decide what we accept and what we reject. Perhaps the most important value that we develop in life is the understanding that there are things in life that matter and that it's a personal duty to uphold them. This is part of the philosophy I embrace—that of living life on purpose. You are not a dry leaf on the surface of a brook: a leaf goes where the brook goes and is at some point submerged. It's important to choose your direction, to know what matters, and to act on it. Our sole possession at birth is free will, the expression of our true selves. Giving up the right (and responsibility) to express the true self is the most self-limiting thing a person can do. Luckily, reclaiming that right is possible: all it takes is a choice.

BEN'S STORY

Ben was born blind. He was raised in a very large family where he felt uncared for and unloved. He developed into an angry young man, mad at the world. He was obnoxious, a façade that covered his deep depression and kept people from getting close to him. He didn't believe in love, never having experienced it. He was a loner in a world that seemed destined to reject him.

As life played out, Ben began to search for some answers to his unhappiness. He went to several different associations seeking someone or something to help him, and he ended up in the front row of one of my seminars on Synergy Life Mastery, looking skeptical and sullen. It was an eight-week course, and pretty soon Ben began to ask very pointed questions, obviously trying to fend off the things I was trying to teach. He practically heckled me, and I looked forward to the end of that class and our association.

I didn't have great hopes for Ben. Once in a while, someone comes along who is so closed to his own potential that he just can't be made to see it. But about halfway through the course, a small miracle occurred: Ben fell in love. He met a girl named Christina, who was also taking the course. I like to think he was subconsciously accepting those same things that he was trying so hard to consciously reject. Something got through to him, some glimmer of hope and possibility.

He was transformed! Suddenly his heart was open. He learned to let go of the past and move on with his life. Christina's unconditional love for Ben changed his life from one of sullen despair to one of purpose, fun, and adventure. In the simple miracle of being loved, Ben learned not only that joy existed, but that he was capable of co-creating it. He's a wild man! Now he does things that most sighted people are scared to try. He sent me a videotape of himself in a tandem skydive, and when I asked him why he decided to take on that particular challenge, he told me, "I wanted to test your idea of living in the present."

"How was it?" I asked.

"Terrific!" he replied with a laugh. "I was totally occupied! All my senses were fully engaged. I felt euphoric!"

Ben is a completely different man. He invites life; he pursues it. Blindness doesn't stop him, and he has no fear of change. He's a happy man, a musical artist, and a public speaker. Best of all, he's now a happily married man and father of a little girl.

Ben may not have been aware of it, but he made a choice. When he met a new girl at a seminar that he didn't like, he could have chosen to remain angry and closed off, but he opened up enough to let some light into his dark world, and that light was so enchanting, so empowering, that he made a decision to risk rejection. He took the chance that someone might find him lovable, and he won. At the start of the class, he probably wouldn't have said openly that he believed in love, and he probably wouldn't have claimed to value it. It was the thing that had always been missing in his life, and he missed it so terribly that the pain almost really disabled him. Realizing that he valued a loving relationship enough to risk himself on it created a place in his life that had never existed before—the joyful place of synergistically connecting with another person.

What Do You Value?

Here's a synergy activity. Set aside a half-hour and go through the Relax-Action process described in Step Four of this book, and then enter the Workshop of Your Mind. Walk through the shower of white light and feel clean and new. Go into the Truth Booth and sit down. Think about the things and people that matter to you, and ask yourself what your values are. Do the values that first spring to mind truly belong to you, or do they really belong to your family, your church, or your own conception of what "a good person" should want?

When you come out of the Workshop, grab a pen and make a list of ten things you value. Write them down here.

MY SYNERGY JOURNAL | *Values*

1._____

2._____

3._____

4._____

5._____

6._____

7._____

8._____

9._____

10._____

Now, place a star by your top four values on the list. Then write yourself a note about your number-one value. What does it mean to you? How do you express it in your everyday life? Is it valued in your original family? Has it ever caused you problems?

A few more questions to consider: Are there things that other people seem to value that you don't? What are they? How do you feel about being different from "everyone else"?

Learning about your real values helps you discover your true life goals and establish a sense of purpose. Now we'll move on to discuss why a sense of purpose matters and how it can transform your life.

A Clear Mission

One of your most important possessions is a mission in life, a clear sense of purpose. If you have a purpose, you're making a deliberate effort to live life on purpose. The best workers, the greatest producers, the most enthusiastic people are those who have the "I-want-to" factor, which I call desire motivation. Desire motivation is just the opposite of an impulsive "I-want-it" accumulation syndrome. Desire motivation is the drive to fulfill life's purpose.

Having a purpose doesn't necessarily alleviate your problems, but it does widen your scope and help put those problems in perspective as you move toward something worthwhile. When you're on the right track, there's a knowledge inside of you that's steadying and comforting even in the midst of troubles.

The enemies of desire and motivation are fear and cynicism. Cynicism is wearying, and even worse, it makes people assume a stance that says, "I'll believe it when I see it." As we've discussed throughout this book, our beliefs have to be wider than our puny physical vision! We create reality from the inside, and waiting for it to manifest itself to us is a self-defeating kind of blindness. When you discover your purpose, don't let your Fear Buddies talk you out of it.

A clear mission creates a context by which to experience life in your own unique way. But how, you might ask, do I discover my mission? One great tool is a mission statement. Creating a mission statement is an act of personal integrity; it's the expression of your true self. A personal mission statement is a short, precise, quotable affirmation that describes your sense of purpose and how you intend to live your life.

✦ MY KEY MISSION STATEMENT

Here's my own personal mission statement:

> My key mission is to focus my mental energy and physical effort into life-enhancing, learning, growing situations and relationships that build a real sense of individual and collective self-worth and purpose.

The things I value most highly are incorporated into my mission statement. The mission statement isn't precise and specific, the way that a goal might be, but it covers what I care about. I feel my best when I'm working with others, helping people, and teaching and learning from the people I meet. So when I wrote my key mission statement, those things went into it. Your mission statement may be longer or shorter, but the important thing is that it's yours. It should contain your most cherished values and wishes. It is a reflection of your purpose.

Creating your mission statement does more than just stating your life's purpose, even though that is terrifically important. It helps you realize and appreciate your unique talents and abundance, and it helps make you feel emotionally secure. Having a mission makes us all more confident of our place in the universe. Your uniqueness secures your place and makes you irreplaceable.

MY SYNERGY JOURNAL | *My Mission Statement*

Take plenty of time to meditate on your purpose and your mission statement. Then compose your mission statement, and feel free to write and rewrite it. The written expression of your life's purpose is an important document, so set aside all the time you'll need.

Use the values list that you created earlier to help you think about what matters most to you. Don't let other people's expectations of you lead you in the wrong direction. Instead, think carefully about what really counts for you. Look at the list of synergy experiences that you prepared for the Synergy Journal exercise in this book's Step One section, and consider what those experiences had in common. Use your experiences of synergy to remind you of not only what you think you *should* want to do or be, but also what actually makes you feel happy, challenged, and immersed. What makes the time fly by? Use everything that you've learned about yourself to create your own mission statement.

_____

_____

_____

_____

_____

_____

Synergy and Purpose

If we look for synergy in everything we do, we discover ways to connect. By practicing synergy, we embrace the idea of growth. If you believe you are the same as everyone else and that it's a dog-eat-dog world, then you will struggle to find synergy, although you won't even value the concept of synergy. But being aware of your values, defining your purpose, and structuring your goals to express that purpose puts you in charge of your life. You have the ultimate power—the power to make choices. And through your choices, you create synergy, which brings you joy.

If teachers who mark kids down for daydreaming knew how important it is to dream, they'd change their grading strategies, and maybe even the curriculum, too! Maybe each school day should start with a session of daydreaming, followed by lessons that teach kids to realize their dreams. Dreams are an expression of mind energy, which is the most powerful thing in the world if it's used effectively—in other words, if it's focused on what we want, not on what we don't want. That's why learning to erase old Playbacks, to replace negative thought patterns with optimistic ones, to use techniques such as the Mental Workshop and positive affirmations, and to discover our true purpose in life are all powerful tools when we're creating a new reality.

Reaching Extraordinary Joy by Achieving Your Goals

Nothing contributes so much to tranquilize the mind as a steady purpose—a point on which the soul may fix its intellectual eye.

MARY SHELLEY

Goals and What They're Good For

If your dreams and intentions are the grassy plain at the foot of a mountain and your mission is a flag at the mountain's very summit, your goals are the steps carved into the mountainside. You might reach the summit without using the steps, but it's a hard climb. It takes longer, is more arduous, and makes you much more tired and liable to quit before reaching the top. Goal-setting sounds harder than it really is, but in fact, the very act of setting goals relieves worry and focuses the mind.

Often we have one major goal, and that's what we focus on. But because it's a big goal, it might seem too difficult, if not impossible, to accomplish. We might make a couple of half-hearted attempts, get discouraged, and file the dream away under "things that will never happen." But it's not that the goal is impossible—it's just that you tried to climb the mountain in the hardest way.

Let's say you're out hiking one day, and you see a man standing at the base of a mountain, beside the stone steps that lead to the very top. He's jumping up in the air over and over again, and although he's a pretty good jumper, he just ends up back on the ground. He's tired and sweaty and dirty from falling down. You watch as he takes another six or seven jumps, and then you can't resist anymore, and you go over to him. "What are you doing?" you ask him.

"I'm trying to get to the top of this mountain," he replies, wiping his forehead, "but it's awfully hard work."

You think he's nuts, right? This guy's never going to get to the top with the method he's using, and he's ignoring the steps that lead directly to the summit. Maybe he thinks that he doesn't have the time to climb them and that if he can just make it in one hop, look at all the time he'll save.

All this is to say that almost any goal worth having is actually made of lots of smaller goals that have to be accomplished first. If your big goal is becoming vice-president of the agency at which you work but you're currently employed in the mailroom, you could apply for the position of VP, but you probably won't get it. That doesn't mean it's an impossible goal, just that you have to take the necessary steps to the top. You might have to attend night school, master the job you now have, take on increased responsibilities, learn more about the organization and the way things are done, get a degree in engineering or business, and steadily work your way up.

✦ "PATIENCE, GRASSHOPPER"

The feeling that there just isn't enough time to accomplish your desired goals is a common de-motivator. When a friend of mine was considering going back to school for a master's degree in English literature, her husband encouraged her. "We have enough money if you make your job part-time," he said.

She shook her head sadly. "Do you realize," she asked him, "that by the time I finish school, I'll be fifty-three years old?"

He thought for a second or two. "How old will you be if you don't finish school?" he asked. She didn't speak to him for a couple of hours, but she applied to graduate school and started the following fall.

Sometimes a goal just isn't worth the effort, in which case it doesn't reflect your true purpose, and it's perfectly okay to let go of it. Other times, the goal is worthwhile: there's a set of steps up that mountain, and it's *your* mountain. It matters to you, you have sacrifices to make, and it will take time.

It's easier to be patient when your minor goals are laid out in an organized way, so that you have recognizable milestones on your journey up the mountain. Don't expect to go for years without a reward because you're saving up for one giant party at the end! Steven Covey frequently reminds his listeners to plan and celebrate the achievement of smaller goals and then use that joy to motivate themselves to continue their achievements.

To achieve your goals, do it one step at a time, but don't lose your focus on the big picture and why you want it. Just keep seeing it. Visualize every detail and take one step at a time. Richard Dreyfus and Bill Murray demonstrated this concept in the movie *What About Bob?* They called it "baby steps." With baby steps, you can achieve just about anything as long you are patient, persevere, and keep the visual image of your goal clear in your mind.

Setting and Achieving Your Goals

The other day, as I was in the airport on my way to present my ideas on synergy to a group in Orlando, Florida, I looked out onto the runway and found myself staring at a Boeing 747. At such close proximity, its size was overwhelming, and I was absolutely struck by the magnificence of this man-made flying machine. It reminded me of how far our technology has advanced. The Wright brothers dreamed of flying, and their homemade flying machine started a never-ending adventurous journey, from walking on the Moon to probes on Mars.

The hardest part of goal-setting is discovering what you want and kicking out the "Fear Buddies" (see page 87) who try to scare you away from achieving your purpose. Sometimes our fears cause us to set our goals too low, to choose goals that will give us only a minimal level of satisfaction.

This may help us cope and survive, but it's the challenging, meaningful, stretching goals that help us achieve greatness.

Buildings need blueprints, and road trips work much better with maps. Life's journey requires even deeper attention. Making plans that help fulfill your purpose can manifest your dreams in physical reality.

Recently, I began a walking program. My purpose and desire were to become healthier, more fit, and more able to cope with my demanding speaking schedule. I was excited and motivated to walk. But on the first day, I saw all these incredibly healthy beautiful people who were much slimmer and more fit than I was. They were running distances that I never thought I could achieve. That was very discouraging, and I really disliked my first few outings. Then I realized what I was doing: I was comparing myself to all those other people, and I was creating a failure feedback loop. Rather than sticking to my original purpose, which was to improve my quality of life, I was thinking, thinking, thinking about all the things I was not. When my mind gets in my own way like that, I call it analysis paralysis. It was causing me to lose sight of my big picture and my present-moment power.

My Fear Buddies were my walking partners, and they harassed me with self-doubt. As soon as I realized that the reason I was finding excuses not to do my walking was analysis paralysis, I threw out my Fear Buddies. I decided to take it one day at a time, one literal step at a time.

A few years ago, a woman decided to break a record by swimming from Catalina Island to the coast of California, a distance of twenty-six miles. She trained for months for the event. She even raised sponsorship money to cover the costs of renting a large yacht and employing professional coaches and athletic medical personnel.

When the big day came, she slipped into the icy waters and began the slow, rhythmic motion she had practiced to utilize her energy to the utmost. At first, she felt extremely confident. She took her time, and she was completely aware of the conditions of the water, her energy level, and her goal. But as time elapsed, she began to feel the pressure of the distance and the coldness of the water. It became foggy, and she began to panic. The fog got so thick that she had to get directions from her coaches, who shouted to her from the yacht only a few yards away.

"A little to the right!" her coach would yell through a megaphone.

"A little to the left!" he shouted when she was off course again.

He needed to keep her on course to avoid the danger of all the boat traffic. This went on for what seemed like an eternity. Suddenly fear, doubt, and panic took over, and she begged to be pulled out of the freezing water, although she was only one mile from breaking the record.

After a few cups of hot tea, she said, "When I started focusing on me, on the temperature of water, and began doubting myself, I let my purpose and my big picture slip away, and everything suddenly seemed impossible."

She had lost her belief and her vision only one mile from fulfilling her dream.

When you set a goal, it's based on your dream, so set a big one. Then break it down into baby steps, the smaller goals that help you climb that mountain. You will work though those small goals, but while you do it, keep your mind on the big one and use it for hope and inspiration. Surround yourself with people who understand and support your purpose, because we all get lost in the fog sometimes and need someone to remind us that the shore is just a mile away.

✦ GET SPECIFIC

When you start setting goals, it's important to be specific about what you want to do, how you want to do it, and when you will complete it. Time is a crucial component of reaching your goals, so write down your goals and be sure to add a timeline. After you've set your goals, take action so that you synergize yourself internally. Don't let yourself get scattered, and don't try to climb the mountain in one jump. By defining goals, you also reinforce your commitment to them, so make sure that all of your talents, focus, and energy are guided toward fulfilling your purpose.

Write It Down

Writing down your goals is vastly important for planning purposes, not only because putting a checkmark next to a goal at the end of the day feels so good, but because written goals act as affirmations. By writing your goals, you give your mind something positive and real to focus upon. At the start of each day, sit down with a dayplanner or a notebook and list the things you need to accomplish. Refer to the list often to keep you on course, and at the end of the day, check off the things that you've done. Move the things that you didn't do onto the next day's list, or choose a time in the near future when you can easily get them done.

Goals are like affirmations and should be written in the present tense, in the here and now. Using the present tense helps you to clarify and more vividly visualize your goals, and it also conditions your subconscious to accept the written statement as reality, as the truth. Then the mind ignites with desire and fuels physical action.

Here are some sample present-tense statements:

+ I am writing a three-page report on employee standards. I plan to have it done by 6 P.M.

+ I am walking two miles tonight after supper.

+ I am checking my daughter's algebra homework tonight and helping her study for her test.

+ I am happy and successful in my position as a dentist.

+ I am picking up the laundry from the cleaners at 6:45.

Several kinds of goals are here: a work-related goal, a health-related goal, a goal related to parenting your child and ensuring her success, a happiness- and success-related affirmation, and a daily-chore goal. The goals are as specific as possible about time, which helps you plan your day.

As you can see, a goal written in the present tense is actually an affirmation of what you want to have, be, or do, and it's also an affirmation that your goals are already realized.

Create a Timeline

Every physical journey we take has a timeline. It takes five hours to fly from the West Coast to the East Coast. It takes twenty minutes to call the airline and make a reservation.

It is good to dream, and it is good to hope. It's wonderful to be and do something great in the present moment, something that builds and stretches us. But actually putting our dreams and hopes into action can be frightening. It's normal to feel some initial dread when facing a sheet of things that you have to do, and sometimes we fill pages with goals, get overwhelmed, and run away from the whole thing. Dealing with your written goals is like getting into the pool: it's cold at first, and you don't want to do it. You can wade in by undertaking the smaller, more manageable tasks and working your way through them each day, or you can plunge in by starting with the goal that you fear most, getting it done, and taking on the small stuff afterward.

Don't let yourself get stuck in the dreaming stage. Visualizing without materializing can be a wonderful escape, but it can also be frustrating and depressing. The greatest satisfaction we have as humans is living in the present, and thus acting on the goals that we set is a happy, creative experience.

Compare setting life goals to sailing. When you sail across a lake, you focus on a specific landmark on the other side. You know where you're going. But sometimes the wind changes and pushes you in a direction that you don't want to go. When this happens, concentrate, alter your sails, adjust the rudder, re-angle your yacht, and continue toward your original destination. When the wind shifts, don't just say, "Oh, well, I didn't feel like sailing anyway," and go home! You have to make changes to get to where you want to go. You plan your life's journey, set timelines, visualize the end result, and then work backward, setting up each goal that you need to achieve.

After you've chosen your goals—for the day or for your entire life—sit down and write out the steps that you'll need to take to accomplish them. Then assess the time that you'll need to accomplish each step, and set a deadline for each step. As you pay fanatical attention to detail and write out the actions that you'll need to take each month, week, and day, you'll start manifesting your dreams. Timelines are important: they help energize us into action because they create a sense of urgency and a do-it-now mentality. A sense of urgency combined with positive energy creates just the right amount of tension, keeping our attention and focus strong. That directed energy fuels the process of creation.

✦ GOALS ARE DAILY TASKS

Break big goals into little goals, and if you can't figure out how to get a big goal accomplished, consult an advisor. Career counselors, nutritionists, personal trainers, life coaches, and mentors may be helpful, depending on your goal. If you hit a wall, your next goal may be "find someone who can help me plan my goals."

Use a Things-to-Do-Today list or a dayplanner to keep your daily goals up-to-date. Don't forget to schedule time (put at the head of your daily list) to actually do the planning, and don't cheat yourself, because proper planning saves you much more time than you spend on it. If a certain goal must be accomplished by a particular time, make sure to include that deadline in your planning. Put stars beside the most important goals on the list so your eye will be drawn to them throughout the day.

As you work toward your goals, you will inevitably encounter interruptions, especially with goals that hinge on someone else's progress, which is invariably hard to predict. Don't drive yourself crazy, and don't expect to always get every goal done. Schedule time in your planner to do things you enjoy, too, and make those activities as legitimate as your work-related goals. Remember that some of your goals should involve keeping yourself on track mentally, physically, and spiritually. Strive for balance as much as you can, and you'll feel more organized and peaceful.

I use what I call the "Easy List System" to stay on track. I begin by listing all the must-dos; then I prioritize those and schedule them into my planner. Next, I schedule the things that I need to do but don't need to accomplish by any deadline. I also schedule the things that I like to do, and I treat those with the same importance as the others.

✦ GOALS ARE REALISTICALLY CHALLENGING

To understand the concept of realistically challenging goals is also to understand the concept of controlled enthusiasm. Controlled enthusiasm means that you have a positive attitude toward your goal but aren't unrealistic. This is trickier than it sounds, because negativity sometimes presents itself as "realistic." On the other hand, I have seen great plans fall apart because people did not consider the skills and abilities needed to reach a goal.

When I began my walking program, I started with a 5-minute brisk walk and repeated that once. Then I walked 7½ minutes, then ten minutes, and then increased my time by increments of 2½ minutes every third time out. This resulted, in a very short space of time, in the ability to walk constantly for 50 minutes. Trying to do 50 minutes my first time out would have been unrealistic and ended in failure. So, to reach your goal, make it realistic and challenging, and work toward it with constant, persistent effort.

✦ GOALS HELP YOU KNOW YOURSELF BETTER

You'll find that the process of setting meaningful goals helps you to know yourself better: it teaches you what you want and need, and it also teaches you about what new skills or behaviors you'll need to acquire in order to transport yourself to success. You'll find that one of the most important new behaviors is controlled, focused enthusiasm. Enthusiasm is spiritual energy, and thus it must be guided. The human mind and body adapt very quickly and are capable of the most exciting and unbelievable feats, but you don't try to eat an elephant at one sitting: you eat the elephant one bite at a time. Make sure that you set goals toward which your progress can be measured: think about what you've accomplished in the past, and plan to surpass those successes in the future. Setting goals that are measurable against past performance can become a success feedback system.

As I said earlier, patience is another vital part of setting and achieving goals, and the more important the goal, the more patience it requires. If you are not a patient person, don't give up hope! Use your Mental Workshop to practice patience. Focus on going slowly and deliberately through the steps of Relax-Action, spend lots of time in front of your mental movie screen, and then use your pent-up impatience to accomplish as many of your goals as you can each day. In Zulu, *Hamba gashle* means to go slowly, but go steady. Use the words *Hamba gashle* as an affirmation when you need to take time to focus.

✦ GOALS HELP YOU GO BEYOND LIMITATIONS

When setting a goal, set it beyond what you actually want. Aim farther than the target.

The brain is the most sophisticated chemical computer in the universe, and the mind is very discriminating and can often read meanings into what we think and do that surprise us. Thus, the way that you write down and think about your goals is of the utmost importance. For example, if you say, "I'll never be able to be happy," that's what you'll get. If you say, "I can never save money," when you do get some, your mind will make sure you lose it quickly. Don't say, "All I want in the bank is $20,000, and that will be enough." Your mind, working like a guided-missile system, will take you directly to that goal, and on arrival, it will stop and shut down its power. Ensure that your goals are stated in a way that gives you more than just the minimum.

How have you communicated with your mind and spirit? Have you allowed the opportunity for greater success to occur? Do you say, "I want no less than X" or "I want only X"? If so, try writing your goal statements this way:

> *By December 31, I will have no less than $2,000 in my savings account.*

It is important to understand that abundance comes to you in direct relation to the prosperity of your thoughts. Reach out for it with your mind, spirit, and body. Don't just plan for enough—plan for more than enough!

✦ GOALS ARE POSITIVELY FOCUSED

Being optimistic about life's journey is probably the greatest tool we can use. Being optimistic is a fun way to live our lives. Being optimistic is choosing life, choosing to be proactive, and choosing to have a creative, building attitude. Life is about what you make, not about what you take.

Setting goals assumes abundance in your life. Setting meager goals, goals based on what you don't want to happen (such as "I'm not going to be unhappy anymore"), is like having a whole supermarket's worth of food to choose from and coming home with a pack of sugar-free gum. Go beyond the determination not to be unhappy and choose to be happy. Go past the intention to avoid heart disease and quit smoking so you can improve the quality of your whole life. It's easy to get caught in the trap of settling for things, of choosing merely to be less miserable, when for the same effort or less you could choose to be joyful. Don't short-change yourself: you deserve so much! All you have to do is decide to have it.

Optimism, like almost anything else, is a habit. When you make optimistic goals, you express confidence in life, and that confidence translates into positive action. You have control of your destiny when you make choices that increase synergy in your life, and your goals—if they're realistic and broken into steps small enough to handle—are the steps that take you toward synergy. Optimistic goals support your intention to live a purposeful, joyous life.

See the difference between goals written from a pessimistic stance and those that are optimistic:

Negative: I'm not going to yell at my kids today.

Positive: I'm going to treat my kids with playfulness and respect today.

Negative: I'm not going to eat fatty foods today.

Positive: I'm going to eat fresh fruit and a delicious salad today.

Negative: I'm going to ignore my colleague's annoying ways today.

Positive: I'm going to see at least three positive things in my colleague today.

Now, write some of your own goals. Invent some pessimistically phrased ones, then rewrite those same goals from an optimistic viewpoint.

When you have written both lists, first read all the negative ones, and jot down how you feel at the bottom of the list. Now, read all the positive ones, and make another note of your feelings at the bottom of that list. See how it works?

Pessimistic

1. _____

2. _____

3. _____

4. _____

5. _____

Optimistic

1. _____

2. _____

3. _____

4. _____

5. _____

My Feelings

_____

_____

_____

_____

My Feelings

_____

_____

_____

_____

✦ YOUR GOALS BELONG TO YOU

Your goals of two kinds—steps that lead toward the expression of your highest purpose, and the stuff that you have to do to keep life running smoothly along. Sometimes your goals involve things you do for other people, but most of the time your goals are yours alone.

If you find yourself moving a goal from one day to the next for weeks on end, take a hard look at it and ask yourself, "Do I really have to do this at all?" Consider whether it's actually your goal, or someone else's, and whether it's worthwhile at all. Sometimes the answer is "no," because the goal wasn't especially rewarding in the first place. It's something you've thought about doing but just haven't gotten to yet. For many people, it might be something such as, "Lay down fresh shelf paper in the kitchen cabinets." Once a goal is written down, urgency takes over and even something totally unnecessary becomes a niggling thought at the back of the mind. Do you really need new shelf paper, or did you write that down after watching Martha Stewart last month? Did your mom change the shelf paper every year, so you feel you should, too? What exactly is shelf paper for, anyway? Who sees it? Does it add to the health and well-being of your family? Once you've asked yourself enough questions, you may realize that shelf paper is a waste of time. There is no dishonor in drawing an X through that goal and getting on with the meaningful things in life.

Goals that belong to you fuel your excitement about your purpose and smooth the path of your life. Goals that don't belong to you are someone else's burdens. Goals are also your private property, so you'll put yourself under less pressure if you don't generally share your goals with other people unless you know those people will be sources of motivation and support. Never share your goals with people you don't especially like or trust.

Five percent of the world's population master life's journey because they innovate, create, and fulfill their purpose by setting clearly defined goals. Fifteen percent criticize, condemn, and/or assist the 5 percenters while they are making their goals happen. Eighty percent don't believe in their own greatness and potential; either they have never heard of goal-setting or they have never taken a chance and tried it.

✦ GOALS BALANCE YOUR LIFE

You can set goals in every area of your life. Just as it's important to balance family with work and personal growth with community and spiritual life, it's important that your goals support you as a whole person. Your life increases in synergy with the number of connections you make, and just as strengthening your abdominal muscles prevents back strain, strengthening yourself in one area results in new strength in others. When you make your list of daily goals, look it over to see if you've left out anything. If you find that all your goals are work-related, stretch yourself a bit by incorporating something personal or spiritual into your list. Don't worry too much about overextending yourself. Trust that the diversity of your goals will result in increased empowerment and synergy.

Family Goals

Parenting is a tough job, a leadership role for which few of us are prepared. However, some basics never change. When setting family goals, remember that the only real control you have in your family (no matter who you are!) is your control of your own actions and feelings. You can hope that your child will grow up to be a physician, and to that end you can choose her schools, buy her her first microscope, and encourage her in that direction. But the choice is really hers, and you may do "everything right" and still be disappointed when she comes to you and says, "Dad, I've decided to be a journalist." So, choose your family goals by thinking of what you can contribute to your family, not what you can get out of it. The main reason to create a family in the first place is to have the satisfaction of helping others grow, and sometimes the growth of your children and partner may not necessarily please you. It's not their job to please you, just as it isn't your job to please them.

As a parent, you can do much to choose your children's activities, and you provide many of their opportunities. Some parents try to give their kids everything, and they may go overboard. Kids need a certain amount of time and space to do what they like to do, to make discoveries about the world, and even to make their own mistakes. Some kids have so many activities that they barely have time for a childhood. Children need a certain amount of structure and parents should provide it, but be careful to gradually increase their responsibilities and opportunities for choice as they grow up so they learn what it is to make their own decisions.

I wanted to be a good tennis player and never became one, so I tried to live this dream through my sons. I encouraged them in that direction, and they became very good. Shand really seemed to enjoy the game and took to it. However, when I went to watch him at a tournament or a match, he didn't play as well as he did when I wasn't there. This worried me a lot. Then I realized the problem. When I was there, he played for me. When I wasn't there, he played for himself, and played better. So, goals and family goals are very important, but they must be individual goals.

Include your family in your own dreams and goals, too. Let them know what's important to you, keeping in mind that what you want may not be what they want. You can't have a goal such as "My wife is going to finish her college degree." Your goals have to be things that *you* will do. In this case, if your wife's goal is to finish her degree, yours might be to help her in any way you can. Your goal would look something like this: "I'm going to help my wife finish her degree by taking over the grocery shopping and cooking dinner three nights a week so she can study."

You might try creating a set of family goals together, but keep in mind how important it is that everyone participates. Some parents try to create family goals, and although their intentions are the best, they become discouraged and frustrated when their partners or children don't seem interested in helping those goals to take shape. If you want people to be responsible and enthusiastic about accomplishing a goal, that goal has to belong to them from its very start. Family goals might center on vacation plans, a large purchase, taking part in a particular activity that interests everyone, or doing something community-oriented together. You might even have a goal meeting at which everyone shares their individual goals and tries to find ways to help one another achieve them. Whatever way you decide to use goal-setting in your family, you'll see that the goal-setting process itself helps your family grow closer as you communicate, tell one another your dreams, and help one another plan.

Jane, a personal friend of mine, explained how including her family in her goals has helped her. "Since I included my family in my goals, something amazing happened. I suddenly have a whole team supporting me. When I get home, they want to know how much I sold today and how much closer we are to going to Hawaii. It is really motivational, and, you know, it seems to give us a platform for communication. Our family is much closer and more supportive since I've included them in my vision for the future."

Career Goals

A few years ago, I employed a gardener. This gardener had little academic education, but he had life intelligence. In no time, he was able to make the garden look really attractive, and in the process, he taught me an important lesson about organization and work.

He had a clear objective for each day that he worked. He moved steadily through each day with incredible focus and attention to detail. Whatever he planted or cared for seemed to grow, grow, and grow.

One day I asked him, "How do you get everything to grow so quickly and become so healthy?"

"These flowers are my children," he said glowingly, "and they make their own children, so I have become their great father. I am creating a world of life, and it gives me happiness in my heart. This is my way to give to Mother Earth."

He was professing all the great laws of the universe. He was ensuring that his role on the planet got the attention it deserved. His life was centralized on a purpose that helped him be organized, focused, and fulfilled. He did not see my garden or his job as a grind or an unnecessary place to which he had to go. He just worked and sang and spoke to the plants until he felt complete. For him, work was not unnecessary hours that linked drinking time and fun time. He wanted to build something, and he wanted that something to reproduce itself. In a simple, most profound way, he lived his purpose with synergy and joy.

My garden lives and flourishes and so does he. He now owns and manages his own prosperous garden-service company.

When we have a sense of purpose and passion, work is never "work" in the derogatory sense. It's a place for fulfillment and achievement. Working isn't hard when you love it. When work is fun and purposeful, it's not "work," it's "work!" The strange thing is that when you love something, the other things you do also seem more enriching and enjoyable. Working with purpose and loving your work adds to your self-respect and self-esteem. Doing a good job feels good, and working with purpose is an expression of hope.

Ten Steps to Career Enhancement

1. **Set your goals high:** When teachers believe their students are bright, students achieve more, whether or not they are actually "bright." Goals should stretch you—it's in the stretching that you grow.

2. **Keep the details of your career goals private:** You are the person most concerned with your career. If your goal is to acquire your boss's job, don't tell coworkers about it. It's great to have friends at work, but unless you trust your friends implicitly, remember that most workplaces are still bastions of competition and that it's best to keep your wishes to yourself.

3. **Be a good team member:** Group synergy is a terrific goal to strive for at work. To achieve synergy, do your part by being helpful and cooperative, and if not everyone has your skills, try to model them. Once enough people understand the value of working as a team, competitive workplaces become more cooperative.

4. **Be kind to your coworkers:** Workplace harmony is an essential part of a joyful, synergistic life. Add to that harmony and your own spiritual growth by being good to the people with whom you work. Not only will it benefit you as a human being in the long run, but it will make work a pleasant place to be.

5. **Work honorably:** Taking pride in your work is important for general self-esteem. It doesn't matter what your job is if you work with the right attitude. Be consistent, creative, and reliable. Do your best, and expect good things from your work.

6. **Review and reassess your direction continuously:** In the work world, there is rarely time to rest on your laurels. Make sure you're doing what you want to do and what you do well. Study up on areas you want to master, look for role models, and stay your course. Make your career planning part of your goals, not just your daily goals but your lifelong ones.

7. **Be flexible:** People who can bend aren't broken by things such as mergers and downsizing. Take every chance to learn new things, and keep an open mind when you're faced with changes. Some people are caught up in resenting their jobs and reactively complain about any new change, even when it turns out to be beneficial. Being rigid and unable to cope with change is one predictor of mental illness; an open attitude is better for your health and happiness.

8. **Learn all you can about the job:** Don't just do your job—create a relationship with it! Learn its history and ups and downs. Read about leaders and current innovations in the field. Attend seminars and classes to help you further your career.

9. **Pay attention to synergy in your work:** If you've already got a job that you like and that meets your economic needs, you are blessed. If, like many people, your job doesn't fit you, or if you need to make more money, your challenge is to remedy the situation. In anything you do, the more synergy that comes to you, the better. You need enough money to live on, but you also need joy in your work, a sense of purpose, and generally good feelings. When you find something that really makes you sing, stay with it!

10. **Acquire some management skills:** In many organizations, moving up invariably means managing projects and people. Very few people are born managers: management is a set of acquired skills. Take a class, read books, and observe the managers around you. If you're shy but your managers speak to large groups of people on a regular basis, consider joining Toastmasters to get some public-speaking practice.

Personal Growth Goals

Personal growth and synergy go hand in hand. The reason that you're reading and working through this book is that you've made a commitment to grow into a more synergistic, joyful life. Personal growth is anything that makes you better as a person. It may encompass learning experiences and physical, emotional, and mental exercises.

The human brain was built to acquire, incorporate, use, and remember new facts, tools, and ideas. We are all learning organisms. We learned to do so much in the early years of our lives: how to drive a car, use a computer. We learned ways to cope with life and to deal with heartache and disappointment. We learned many day-to-day things that became habits. Think back to the time you were learning to read and write: do you remember how hard and complicated it seemed? Now it seems that you were born with those skills, but you weren't. There was a time when reading and writing were utterly impossible for you. Imagine that!

As we age—and this is especially true for people who are highly educated—we may tell ourselves that we have completed our schooling and that there's no reason to learn any more. Usually, fear, fatigue, or lack of interest is behind this idea. Stay open to learning, and if you've already got a couple of degrees and are feeling jaded and bored, consider learning something that is pure fun. Build model ships, take up needlepoint, or study Japanese. Broaden your horizons and seek out things that fascinate you. If, on the other hand, you're not satisfied with the amount of traditional learning you have, you can certainly acquire new knowledge, even if you do it one night class at a time.

As I noted above, there are all kinds of exercises that help you with personal growth: physical ones, mental ones, and emotional ones. Here's some information on the benefits of each kind of exercise; try to make each type a regular part of your personal-growth goals.

Physical exercise: Maintaining physical fitness can be a great challenge, but you must realize that your body is an important part of who you are and that its health is necessary to your goals and ultimate purpose. Thirty minutes of moderate exercise each day strengthens the skeletal and muscular systems and improves movement and flexibility. Physical exercise helps the cardiovascular system to supply blood to the entire body and enhances the respiratory system. The increase in activity and oxygen stimulates the brain's neurotransmitters to fire electrical impulses that travel along the axon terminals and stimulate the various hormonal systems of the body, which in turn release endorphins and other happiness hormones that keep the body's chemical system in balance. Finally, our digestive and gastrointestinal systems are cleansed naturally and regularly through physical exercise.

Physical fitness affects your mental and physical health, and it gives you a new perspective. It's also a good use of time because you can often do more than one thing when you're exercising. Playing basketball is great cardiovascular exercise, but it's also a good way to socialize. You can practice affirmations while swimming or lifting weights, or catch up on your reading while riding an exercise bike. Hiking with friends or family members brings you closer together as you share the small adventures of getting lost, running from snakes, or discovering a waterfall.

Emotional exercise: Exercising our positive emotional responses, such as laughter, joyfulness, gratitude, and bliss, validates and nourishes our authentic selves. Being sentient means being open to sadness and sympathy, so you may find yourself crying at sad movies, and loving it. Awareness of your own emotions and empathy for others brings a better understanding of your own and others' behavior. Making it a point to laugh every day stimulates the immune system, releases stress, and fills your life with joy.

We know that we are waking up when we become more sentient (in touch with our innermost feelings). As Ramakrishna once said, "If tears of ecstasy come spontaneously to your eyes or if the sensation of weeping springs forth secretly in your heart, ... this is authentic confirmation that you are awakening." A sentient person is unafraid of the personal search that leads to identifying and overcoming fears, prejudices, excuses, false fronts, and phantom inhibitors that, all too often, cast a dismal shadow over our rightful inheritance: extraordinary joy.

Mental exercise: Mental exercises, such as reading, journaling, visualizing, intellectual conversation, and the development of new skills and challenging tasks—and even working through this book!—help us move purposefully toward Mind Mastery.

Spiritual Goals

Growing as a spiritual being takes as much planning as furthering a successful career does. Spiritual goals may involve becoming more closely connected to the universe or to your god through prayer or meditation. You may decide to increase compassion in your life through service, so your goals may include volunteering. Sometimes we just want to be kinder, gentler, or more giving, and there's no reason that these desires can't be put into action in a planned way, too.

Taking time to be alone, to think about what you believe and ways to put your beliefs into action, is more important than many people realize. How many people do you know who make it a point to get to the gym at least three times a week for an hour? On the other hand, how many people do you know who make it a point to spend three hours a week in prayer or meditation? Although many people think you have to be a fanatic to want to spend considerable time practicing and enhancing your spirituality, you might be surprised by the benefits you receive.

Paying adequate attention to the state of your true self might not take three hours of concentrated effort each week, and there are certainly many ways to get in touch with the spiritual side of life. Sometimes just doing something nice for someone else enriches that person's life as well as that of the giver. Giving someone a break could be considered a highly spiritual act: what could be kinder and more compassionate than not judging someone else? There are lots of ways to enhance the soulful part of your life, including spending time in nature, reading the work of spiritual teachers, paying attention to your dreams, and participating in rituals that give structure and meaning to life's milestones.

If you are a believer of any religion, you have an enviable source of strength. The security of knowing what you believe is right, of having accessible spiritual leaders and the comfort of a religious community, is something many people have given up in the name of personal freedom or intellectual rigor. But if your faith nurtures and supports you, it is something to be cherished.

Synergy and Following Through

At first, keeping track of goals is tough. You forget to write them down at the start of the day, you leave your dayplanner under your chair at seminars, and you forget to consult it when you finish one thing and get ready to start something new. The good news is that if you can hang in there for a month or so, you'll find the planning habit becomes easy, then natural, then even necessary. Over time, you'll find your thought processes become more logical, and you'll remember to follow up on things others may forget. You may find your life getting simpler as you find new ways to schedule things that once seemed beyond your control.

As planning becomes a part of your skill set, you'll become more organized. You'll start to save time that you once lost in looking for information and trying to jog your memory about names, dates, and meetings. The psychic energy you'll gain will become part of the synergistic process, since you will be calmer and more in control. After a few months, you'll feel the contribution of organization to your self-confidence. Confidence, calmness, and control in your life create more opportunities for synergy, as you can use your energy to focus on what matters to you.

MY SYNERGY JOURNAL | *Goals*

Use the space on the next page to state your three major goals in each of four areas: family, career, personal growth, and spiritual growth. Remember that these are your major goals, so you will probably want to use another sheet of paper to list the subgoals that contribute to each major goal—the steps you need to reach the top of the mountain. In addition, you may want to look at all the major goals that you list and prioritize them in order to decide which to work on first. Don't attempt to work on more than one or two major goals at once, or you may become overwhelmed!

Family Goals

1._____

2._____

3._____

Career Goals

1._____

2._____

3._____

Personal Growth Goals

1._____

2._____

3._____

Spiritual Growth Goals

1._____

2._____

3._____

STEP SEVEN

Staying Connected— with Joy

Synergy, Choice, and the Seven Steps to Joy

Every time you connect with synergy, you feel joy. The choices you make enable you to access the stream of synergy any time you want. I started this book by discussing synergy and choice because I believe they are the two necessities for creating a joyful life. Replacing Inhibiting Thoughts and cleansing your Inner Ecology are ways of preparing to make authentic choices, set and achieve goals, and ultimately express your higher purpose— the deepest desire of your true self.

The tools in this book are many and varied—you may find that some work especially well for you. One choice you make daily is to do what works for you, and, of course, that applies to this book as well, so choose the strategies that best fit you.

Troubleshooting

We've covered a lot of ground in this book, and I hope you'll keep it near you in years to come. It's normal to get distracted, to backslide from well-intentioned plans, and even to forget what once made us happy. When trials come to you, return to the basic ideas of synergy and choice. Remember that you have the power to make different choices, and if one choice hasn't been working for you, use the tools of envisioning and imagining to come up with new choices. Visit your Mental Workshop, take extra time to reflect on what you need, and drag your mind away from pessimistic thoughts. As soon as you can do it properly, make a plan, write down your goals, and take action. One of the most helpless feelings in the world is to do nothing, so, at the very least, force yourself to exercise until you've got a plan that addresses your current problem.

When trouble comes, help yourself all you can, and don't forget to give others the opportunity to help you as well. Don't let independence isolate you from friends or family members who want to help you back to happiness. Take help with gratitude, because it too is a way to connect with others. And as soon as you can, help someone else.

Daily Reconnecting

Make sure you include something spiritual in each day's goals. Spend time with people you love, and make it special. Hug and kiss your family, your sweetheart, your cat. Love as much as you can, because it's love that gets you through the horrors. Sit in the park or take a walk so you can connect with nature and remind yourself of how awesome it is. Pray, meditate, contribute something of yourself to someone who needs it.

Another part of daily reconnecting is doing kindnesses. Stop for pedestrians, smile at the kid who serves your coffee, compliment a coworker. Bring muffins to the office for no special reason. Daily reconnecting is important to the people who are touched by your actions, and it is vital for you. You are doing more than "nice things"; you are building a reserve of good feeling in the world and contributing to synergy. You are making good choices and meeting life creatively and on your terms. Slipstream into the flow of life's re-creative power, and bring others with you.

Connection is a primal human need. We spend the first part of our lives making connections, such as the ones we make with our children or parents, but the first time your ten-year-old says to you, "Oh, Mommmm!" in that condescending tone of voice, you hear that connection break and have to wonder if it's all downhill from here. It's not downhill, not by a long shot! But connecting with others takes effort and needs to be a priority.

Anything that puts group synergy into place is an avenue for connection: volunteering, joining groups and clubs, exercising with a lot of other folks, traveling. As we age, we have to make more of an effort to create and maintain our connections; we may feel less need for connection, and we may slow down physically, taking up hobbies that are less active and more solitary. It doesn't have to be that way, though: readers can join book clubs, and people who like to sew can work on quilts in a group. Stay connected to possibilities for group activity in the community by subscribing to the local paper and reading the community section that lists all the readings, exhibits, club meetings, and school plays. Choose events to attend each week.

DELORES'S STORY

Delores is a sweet soul and a tough lady. She's a therapist for the Emancipated Youth Program, a wilderness training program that helps foster kids who are turning eighteen transition to living on their own as adults. A lot of these kids have been hardened by a lifetime of neglect and abandonment, moving from home to home. They're much too old in some ways, naïve and backward in others. Delores is a terrific success coach for these young people. When a kid acts tough and scary, Delores responds with, "Don't flirt with me! We're going to talk about how to improve the quality of your life, so sit down!" And they sit down.

Maybe Delores will retire some day, when she's ninety or one hundred. Probably not much before that—she's eighty-five now.

Connecting with Nature

One of the most powerful things I do to reconnect is to go into the canyons around my home and watch hawks riding the thermal layers and being chased by swallows fearful for the safety of their nests. The smell of papery-barked eucalyptus trees, with their waxy, camphorated blossoms, soothes my mind and relaxes my body, and troubles seem to melt away from me. Probably the best thing one can do in the world is to be in the world!

I think computers are magnificent examples of humankind's ingenuity. I also think we are spending too much time in front of computers and not nearly enough time lying under the trees or looking up at the sky. I have a hard time believing that children benefit more from additional school computers than they do from trips to the beach, and I wonder what values they are learning about nature when nature is removed from their education. The grandest adventures are to be had out of doors, though they might be as simple as visiting a local park or as complicated as tagging polar bears in the Canadian Arctic. Whenever you need to reconnect, whenever synergy and joy seem to have disappeared from your life, go outside. Even in the city it's possible to marvel at a tree or admire the flowers in a windowbox.

Connecting with nature means casting aside the idea that we must be productive at all times to be valid. Observing and appreciating nature is about what goes on inside you as a result of your interaction with the world. Wind, water, earth, and sun belong to us all, and there is a primal human need for contact with the elements. This contact is something that you might feel is missing from your life even if you can't name exactly what it is. When you feel depleted or harassed, leave the cell phone at home and give yourself the gift of time spent in nature. Don't allow deadlines, guilt, or the expectations of others to rob you of your rightful place in the natural world.

The Joy Prayers

Joy prayers are inner ecology treatments that strengthen and build inner peace, love, and joy. Joy prayers are life-enhancing affirmations and confessions of your deepest, most intimate yearning and desires. Joy prayers work from the inside out by helping you to to seek synergy spiritually through connections that create harmony, unity, and healing.

We invite our readers to forward their individual "Joy Prayers" to extrajoy@pacbell.net for posting on our website.

A PRAYER FOR MENTAL HEALTH

Dear God (Divine Presence, Spirit),

*I come to you searching for peace of mind. I let go and
hand my worry, fear, uncertainty and doubt over to you.*

*Bless me with clarity of thought and help me each day
to think divine thoughts of love and joy.*

*Give me the power to make wise decisions and to understand
that knowledge is more important than strength.*

*And teach me to be alert and aware of Your messages
in everything I think, feel, and do so that I may learn
to create joy from this day forward.*

Please show me the way. Amen.

A PRAYER FOR PHYSICAL HEALTH

Dear God (Divine Presence, Spirit),

I come to you searching for physical health and well-being.

*I let go and hand over my ailments to you and ask you
to help me remove the root cause of my problems.*

*Bless me with the power to appreciate the blessing
of physical health.*

*Teach me good lifestyle habits so that I may learn
to create joy from this day forward.*

Please show me the way. Amen.

A PRAYER FOR EMOTIONAL HEALTH

Dear God (Divine Presence, Spirit),

I come to you searching for emotional balance.

I let go and hand my anxiety, guilt, nervousness, and emotional pain over to you and ask you to help me calm my inner turmoil.

Help me to learn the power and comfort of prayer and meditation.

Teach me to reduce my physical stress levels and give me rest and peace so that I may face each day renewed.

And finally, may I learn to create joy from this day forward.

Please show me the way. Amen.

A PRAYER FOR SPIRITUAL HEALTH

Dear God (Divine Presence, Spirit),

I come to you searching to satisfy an emptiness that I feel deep within me.

*I want to let go of all manmade religious ideas and open my heart
and my mind to your infinite well of love.*

*Teach me to know deep within me that the first expression
of spirituality is love.*

*Bless me with loving thankfulness, gratefulness,
and a merry disposition so that I may learn
to create joy from this day forward.*

Please show me the way. Amen.

Selected Bibliography

Albion, Mark. *Making a Life, Making a Living.* New York: Warner Books, 2000.

Allen, James. *As a Man Thinketh.* Mount Vernon, NY: Peter Pauper Press [n.d.].

American Bible Society. *The Good News Bible.* Glasgow, Scotland: William Collins, 1976.

Attenborough, David. *Life on Earth.* Boston, MA: Little, Brown, 1979.

Bennis, Warren. *On Becoming a Leader.* Reading, MA: Addison-Wesley, 1989.

Berne, Eric. *Games People Play.* New York: Grove Press, 1964.

Blanchard, Kenneth, and Spencer Johnson. *The One-Minute Manager.* New York: Berkley Books, 1982.

Borysenko, Joan, and Miroslav Borysenko. *The Power of the Mind to Heal.* Carlsbad, CA: Hay House, 1996.

Buscaglia, Leo F. *Living, Loving & Learning.* New York: Ballantine Books, 1983.

Butler, Gillian, and Tony Hope. *Managing Your Mind.* New York: Oxford University Press, 1995.

Capodagli, Bill, and Lynn Jackson. *The Disney Way.* New York: McGraw-Hill, 1999.

Castaneda, Carlos. *The Teaching of Don Juan . . . A Yaqui Way of Knowledge.* New York: Pocket Books, 1977.

Chopra, Deepak. *Return of the Rishi.* Boston, MA: Houghton Mifflin, 1991.

———. *Unconditional Life.* New York: Bantam Books, 1992.

———. *To Know God.* New York: Harmony Books, 2000.

Covey, Stephen R. *Principle-Centered Leadership.* New York: Simon & Schuster, 1992.

Csikszentmihalyi, Mihaly. *Flow: The Psychology of Optimal Experience.* New York: Harper & Row, 1990.

The Dalai Lama. *The Joy of Living and Dying in Peace.* New York: HarperCollins, 1991.

————. *The Art of Happiness.* New York: Riverhead Books, 1998.

Davis, Phyllis K. *The Power of Touch.* Carlsbad, CA: Hay House, 1991.

Dyer, Wayne W. *Wisdom of the Ages.* New York: HarperCollins, 1998.

Elkin, Allen. *Stress Management for Dummies.* Foster City, CA: IDG Books Worldwide, 1999.

Exley, Helen. *In Praise and Celebration of Love.* New York: Exley Publications, 1995.

Foundation for Inner Peace. *A Course in Miracles.* Huntington Station, NY: Foundation for Inner Peace, 1979.

Fuller, R. Buckminster. *Synergetics—Explorations in the Geometry of Thinking.* New York: MacMillan, 1975.

Gallo, Fred P. *Energy Psychology.* Boca Raton, FL: CRC Press, 1999.

Goleman, Daniel. *Emotional Intelligence.* New York: Bantam Books, 1995.

Greenleaf, Robert K. *On Becoming a Servant Leader.* Don M. Frick and Larry C. Spears, eds. San Francisco, CA: Jossey-Bass, 1996.

Harris, Judith Parker. *Conquer Crisis with Health-Esteem.* Beverly Hills, CA: Saywrite Publications, 1998.

Harvey, Andrew. *Teachings of Rumi.* Boston, MA: Shambhala Books, 1999.

Hay, Louise L. *Heal Your Body.* Carlsbad, CA: Hay House, 1988.

Hill, Napoleon. *Think and Grow Rich.* North Hollywood, CA: Wilshire Book Company, 1966.

————. *The Law of Success.* Chicago, IL: Success Unlimited, 1979.

Hillman, James. *The Soul's Code.* New York: Random House, 1996.

Hogan, Eve Eschner, with Steve Hogan. *Intellectual Foreplay.* Alameda, CA: Hunter House, 2000.

Holmes, Ernest. *The Science of Mind.* New York: Dodd, Mead, 1938.

Jampolsky, Gerald. *Love Is Letting Go of Fear.* Berkeley, CA: Celestial Arts, 1979.

Keen, Sam. *To Love and Be Loved.* New York: Bantam Books, 1997.

Kuhn, Robert Lawrence. *Closer to Truth.* New York: McGraw-Hill, 2000.

Lindbergh, Anne Morrow. *Gift from the Sea.* New York: Pantheon, 1955.

Malta, Maxwell. *Psycho-Cybernetics.* Hollywood, CA: Wilshire Book Company, 1965.

Mandino, Og. *The Greatest Salesman in the World*. New York: Bantam Books, 1968.

———. *The Greatest Miracle in the World*. New York: Bantam Books, 1975.

———. *The Greatest Salesman in the World, Part II*, New York: Bantam Books, 1988.

McBryde, Linda. *The Mass Market Woman*. Eagle River, AK: Crowded Hour Press, 1999.

McWilliams, John-Roger, and Peter McWilliams. *Life 101: You Can't Afford the Luxury of a Negative Thought*. Los Angeles, CA: Prelude Press, 1988.

———. *Life 101*. Los Angeles, CA: Prelude Press, 1991.

Montrose, Philip. *Getting Through to Your Emotions with EFT*. Sacramento, CA: Holistic Communications, 2000.

Moore, Thomas. *Original Self*. New York: HarperCollins, 1981.

Nerburn, Kent. *The Soul of an Indian*. San Rafael, CA: New World Library, 1993.

Nerburn, Kent, and Louise Mengelkoch. *Native American Wisdom*. San Rafael, CA: New World Library, 1991.

Noel, Brooke. *Back to Basics*. Beverly Hills, CA: Champion Press, 1999.

Novak, Philip. *The World's Wisdom*. Edison, NJ: Castle Books, 1996.

Ornish, Dean. *Love and Survival: The Scientific Basis for the Healing Power of Intimacy*. New York: HarperCollins, 1998.

Palmer, Parker J. *Active Life*. San Francisco, CA: Jossey-Bass, 1990.

———. *Let Your Life Speak*. San Francisco, CA: Jossey-Bass, 2000.

Pearsall, Paul. *The Pleasure Prescription*. Alameda, CA: Hunter House, 1998.

Peck, M. Scott. *The Road Less Traveled*. New York: Simon & Schuster, 1978.

Pert, Candace, and Deepak Chopra. *Molecules of Emotion*. New York: Scribner, 1997.

Pope John Paul II. *Crossing the Threshold of Hope*. New York: Random House, 1994.

Powell, John. *Unconditional Love*. Allen, TX: Argus Communications, 1978.

Redfield, James. *The Celestine Prophecy*. New York: Warner Books, 1993.

Robbins, Anthony. *Awaken the Giant Within*. New York: Summit Books, 1991.

Russell, Peter. *The Brain Book*. New York: Penguin, 1979.

Simon, David. *Vital Energy*. New York: John Wiley, 2000.

Stanley, Andy. *Visioneering*. Sisters, OR: Multnomah Publishers, Inc., 1999.

Star, Jonathan. *Rumi*. New York: Penguin Putnam Inc., 1997.

Thich Nhat Hanh. *Living Buddha, Living Christ*. New York: Riverhead Books, 1995.

Thomas, R. David. *Dave's Way*. New York: Berkley Books, 1992.

Thoreau, Henry David. *Walden and Other Writings*. New York: Barnes & Noble Books, 1993.

Tracy, Brian. *The 100 Absolutely Unbreakable Laws of Business Success*. San Francisco, CA: Berrett-Koehler Publishers, 2000.

Weil, Andrew. *Spontaneous Healing*. New York: Ballantine Books, 1996.

Wheatley, Margaret J., and Myron Kellner-Rogers. *A Simpler Way*. San Francisco, CA: Berrett-Koehler, 1996.

Wigginton, Eliot, ed. *The Foxfire Books: Hog Dressing, Log Cabin Building, Mountain Crafts and Foods, Planting by the Signs, Snake Lore, Hunting Tales, Faith Healing, Moon*. New York: Anchor Books, 1972.

Wolf, Fred Alan. *Mind into Matter*. Portsmouth, NH: Moment Point Press, 2001.

Ziff, Lazer. *Ralph Waldo Emerson—Selected Essays*. New York: Penguin, 1984.

Zukav, Gary. *The Seat of the Soul*. New York: Fireside, 1989.

Index

WRITING FROM WITHIN: A Guide to Creativity and Life Story Writing *by* Bernard Selling

Writing from Within has attracted an enthusiastic following among those wishing to write oral histories, life narratives, or autobiographies. Bernard Selling shows new and veteran writers how to free up hidden images and thoughts, employ right-brain visualization, and use language as a way to capture feelings, people, and events. The result is at once a self-help writing workbook and an exciting journey of personal discovery and creation.

320 pages ... Paperback $17.95 ... Third Edition

MAGICAL MANDALA COLORING BOOKS
42 Mandala Patterns Coloring Book
42 Indian Mandalas Coloring Book
42 Seasonal Mandalas Coloring Book

by Wolfgang Hund and Monika Helwig

Mandalas represent wholeness and life. The designs contain themes and patterns taken from geometry, nature and folk art. Made up of simple elements, yet often marvelously complex, they fascinate children and adults alike. Mandalas have been found on the walls of prehistoric caves, in ancient tapestries and stained glass windows and in the artistic expression of people all over the world.

These three books of mandalas can be used anywhere—all you need is a set of colored pens, pencils and crayons.

Mandala patterns—circles of life

These mandalas are drawn from the entire world of design and nature, mixing traditional and modern themes. They include nature elements and animals and are a perfect introduction to the joy of coloring mandalas.

Indian mandalas—traditional household and village art

These mandalas are based on ornamental patterns created in India. Traditionally made of colored rice powder, flower petals, leaves or colored sand, they are used to decorate homes, temples and meeting places.

Seasonal mandalas—windows into nature's cycles

The mandalas in this book mix Eastern and Western themes and include fruit, flowers, leaves and snowflakes, while more whimsical patterns include bunnies and spring chicks, jack-o-lanterns, Christmas scenes and New Year's noisemakers.

All books 96 pages ... 42 drawings to color ... Paperback $9.95ea.

To order or for our FREE catalog call (800) 266-5592

LOVING YOUR PARTNER WITHOUT LOSING YOUR SELF

by Martha Beveridge, MSSW

This book explains how to maintain your sense of self in a relationship. Beveridge, an experienced therapist, shows why romantic relationships often deteriorate from intense love into day-to-day struggles that tear couples apart, and gives practical and unique strategies for transforming these struggles into deeper intimacy. These include:

– getting past the ABCs (Attacking, Blaming, Criticizing)

– recognizing the symptoms of poor boundaries (clinging, jealousy, acting single, running away)

– dealing with the smokescreen issues: time, money, sex

256 pages ... Paperback $14.95 ... Hardcover $24.95

INTELLECTUAL FOREPLAY: Questions for Lovers and Lovers-to-Be *by* Eve Eschner Hogan, M.A., with Steven Hogan

Do you want to find out whether a romantic partner is "the one"? Practice intellectual foreplay! This book of open-ended questions is arranged in thirty-four chapters ranging from *Romance and Sex* to *Values and Beliefs,* from *Sports and Hobbies* to *Money, Home, and Children.* It can help you get to know a partner—and yourself—in a deep, practical way, and improve your chances of finding the right partner while avoiding the wrong one.

Intellectual Foreplay includes guidelines for working with a partner's responses and steers you through a decision-making process, making it an exciting tool for discovery and growth.

288 pp. ... Paperback $13.95 ... as seen on MatchNet.com

VIRTUAL FOREPLAY: Making Your Online Relationship a Real-Life Success *by* Eve Eschner Hogan, M.A.

Entering the world of online dating can be intimidating. What do you want? What should you say about yourself? How do you transition from the virtual world to real meetings? These are just a few of the questions that are addressed in *Virtual Foreplay.* This book will help you define and reveal your values and goals, improve your online presentation skills, and build confidence and self-esteem both online and off. The book also acts as a guide to learning about yourself and what you want in a relationship.

224 pages ... paperback $13.95 ... as seen on MatchNet.com

All prices subject to change

THE PLEASURE PRESCRIPTION: To Love, to Work, to Play—Life in the Balance *by* Paul Pearsall, Ph.D.
NEW YORK TIMES BESTSELLER!

This bestselling book is a prescription for stressed out lives. Dr. Pearsall maintains that contentment, wellness, and long life can be found by devoting time to family, helping others, and slowing down to savor life's pleasures. Pearsall's unique approach draws from Polynesian wisdom and his own 25 years of psychological and medical research. For readers who want to discover a way of life that promotes healthy values and living, *The Pleasure Prescription* provides the answers.

288 pages ... Paperback $13.95 ... Hard cover $23.95

WRITE YOUR OWN PLEASURE PRESCRIPTION: 60 Ways to Create Balance & Joy in Your Life
by Paul Pearsall, Ph.D.

For the many readers who have written asking for ways to translate the harmony of Oceanic life to their own lives, Dr. Pearsall offers this companion volume. It is full of ideas for bringing the spirit of aloha—the ability to fully connect with oneself and with others—to everyday life. Pearsall encourages readers to feel the pleasure that comes from making joy a part of each day.

224 pages ... Paperback ... $12.95

PARTNERS IN PLEASURE: Sharing Success, Creating Joy, Fulfilling Dreams—Together *by* Paul Pearsall, Ph.D.

In this new book, Dr. Pearsall introduces what he calls "*naupaka* love" or *aloha kakou*—love shared, profound companionship, surrendering to a relationship and embracing it as a journey of discovery and mutual pleasure. A uniquely warm combination of oral wisdom and psychological research, *Partners in Pleasure* is nothing less than a re-visioning of marriage. It offers eight lessons in *mahele* (sharing)—pleasure prescriptions for partners, from dreaming the same dream to becoming one body. Woven throughout are life and relationship lessons from Hawai`i's foremost *kupuna* (elders) and *kahuna* (healers or priests).

Pearsall returns couples to the task of becoming the right partners together, a lifelong adventure that strengthens and sustains each partner even as it brings harmony and peace to all those around them.

288 pages ... Paperback ... $14.95 ... Hardcover $24.95

To order see last page or call (800) 266-5592

ORDER FORM

10% DISCOUNT on orders of $50 or more —
20% DISCOUNT on orders of $150 or more —
30% DISCOUNT on orders of $500 or more —
On cost of books for fully prepaid orders

NAME

ADDRESS

CITY/STATE   ZIP/POSTCODE

PHONE   COUNTRY (outside of U.S.)

TITLE	QTY	PRICE	TOTAL
Creating Extraordinary Joy (paperback)		@ $15.95	

Prices subject to change without notice

Please list other titles below:

		@ $	
		@ $	
		@ $	
		@ $	
		@ $	
		@ $	
		@ $	
		@ $	

Check here to receive our book catalog ❑   free

Shipping Costs

First book: $3.00 by bookpost, $4.50 by UPS, Priority Mail, or to ship outside the U.S.
Each additional book: $1.00
For rush orders and bulk shipments call us at (800) 266-5592

TOTAL	_____
Less discount @_____%	(_____)
TOTAL COST OF BOOKS	_____
Calif. residents add sales tax	_____
Shipping & handling	_____
TOTAL ENCLOSED	========
Please pay in U.S. funds only	

❑ Check ❑ Money Order ❑ Visa ❑ Mastercard ❑ Discover

Card # _____ Exp. date _____

Signature _____

Complete and mail to:
Hunter House Inc., Publishers
PO Box 2914, Alameda CA 94501-0914
Website: www.hunterhouse.com
Orders: (800) 266-5592 or email: ordering@hunterhouse.com
Phone (510) 865-5282 Fax (510) 865-4295

CEJ - 12/2001